MARC DIVINÉ

B2B MARKETING
16 DECISIONS

A2Z Innovation

B2B Marketing: 16 Decisions, 86 Tools, by Marc Diviné.
Copyright 2015 by A2Z-Innovation.
Published by A2Z-Innovation,
47 rue de l'Yser, 92330 Sceaux, France.

Cover and interior design by Lucille Schmitt (lucilleschmitt14@gmail.com)

All rights reserved. This book may not be reproduced, in any form or by any means, without permission in writing from the publisher. All trademarks, service marks, registered marks, and registered service marks are the property of their respective owners and are used herein for identification purposes only.

ISBN: 9782955375310

INTRODUCTION

Business-to-business (B2B) marketing managers work for companies that sell their products or services to organizations. This book is dedicated to them. Their decisions have a large impact on the world economy. In fact, among the 30 companies that are members of the Dow Jones in 2015, 11 are considered B2B companies: 3M, Boeing, Caterpillar, Chevron, Cisco, DuPont, Exxon, General Electric, Intel, IBM, and United Technologies. If we also consider Goldman Sachs, JP Morgan, Verizon, Microsoft, four others have important B2B activity. So half of the Dow index depends widely on B2B performance. Out of the 10 largest companies in the world mentioned in Fortune 500 in 2015, six are involved in B2B: Royal Dutch Schell, Sinopec, China National Petroleum, Exxon, BP, and Glencore.

The first objective of this book is to describe the global mechanics of B2B marketing decisions and their interdependence. The second is to provide an array of tools that suggest decision-making methods. B2B managers will find definitions of the necessary concept as well as practical means of addressing their day-to-day issues. This book offers a vision of strategic and operational B2B marketing activities. It lists the 16 major decisions and their choices and provides 86 tools to help manage them.

Marketing or engineering master's students interested in the B2B field will discover the global rationale for the position and the type of decision-making work that characterizes this exciting job. In order to benefit from this book, the reader should preferably have basic marketing knowledge. This book is not an academic B2B marketing synthesis, however. Despite the fact that some of tools mentioned are drawn from research, it is focused on their practical application. Each chapter is aimed at answering a "How to" B2B marketing question and using the proposed tools. Each tool focuses on a decision. Each tool description contains an introduction, a presentation, a "how to use" section, and an explanation of the strengths and limitations. When needed, a tool's description may begin with definitions.

Chapter 1 provides tools to discern the difference between B2B and B2C marketing issues, and provides an overview of global decision mechanisms. The following four chapters analyze and help construct comprehensive models of the environment and the company. The next six chapters cover the strategic decision questions and tools: strategy definition, design of the value proposition, and management of the global product range. The go-to-market and customer life management activities require tools concerning the management questions of the distribution, the marketing support to the sales force, the communication, the brand management, and the customer life management. They are covered in the following four chapters. A chapter is dedicated to decisions linked to surveys, an area with a vast amount of choice. The last chapter presents tools to help decide on a marketing structure, a dashboard, and the design of marketing plans.

Each tool suggests a panel of choices and proposes a logical way of decision making. The tools can also be considered a simple way to direct one's thoughts and find an appropriate method. Additionally, the user may build his or her own customized tool by maintaining the same logic. In practice, tools may often need modification, given the variety of B2B companies in existence.

Table of Contents

Chapter 1: What B2B Marketing Decisions Are Needed
Tool 1: The B2 Constellation
Tool 2: The B2C-B2B Marketing Profile Questionnaire
Tool 3: The Decision Gearwheel
Tool 4: The Closed Loop Marketing Tool

Chapter 2: How to Create a Macro Model of the Environment
Tool 5: The Role Map of Business Field Actors
Tool 6: The Business Field Connection Model
Tool 7: The Business Field Value Chain Breakdown
Tool 8: The B2B SPECTRED Analysis
Tool 9: The Porter Six Forces Model
Tool 10: The Market Segmentation Criteria Families
Tool 11: The Segmentation Matrix

Chapter 3: What Micro-Environmental Analyses Are Necessary
Tool 12: The ARA Model
Tool 13: The IMP B2B Interaction Model
Tool 14: The Technology Marketing Photograph
Tool 15: The Competition Value Proposition Photograph
Tool 16: The Value Disciplines Model

Chapter 4: How to Make a Model of B2B Customer Behavior
Tool 17: The Buying Center Criteria Identifier
Tool 18: The Buying Center Map
Tool 19: The Purchase Process Model

Chapter 5: How to Analyze the Internal Status of the Company and Synthesize
Tool 20: The Enterprise Resource Chart
Tool 21: The Porter Value Chain
Tool 22: The SWOT Matrix

Chapter 6: How to Select the Global Company Strategy
Tool 23: The Maturity-Competition ADL Matrix
Tool 24: The Dual Attractiveness Matrix
Tool 25: The Ansoff Matrix
Tool 26: The BCG2 Matrix
Tool 27: The Risk Management Matrix
Tool 28: The Six P Strategy Mix
Tool 29: The Five Business Models Mix
Tool 30: The Positioning Mix

Tool 31: The Canvass Model Adapted to B2B
Tool 32: The Brand Identity and Naming Charter
Tool 33: The B2B Marketing 4SRs
Tool 34: The Hybrid Offerings Model

Chapter 7: How to Initiate New Product or Service Generation

Tool 35: The Ideation Star
Tool 36: The Creativity Method Chart
Tool 37: The Standardization-to-Customization Scale
Tool 38: The Flower of Services
Tool 39: The Kano Graph
Tool 40: The Specification Section Table
Tool 41: The Business Plan Content and Source Map

Chapter 8: How to Price a Product

Tool 42: The Priority Pricing Method
Tool 43: The Pricing Process Model
Tool 44: The Customized Product and Project Pricing Process
Tool 45: The International Pricing Breakdown

Chapter 9: How to Support the New Product Generation Process

Tool 46: The Five New Product Project Structure Models
Tool 47: The Combined Process-Gate and Chain-Linked Idea-to-Launch Model
Tool 48: The Innovation Sources and Validation Tool
Tool 49: The Launch Book Pattern

Chapter 10: How to Manage the Product Portfolio

Tool 50: The Offerings Cube
Tool 51: The Product Cycle Pattern
Tool 52: The Maturity Matrix and Scales
Tool 53: The Technology-Product Road Map
Tool 54: The Product Platforms Tool
Tool 55: The BCG1 Matrix
Tool 56: The Project Scoring Tool
Tool 57: The Marketing and Non-Marketing Project Priorities Tool

Chapter 11: How to Select and Support the Distribution Model

Tool 58: The Alternative Distribution Model
Tool 59: The Dealer Category Matrix
Tool 60: The Coverage-Base Matrix
Tool 61: The Customer Rotation Matrix

Chapter 12: How to Manage the Customer Experience

Tool 62: The Deal Category Matrix
Tool 63: The Circle of Customer Relations

Tool 64: The Customer Experience Blueprint

Chapter 13: How to Model the Sales Meeting and Support the Salesperson
Tool 65: The Customer-Facing Triangle Method
Tool 66: The Diamond of Supplier-Customer Relationships
Tool 67: The Business Developer Sales Tool Series
Tool 68: The Business Developer Training Schedule
Tool 69: The Sales Commissioning System

Chapter 14: How to Decide the Media Mix and Customer Experience
Tool 70: The Media Support and Influence Matrix
Tool 71: The Product and Deal Media Fit Tool
Tool 72: The Media Mix and Lead Processing Model
Tool 73: The Media Mix Blueprint
Tool 74: The Website Content and Function Spectrum

Chapter 15: How to Manage the Customer Lifecycle
Tool 75: The Magical and Critical Moments Tool
Tool 76: The CRM Content and Use Map
Tool 77: The Customer Value and Acquisition Cost Perspective
Tool 78: The LNA Care Program
Tool 79: The Medium-Sized Enterprise Care Program
Tool 80: The SoHo and Small Business Care Program

Chapter 16: How to Select and Conduct Surveys
Tool 81: The Survey Selection Guide
Tool 82: The Survey Protocol Designer
Tool 83: The Survey Protocol Optimization Tool

Chapter 17: How to Design and Monitor the Marketing Organization
Tool 84: The Marketing 3Y Strategic Plan
Tool 85: The Marketing Plans Structure
Tool 86: The B2B Marketing Global and Digital Dashboards

References
Abbreviations
Glossary
About This Book and the author

CHAPTER 1
WHAT B2B MARKETING DECISIONS ARE NEEDED

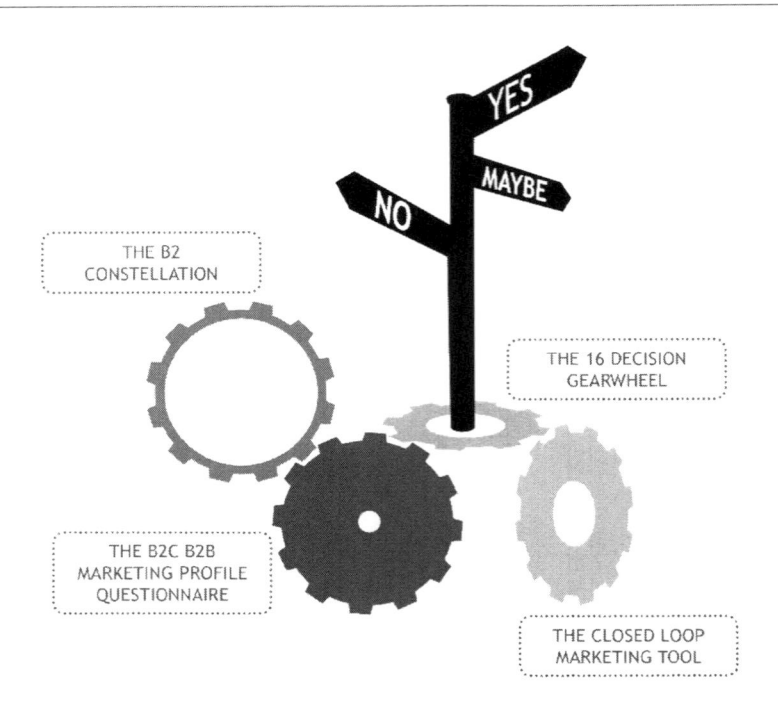

The basis of B2B marketing is the same as B2C marketing: It is a universal activity to identify customer segments and to define what to sell and how to sell it. However, it varies in many respects.

Among them:
- Products or services may be invisible ingredients whose brands are not mentioned in the end user final product.
- Their value proposition and customer purchase criteria often have complex technological content.
- Their customers are usually expert buyers who may want to create their own solution.
- The deals and relations may take only a few seconds or may last for long periods of time, involving a number of people.
- Sales contacts are a mix of face-to-face meetings on the customer's premises and online contact.

- Their competitors may be also be customers or partners in some projects.
- Deals include negotiation tactics and discounts.

In this environment, what are marketing managers' global objectives?

According to the Institute for the Study of Business Markets (Malaval & Benaroya, 2013), their strategic responsibilities include three activities:
1. The business field and market comprehension, delivered to the executive management and sales force.
2. The definition of the strategy with the targeted segments, the business model, the positioning, and the marketing partnerships to the executive management
3. The definition and management of the value proposition delivered to R&D and the sales force.

Their operational responsibilities include two activities:
1. The management of products and services and the go-to-market through the sales force.
2. The customer life management made through communication and the sales force.

Who are marketing managers' customers and to whom do they deliver value?

Marketing managers are suppliers to many groups:
- To executive management, their value is a defined vision, product range, or customer experience.
- To customers, they produce brand and value awareness.
- To the sales force, they launch products and provide sales support.
- To R&D and the supply chain, they deliver specifications and product evolutions.
- To marketing partners, they conclude win-win agreements.

This chapter proposes fives tools to accurately define B2B marketing, its differences from B2C, and the associated cycles of decision-making. Marketing managers should be able to define their own business parameters for decisions.

- Tool: The B2 Constellation
- Tool: The B2C-B2B Marketing Profile Questionnaire
- Tool: The 14 Decision Gearwheel
- Tool: The Closed-Loop Marketing Model

Tool 1: The B2 Constellation helps identify the type of relation of the firm

DEFINITIONS

Business to business (B2B or B to B) is the business of selling products or services to organizations. *Business to consumers* (B2C or B to C) is the business of selling products or services to individuals. Most B2C companies sell their products to retail organizations, which then sell to consumers. Business to administrations (B2A to B to A) is a part of B2B limited to business conducted with public authorities, including federal, national, state, and local authorities. When the products sold to administrations are used by citizen, the business is *business to user* (B2U or B to U). *Business to business to consumer* (B2B2C or B to B to C) refers to companies that produce products and sell them to other companies, which further develop the products and sell them to consumers. Such companies differ from "pure B2B" companies whose products are used or consumed by organizations. *Business to employees* (B2E or B to E) refers to products developed specifically for employees. As such, B2E will not be covered in this book, nor will consumer-to-consumer (C2C) marketing, which has been developing in Internet marketplaces (Malaval & Benaroya, 2013).

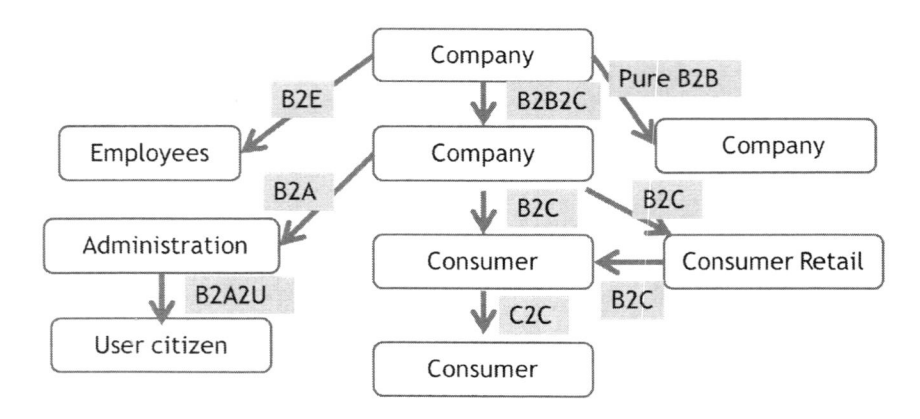

FIGURE 1.1 *THE B2 CONSTELLATION.*

How to use the tool?

First, identify the profiles of the actors or consumers—individuals, companies, administrations, employees, citizens, etc. Then, identify their relationships. Each actor's primary relationship will help to understand its B2 type, which triggers management strategies.

Strengths and limitations of the tool

Many companies sell to both individuals and companies and administrations, so they have B2B, B2A, and B2C activities. They would be classified where the activity is the most important, which is a limitation. The benefit of the tool is primarily to point out the different types of business know-how required for each B2 activities. The same product sold to companies and to consumers may generate different business activities, which should be separated.

Tool 2: The B2C-B2B Marketing Profile Questionnaire raises strategy and operations issues

DEFINITIONS

Customization is the design of tailor-made products or services for each customer. *Criticality* is the level of impact of the purchase on customer performance. *Customer acquisition cost* refers to the total cost of sales, communication, discount and pre-sales technical support necessary for the first deal. *1:1 media* is media developed for personal interactions with consumers (e.g., personal messages). *Customer predictability* is the ability to predict customer purchases. *Product value* is the customer perception of the benefits it can bring.

There are many differences between B2B and B2C markets. The Marketing Profile Questionnaire includes 20 questions to help differentiate between these two markets. The markets are not always mutually exclusive: Features of B2C markets can appear in specific B2B markets, and vice-versa. There are several opportunities to integrate the know-how of B2B and B2C marketing. This tool helps to provide a marketing profile of the company and offers alternative marketing questions.

TABLE 1.1 *B2C-B2B Marketing Profile Questionnaire.*

DIFFERENCES	B2C	B2B	MARKETING QUESTIONS
Product feature richness and technicalities	Generally low	Low to very high	How can the product be richer and simpler to use?
Product and service customization	Rare	Frequent	To what extent should the product be customized?
Product use criticality	Not critical	The product is integrated into a process of the company that is critical to its performance	How can use of the product be more important to the customer?
Product or service value to the customer	Generally a mix of product benefits and brand image	Generally an impact on cost reduction and company productivity brought by the product	How do you increase the product value to customers?
Product price	Fixed and low	Negotiated from low to very high	How do you increase the price bracket per customer segment?
Description of customers	Area, age, social category…	Starts with area, size, business field	How can we describe customers using the available data?
Number of customer	Up to hundreds of millions	Up to hundreds of thousands	How can we build a comprehensive list of prospects?
Customer needs	Generally simple and similar in a segment	Generally complex and variable per customer	How can we identify the customers' needs and preferences?
Customer predictability	Limited, impulse-based	Possible with purchase and re-purchase cycles and schedules	What events generate purchases and how do we build life cycle models?
Customer brand loyalty	Low	Often high, as customers look for low risk, so relationships are stable	How do you secure long-term relationship?

TABLE 1.1 *(Continued).*

DIFFERENCES	B2C	B2B	MARKETING QUESTIONS
Customer purchase power	Low	Low to very high	How do we strengthen the brand to counterbalance customer purchasing power?
Customer purchase process	Simple, one person consults and buys	Complex, several persons involved in a series of operations and different motivations	How do you help to improve the customer purchase process and productivity?
Customer acquisition cost	Low, mainly the distributor margin	High, particularly with complex products; includes the salespeople, the lead generation, pre-sales technical support and the discount	How can we reduce the customer acquisition cost?
Customer relationship	Fast, with a mix of mass and 1:1 media	Long duration, with face-to-face and 1:1 media	How can we optimize the customer relations media path?
Sales tools	Limited to packaging	Many sales tools used at different times	How do you create the best sales tools mix?
Customer revenue	Equal to product price	Measured over a period of time with several purchases	Which period is the most critical for measuring customer value?
Internet operations	Mainly used for transactions and conversations	Mainly used before and after the deal	How can the Internet improve customer life experience and company sales productivity?
Distribution structure and competencies	Short path from manufacturer to consumer	Direct and indirect paths according to distribution means and competencies required	What is the best distribution mix per segment?
Support to distribution	Point of sale communication	Training, lead generation, sales support programs	What marketing support should be provided to distributors?
Market knowledge	Statistics are available	Deals and discounts information is not available	How can we track the market deals?

The table highlights the differences between B2B and B2C marketing. For example, the purchase process is more complex, rational, and organized in B2B. However, nothing is fixed. The process is not definitive and there is room for creativity in purchase processes, which can serve to generate newer, simpler, more efficient procedures.

How to use the tool?

First, the list of questions should be adapted to the business field and completed as necessary. Then, for the most important questions, surveys and consultation may be required. The result can be a full marketing transformation program.

Strengths and limitations of the tool

The tool gives fundamental directions for the addition of B2B marketing value. It triggers a program of necessary analyses in order to define a strategy and operations. A limitation of tool is that the questions are non-exhaustive; also it may require excessive time and resources from marketing managers.

Tool 3: The Decision Gearwheel lists the main B2B marketing decisions and their interrelationships

DEFINITIONS

The *business model* is the strategic plan for operations, including sources of revenue, the intended customer base, products, alliances, and financing details ("Business Model," n.d.). The strategy defines the "what" and to "whom" to sell. It includes the segmentation, identification of the target market, positioning, marketing mix elements, and expenditures (American Marketing Association, 2015). The *operations* are the "how to sell" actions. *Customer relationship management* (CRM) is the system and management of customer contacts. *Customer life management* (CLM) includes the procedures for managing customer events.

The Decision Gearwheel tool describes the mechanics and rationale for B2B marketing decisions. Two decisions precede all others: (a) the type of surveys, and (b) the choice of the models of the environment. These decisions will inform all others. Then, four strategic decisions are made, which allow for the four distribution and seven customer operational decisions. All decisions are detailed with specific tools in this book.

Strategic Information processing
- The type of surveys
- The models of the environment

Strategic decisions
- The global strategy mix
- The business model mix
- The products and service offered and value proposition
- The business partners

Distribution operational decisions
- The distribution mix
- The support to distribution
- The support to sales force

Customer operational decisions
- The customer information content
- The choice of media and customer blueprint
- The program of campaigns
- The website content and functions
- The CRM information
- The CLM procedures
- The marketing organization

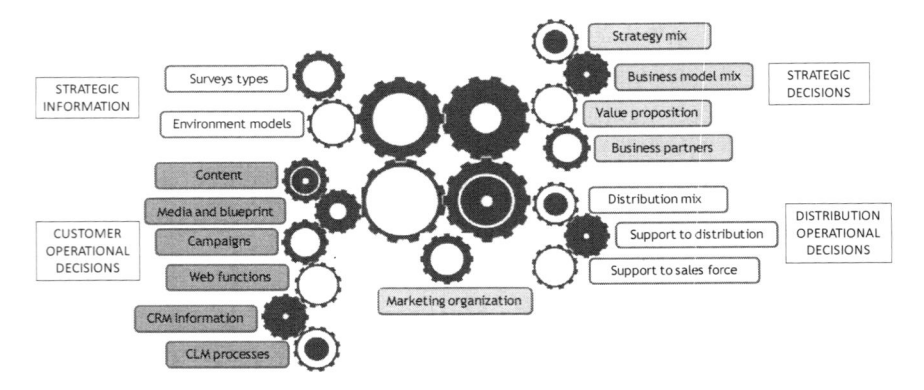

FIGURE 1.2 *The Decision Gearwheel*.

How to use the tool

The global and detailed scope of the tool shows the chronology of particular decisions. The strategy mix choice—for example, the targets, positioning, push/pull—will influence the business partners' choices. Similarly, the support to sales force—such as the training and the sales tools production—will be the consequence of all the strategic decisions, as well as the distribution mix decision.

Strengths and limitations of the tool

The tool displays the spectrum of choices. The process and the connections between the decisions are made clear and reflect the organization of the main chapters of this book. It gives direction for the marketing tasks and organization. The drawback, however, is that managers may have to take on additional responsibilities based on their marketing job descriptions. For instance, special programs are often given to marketing managers.

Tool 4: The Closed Loop Marketing Tool identifies the basic quality processes of customer management

DEFINITIONS

Closed-loop marketing is the process of bridging marketing and sales activities. It relies on a permanent feedback loop including 360° information on customer relationship management (CRM) from both organizations. *CRM* is the system and management of customer contacts. The *buying center* is the group of individuals that consists of all organizational members who are involved in any way, to any extent, in any phase of a specific buying decision (American Marketing Association, 2015).

The Closed loop Marketing Tool originated from efforts to improve B2C Internet purchases. Adapted to B2B, the loop focuses on five phases. First, the source of the customer marketing contacts is carefully tracked. Second, customer interest is evaluated. Third, the customer buying center is identified and the information is passed on to the sales force. Companies can be identified using IP addresses. Fourth, the lead and all the future relations are tracked, including purchase history and communication channels. Fifth, interaction efficiency is analyzed for each customer and the process is revisited and customized.

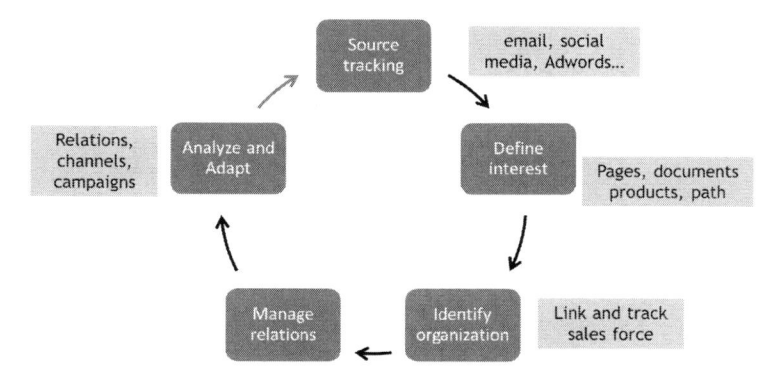

FIGURE 1.3 *The Closed-Loop Marketing Model.*

How to use the tool?

The tool can be used if a complete view of customer relations is outlined. Then the five-phase process can start and never finishes, as long as the customer is targeted. This cycle serves as the basis of customer operations marketing management.

Strengths and limitations of the tool

Thorough tracking and real-time adaptation of customer relations improves the lead-to-sale conversion rate. Channels are better chosen; the marketing budget is better allocated; the customer saves time searching and reading, and is more satisfied; and, most importantly, campaign ROI is improved.

There are two limitations of this tool: (a) some individuals may be resistant to providing detailed information, and (b) it may not have the capacity to generate 1:1 customer-specific relations. Micro-segmentation helps to create groups of customers and the sales force helps to generate leads by providing customers' information.

CHAPTER 2

HOW TO CREATE A MACRO MODEL OF THE ENVIRONMENT

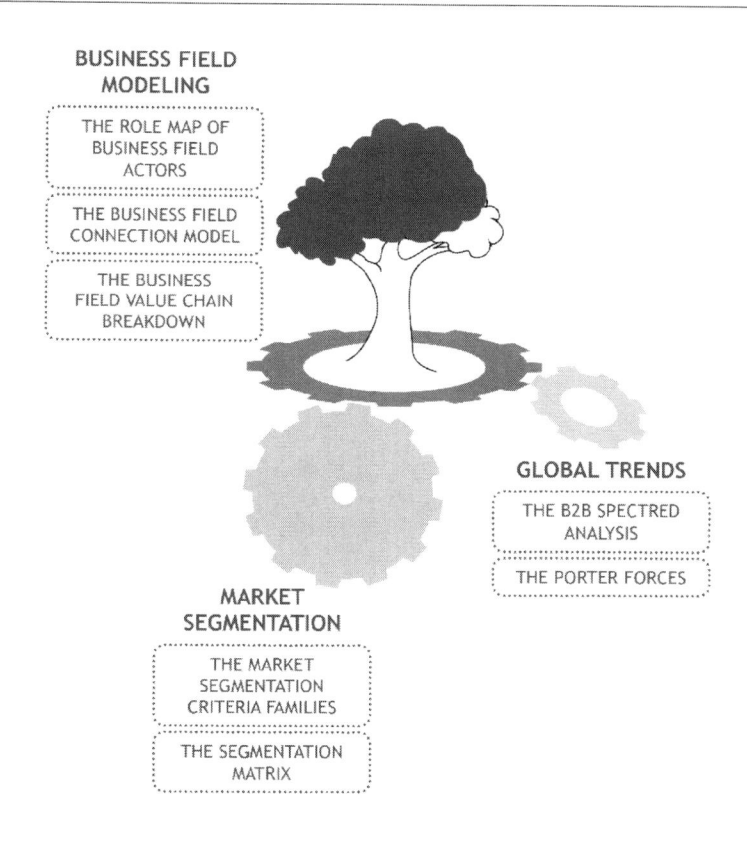

BUSINESS FIELD MODELING
- THE ROLE MAP OF BUSINESS FIELD ACTORS
- THE BUSINESS FIELD CONNECTION MODEL
- THE BUSINESS FIELD VALUE CHAIN BREAKDOWN

GLOBAL TRENDS
- THE B2B SPECTRED ANALYSIS
- THE PORTER FORCES

MARKET SEGMENTATION
- THE MARKET SEGMENTATION CRITERIA FAMILIES
- THE SEGMENTATION MATRIX

The enterprise environment triggers strategy and marketing activities. Customers, customers' customers, competitors, regulators, business enablers, partners, and so on, all influence the environment. The dynamics of the environment continuously influence targeted segments, positioning, value proposition, distribution tactics, and customer relationships.

What is specific to B2B?

The B2B environment is often very different from the B2C environment:

- The volume of interaction is far more important in B2B between two firms than in B2C between suppliers and consumers.
- The number of actors involved can be very large between the two organizations.
- The processes can be very complex, requiring several activities and resources.
- The duration of the relationship can last several years.

These elements are specific to each B2B business field. They justify a careful environmental analysis, with a process that follows the mechanics. The design of a macro model of the B2B environment includes four elements: (a) business field, (c) global trends, (c) forces of the actors, and (d) market segmentation. Seven tools are proposed in this chapter to create a model of the B2B environment.

- Business field modeling
    - Tool 5: The Role Map of Business Field Actors
    - Tool 6: The Business Field Connection Model
    - Tool 7: The Business Field Value Chain Breakdown
- Global trends
    - Tool 8: The B2B SPECTRED Analysis
    - Tool 9: The Porter Forces
- Market segmentation
    - Tool 10: The Market Segmentation Criteria Families
    - Tool 11: The Segmentation Matrix

Tool 5: The Role Map of Business Field Actors helps to identify the roles of important players

DEFINITIONS

The business field or is the group of actors or professional organizations whose actions impact the enterprise strategy and results. *Tier 1* providers are direct providers to the company. *Tier 2* providers supply Tier 1, Tier 3 providers supply Tier 2, and so on.

The ecosystem of organizations is made up of several organizations with different roles. The Business Field Actors Map proposes a typology that helps to build the strategy and organize the tactics, processes, communication, and resources. Use of the tool involves naming the main organizations that have an impact on the enterprise strategy and results. Then, one or several roles are given to each player. This exercise is an opportunity to define the common roles for management.

TABLE 2.1 *Definitions of Business Field Actors.*

ACTORS TYPES	ROLES
The customer	The organizations that buy the enterprise products or services. Buying means ordering and paying.
The user	The organizations that use the products or services. They may be different from the customer. For example, a subsidiary of the customer.
The customers' customers	The organizations that buy products or services from customers. The company is a "Tier 2" provider of these final customers. The customers' customer knowledge may have an impact on the company strategy. For example, their technology preference can modify components sold by Tier 2 providers. B2B managers can analyze this global value chain.
Competition	Organizations that sell products or services that answer to the same type of need, and give an alternative choice to customers. They may answer part of the need, or the entire need. This is a strategic decision. The organizations can also serve as partners is some specific deals.
Distributors	Independent organizations that buy products and sell them. Their know-how includes the identification of prospects, communication, customer relations, closing of one or multiple deals, and management of customer lifespan. They can be dedicated to one supplier, exclusive to a few suppliers, or have a very large range including hundreds of suppliers that cover various needs.
Value-added resellers (VARs)	VARs are distributors that deliver a larger value to customers than reselling products. They can create a global solution including several products, services, customization, and support to purchase managers and users.
Competition	Organizations that sell products or services that answer to the same type of need, and give an alternative choice to customers. They may answer part of the need, or the entire need. This is a strategic decision. The organizations can also serve as partners is some specific deals.

ACTORS TYPES	ROLES
Distributors	Independent organizations that buy products and sell them. Their know-how includes the identification of prospects, communication, customer relations, closing of one or multiple deals, and management of customer lifespan. They can be dedicated to one supplier, exclusive to a few suppliers, or have a very large range including hundreds of suppliers that cover various needs.
Value-added resellers (VARs)	VARs are distributors that deliver a larger value to customers than reselling products. They can create a global solution including several products, services, customization, and support to purchase managers and users.
Agents	Agents are organizations that know a particular market and find distributors. They can be commissioned on a deal, and are intermediaries in complex markets.
Central purchasing agencies	Also known as *trading groups* or *buying agencies*, this type of actor buys large quantities and sell to distributors.
Influencers	An organization or individual who advises the buyer in choosing a supplier. The advice can be about the type of solution, the product, the suppliers, making contact with another actor, etc.
Prescribers	The prescriber is an organization or individual who advises the buyer on the choice of product or service. They can prescribe a technical solution and specific supplier, or a list of suppliers. The level of influence can range from a simple suggestion to an obligation.
Lead providers or referrals	Lead providers, or referrals, are organizations or individuals who provide the names of companies that may be interested in their products. They may receive commission if the deal is closed. They avoid the cost of lead generation communication to the supplier.
Strategic suppliers	Strategic suppliers deliver to the company or its competitors components that are key to the value proposition. The scarcity, the price competitiveness, the technology, or the performance of the components can generate strategic suppliers, who can sell to several competitors.
Business enablers	Business enablers deliver an expert service that allows the deal to be carried out. They can write tenders, find partners, provide financing solutions, get certifications, and provide consultancy in many different areas.
Partners	Partners are organizations that have collaboration contracts with the company or its competitors. Such alliances can be involved with technology development, product co-development, project engineering, as well as the sharing of distribution expenditures. Partners can help to create joint ventures, networks, or other frameworks.

Communities	Communities are informal organizations of individuals who have common professional interests. They often meet in virtual space in social networks, but can have events in real life as well. They debate best practices, technology, solutions, supplier choices, market trends, deal opportunities, etc. Their buzz can have a considerable impact on company image, awareness, revenue, and strategy.
Opinion leaders	Opinion leaders are organizations or individuals who have an audience and inform actors in the business field. They can be official press journals or experts who blog about specific topics.

TABLE 2.2 *The Business Field Actors Map.*

BUSINESS FIELD ACTORS	ROLES						
	Customer	User	Customers' customer	Competition	Distributor	VAR	Etc.
...							
...							
...							

How to use the tool?

Start the process by creating a list of the actors who influence the enterprise strategy. Then, analyze the roles of each after completing the table. Each actor can play several roles and can be mentioned several times.

Strengths and limitations of the tool

This tool is a powerful means of visually representing the positions of each business field actor. It serves as a starting point for an analysis of the environment. A limitation is the feasibility of the process. Identifying actors and their roles may be difficult, as they may be numerous, remain unknown, or work in relative secrecy. Further, identifying the parameters for actions may be complex due to actors' multiple roles.

Tool 6: The Business Field Connection Model maps the environment actors' strategies

DEFINITIONS

From a marketing perspective, the *business field* is the group of actors or professional organizations that influences the company strategy and results.

The B2B ecosystem is comprised of several, interrelated actors, each with a different purpose. The ability to identify actors creates opportunities for strategic partnerships, can help to generate lead provider agreements, and may help to develop tactics to manage competition. The Business Field Connection Model is a map of the interrelationships among the actors, which is important for the sector of the company. The vertical structure of the tool serves to identify the succession of a purchase: Suppliers sell to Level 1 customers, who in turn, become suppliers and sell to the Level 2 customers, and so on. Several levels appear until the end user, who does not sell the product, but rather, consumes or uses it. Actors serve as customers or customers' customers; others are influencers, partners, certification authorities, etc. They are grouped per type at the same level of the model. Six types of relationships can appear: (a) sell, (b) subcontract a custom-made element of the product, (c) influence the purchase, (d) inform the buyer, (e) authorize, (f) integrate several sellers' products with its support, or (g) make an alliance.

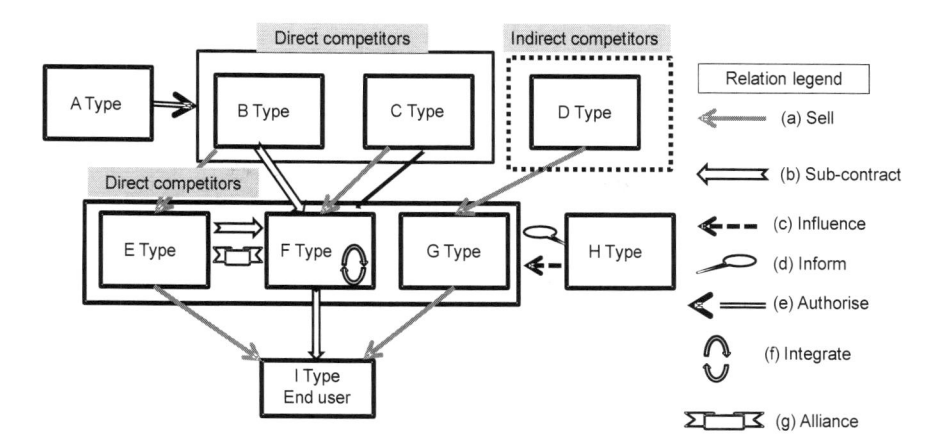

FIGURE 2.1 *The Business Field Connection Model (Example 1).*

Figure 2.2 is an example of a software company that wants to evaluate at which levels it can sell its products. Its customers can be subcontractors, manufacturers, or application editors. The tool shows that its value proposition should be compatible with the activity of the customers' customers in terms of integration, service, maintenance, etc. Based on customers' choices, other actors—such as manufacturers, system integrators, IT service providers, or even end users—should contribute to the end-user product value.

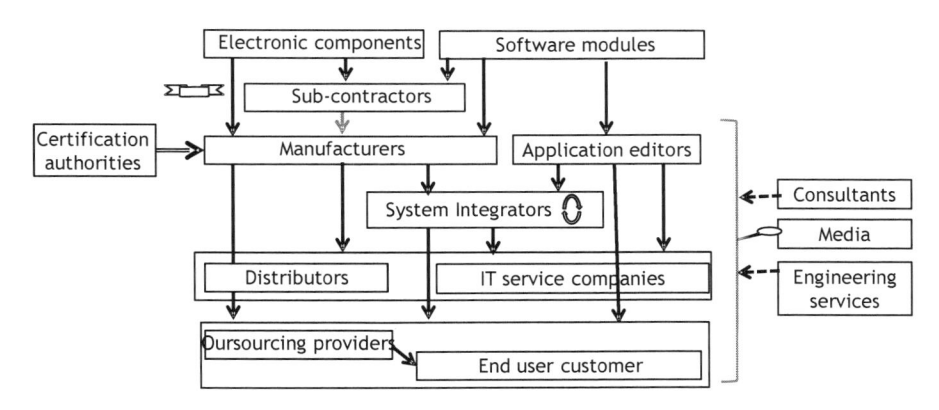

FIGURE 2.2 *The Business Field Connection Model (Example 2).*

How to use the tool?

First, create the list of business field actors. Only actors who have an influence are kept. Then, describe their roles and relationships in a chart. It is easier to start with the end user and see from whom they buy. Work backwards and identify from whom each actor buys at each tier. Then, position the enterprise: Make the decision about who to sell to and with whom to communicate.

Strengths and limitations of the tool

This tool provides a strategic vision of the business field. The act of agreeing upon the mapping is a valuable marketing exercise. It helps to develop a common understanding of the competition, indirect competitors, alliances, and so on. It aids in deciding to whom to sell and with whom to communicate. It requires a thorough knowledge of the field. Far-reaching consultation may be necessary to build it, including the sales force, R&D, purchase managers, communication managers, customers, etc. Using this tool may also help to define new types of relationships not present in the existing business field.

Tool 7: The Business Field Value Chain Breakdown reveals areas of potential profit

DEFINITIONS

The *added value* of a company is its revenue minus its purchases, sometimes called the gross margin. More broadly, added value refers to all of the benefits a company brings to its customers beyond the benefits brought by suppliers. The *EBIT* is the earnings before interest and tax; the *EBITDA* is the earnings before interest, tax, depreciation, and amortization. Both are key indicators of profit.

The value chain analysis of the business field helps to identify which actors are generating significant added value or profit. For example, it shows opportunities for growth by vertical integration of suppliers or distributors, or by horizontal integration with competitors. The Business Field Value Chain Breakdown is a chart that describes the split of the added value from different actors. In Table 2.3, each actor is the supplier of the actor on its right and the customer of the actor on its left. The supplier of a manufacturer is named Tier 1. The supplier of a Tier 1 is a Tier 2, and so on. For each actor, the price of their product is split among the purchase to the previous actor, the purchase to all other providers not listed in the tool, and the added value. The selling price of an actor is the main purchase of the next actor. For Tier 1 in Table 2.3, D1 = A0 + C1. The added value is equal to the selling price minus the total purchase, E1 = B1 − D1, and so on for the "Manufacturer," E2 = B2 − D2, and other actors. What is key is the added value compared to the percentage of the price: F1 = E1/B1. In the case below, an intermediary exist between the manufacturer and the dealer. The breakdown shows where the profit is made and helps to decide to whom to sell; it also helps to identify vertical integration opportunities.

TABLE 2.3 *The Business Field Value Chain Breakdown.*

ACTORS	Tier2	Tier 1	Manufacturer	Intermediary	Dealer
Price	A	B1	B2	B3	B4
Other purchase		C1	C2	C3	C4
Total purchase		D1	D2	D3	D4
Added value		E1	E2	E3	E4
% Added value		F1	F2	F3	F4

Other information can be added for each type of actors, such as the average EBITDA, number of companies, breakdown of nationalities, etc. Companies that cover more than one activity can be mentioned. Below is an example of a specific consumer product in the chemical industry. Actors in the business field range from oil companies to retailers. In this case, a chemical company or manufacturer may consider becoming a formulator when the profit is high.

TABLE 2.4 *The Business Field Value Chain Breakdown.*

ACTORS	Oil	Refinery	Chemical	Formulator	Manufacturer	Retailer
Price (base end user100)	35	45	55	80	95	100
Other purchase	25	6	7	16	15	1
Total purchase	25	41	52	71	95	96
Added value	10	4	3	9	5	4
% Added value	28%	9%	5%	11%	5%	4%
Number of actors	tens	tens	hundreds	tens	hundreds	thousands

How to use the tool?

First, the business field actors are grouped by level and type—Tier 2, Tier 1, distributor, etc.—in chronological order based on purchases. Then, the value additions are calculated, with the average value for each group. The last step is to interpret the figures, which can show common revenue growth and profit profiles for the different groups.

Strengths and limitations of the tool

A particular strength of this tool is that it helps to identify whether a company is well-positioned inside the value chain. It can help strategic planning based on the profits of actors in the business field. A limitation is that use of the tool may require extensive analysis of company accounts, which may be difficult for companies with diversified activities. The tool is valuable if there is a relative homogeneity of value addition among similar types of actors. Large differences among actors would indicate that there is no significance to the average values interpretation.

Tool 8: The B2B SPECTRED Analysis provides the key environmental areas to survey

DEFINITIONS

Triangulation refers to checking information or making estimations by using several sources.

The old PESTLE analysis model covers the following topics in an environmental analysis, as indicated by the acronym: political, economic, social, technological, legal, and ecological. Two topics—cultural and demographics—were later added, resulting in the new acronym, SPRECTRED. Adapted for B2B, the B2B SPRECTRED Environmental Analysis examines five elements per topic. It focuses on company dynamics and constraints. For example, the demographics items include business creations, large and national account (LNA) presence. For the cultural element, it is necessary to know the B2B media preference and purchase processes.

DEMOGRAPHIC
- XY generation
- Business population
- Sector presence
- LNA presence
- Company creations

POLITICAL
- Tax policy
- Barriers to competition
- Monetary policy
- Business support
- Lobbying efficiency

ECOLOGICAL
- Green regulation
- Energy availability
- Recycling
- Local sensitivity
- Associations power

SPECTRED Environmental Analysis

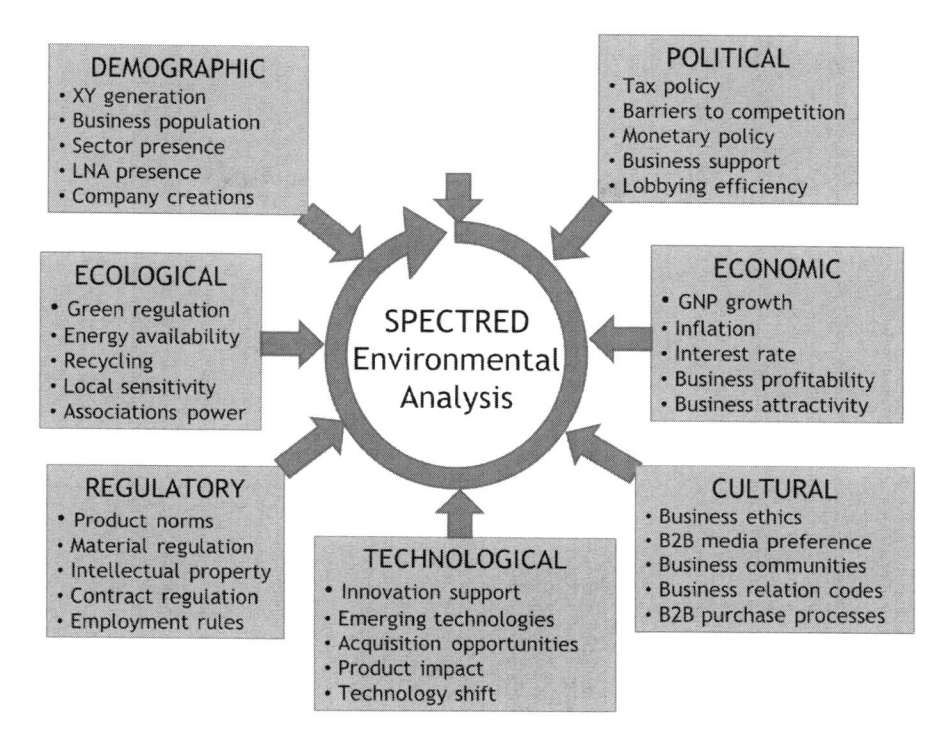

ECONOMIC
- GNP growth
- Inflation
- Interest rate
- Business profitability
- Business attractivity

REGULATORY
- Product norms
- Material regulation
- Intellectual property
- Contract regulation
- Employment rules

TECHNOLOGICAL
- Innovation support
- Emerging technologies
- Acquisition opportunities
- Product impact
- Technology shift

CULTURAL
- Business ethics
- B2B media preference
- Business communities
- Business relation codes
- B2B purchase processes

FIGURE 2.3 *The B2B SPECTRED Environment Analysis.*

The tool suggests information to evaluate. Each company can add the specific data required for its particular field of business. For example, a company can focus on the demographics of customers in targeted business segments. The tool can emphasize product norms in relation to the business field.

How to use the tool?

The tool lists eight areas to be analyzed. The first step is to prioritize the order according to the business field, foreseen risks, and recent events. Then, identify the information wanted for each area. Finally, the information sources are researched and triangulation is used to check them.

Strengths and limitations of the tool

SPRECTRED is a basic tool that provides a picture of the environment. Its spectrum is large enough to cover the most important factors. However, each item requires a customized list of information according to the purpose of the analysis. Some information is easy to find, but the accuracy is often poor; other information may not be available, or may be estimated.

Tool 9: The Porter Six Forces Model underlines the pressures on the firm

DEFINITIONS

The *switching costs* are the customer technical costs and organizational costs of change from one supplier to another.

The Porter Six Forces Model evaluates the environmental pressures in the business field and therefore the sector attractiveness. Porter (1985) divided pressure into five dimensions, later extended to six (see Figure 2.4). The thickness of arrows indicates the level of pressure. Horizontally, the first dimension is the bargaining power of suppliers. This depends on the number of suppliers, the unique features of their products, the product and service delivery capacity, and mutual dependence. The second is generally the most important—competitive rivalry. Number of firms, differentiation, and marketing expenditures also contribute to pressure. The last is the bargaining power of customers, which depends on the number of local suppliers, purchasing volume, switching cost, and the criticality and risk of the purchase. Vertically, the first dimension is the threat of potential new entrants, which depends on the profits and competition level of existing companies, and entry barriers. If the business field attracts new enterprises, competition pressure can increase and market shares can decrease. Local manufacturers often see multinational companies as new entrants. The second threat comes from substitute products or distribution channels, which differ totally from those offered by existing competitors. This dimension depends on competitive technologies and the different types of solutions that customers need. The additional sixth dimension includes pressure from regulators. The acceleration of production, regulations, norms, certifications, and compulsory compliances are permanent pressures in many industries. Figure 2.4 presents a case in which the competitors face maximum pressure—as indicated by the thickness of lines—and buyers have a limited impact.

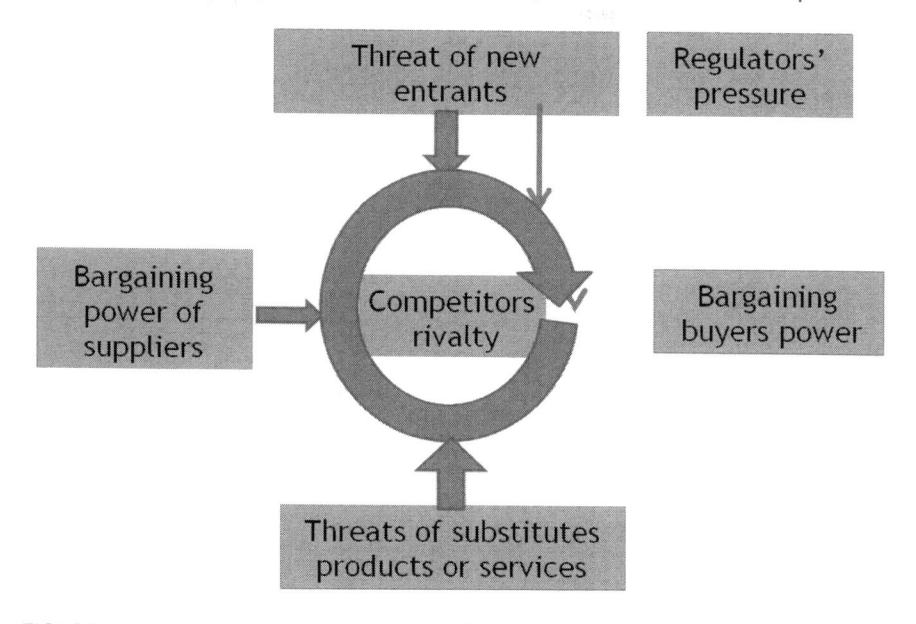

FIGURE 2.4 *The Porter Five Forces Model.*

How to use the tool?

The first step is to list the individuals in contact with the five types of external players. An interview will then help to measure the pressure. Researching documents related to deals will help to understand supplier and customer price pressure, as well as the percentage of lost deals to entrants or substitutes. Finally, the impact of regulation on offerings, for example with norms announcement, will show the regulator pressure. Use of the tool will help to get a full picture of forces of pressure.

Strengths and limitations of the tool

The tool is helpful to identify areas of risk and to define strategies to combat suppliers, customers, competitors, entrants, and substitute producers. A limitation of the tool is that the different labels suggest a simplified process. However, in B2B, it is frequently the case that the same company is a competitor and a partner. Two companies can be both suppliers and customers. Substitutes and replacements of products are not always easy to identify. Thus, companies that are at several points of the matrix often require different decisions and special treatment.

Tool 10: The Market Segmentation Criteria Families help group customers to optimize the strategy and expenditures

DEFINITIONS

Segmentation is the process of subdividing a market into distinct subsets of customers who behave in the same way or have similar needs (American Marketing Association, 2015).

Segmentation is necessary when customers are numerous and the company must find synergies and optimize resources in product design, production, or distribution. The segmentation criteria have a dual use. In the first step, they provide the readability of the market to choose the customers or the end users to address. We can call them macro-strategic segments. In the second step, when the product is on the market, they help define the precise list of customers to address at each opportunity over time. The Market Segmentation Criteria tool proposes five families of segmentation criteria: company, solution, support, process, business. The process includes project management, which shows how the product will be designed and delivered. Aligning with the specific marketing intention, a combination of segmentation criteria is used. For example, if the company has a capacity limit to design products, it may use the segmentation criteria in the Solution family, and choose a different performance and usage. If the company has a limit in its distribution capacity, it may focus on the purchase process criteria and choose to target companies that purchase via the Internet or phone.

COMPANY	SOLUTION	SUPPORT
Size	Technology	Expertise
Duration	Performance	Delivery
Business field	Features	Integration
Location	Quality	Co-design
Number of sites	Durability	Services to buyer
Profit	Modularity	Services to user
Nationality	Usage	Financial services
Alliances	Application	Online services
Capacities	Customization	On site services
Service		**Design**
Distribution	**Design**	**Service**
Partnership	**Production**	**Distribution**

PROCESS	BUSINESS
Centralization	Previous purchase
Purchase criteria	Competition sales
Purchase media	Purchase budget
Purchase cycle and emergencies	Terms of payment
	Acquisition cost
Technical requirements	Discount and ROI
	Customer value
Purchase volume	Lease status
Lobbying	Opportunities
Project man.	
Distribution	**Distribution**

FIGURE 2.5 *The Market Segmentation Criteria Families and Their Six Optimizations (Example).*

The families of criteria show the opportunities for synergies. The use of the criteria linked to Support, for example, will trigger synergies in distribution and services. The same services to buyers and users will be searched in large groups of customers. As another example, the criterion *lease status* in the business criteria family, may save distribution resources if several customers who are at the end of their leases require the same sales method.

How to use the tool

In practice, the strategic criteria are ideal, though they may be not operational (i.e., the information that they require may not be available). In such instances, either the customer database information is confirmed by calling the customer, or the strategic criteria are approximated given the available information. For example, the criterion *long duration in terms of payment*, may be approximated using a combination of sector and size, such as "local authorities below 100,000 persons" and "company with less than 2 years in operation."

Strengths and limitations of the tool

Segmentation is the key strategic activity. The tool displays the different approaches according to intent and provides over 40 possible criteria across six families. It helps to link the choice of criteria to the six benefits of synergy optimization. Each business has to define its criteria per synergy potential. A limitation, however, is the duration of use. A segmentation to help design a product range should be stable and should be adapted to the product life cycle. It is critical to update the criteria without interfering with R&D teams.

Tool 11: The Segmentation Matrix groups the segmentation criteria and defines targets

The number of segmentation criteria can inflate such that the readability of the market and the choice of targets may be an issue. The Segmentation Matrix groups the criteria together, connecting a limited number of segments. Three groups are made with the technical criteria, which exclude the company and place it at the same level or better than the competition. They come from the Solution family in the tool Market Segmentation Criteria Families. One group concerns the deal revenue and profit provision, which come from the Process, Business, and Support families; for example, average revenue per customer and the net margin (i.e., margin minus cost of acquisition). The last group comes from the Profile family with, in particular, the basic universal information on size, sector, and location. One can arrive at target choice more easily by prioritizing customers with better solutions and better revenue and margin. In order to find them easily, they will be translated into micro-segments (i.e., combinations of size, sector, and location if no other information is available).

Families	Profile				Solution						Support Business Process	
Groups of criteria	Profile				Below competition		As competition		Better than competition		Revenue & Margin	
Criteria	Size	Sector	Place	# Sites...	Feature 1.1	1.2...	Feature 2.1	2.3...	Feature 3.1	3.2	3.3	High	Low
Seg. 1													
Seg. 2													
Seg. 3													
Seg. 4													
Seg. 5													
Seg. 6													
Seg. 7													
Seg. 8													
Seg. 9													

FIGURE 2.6 *The Segmentation Matrix.*

In this example, three feature—3.1, 3.2 and 3.3—are better than the competition, in order of importance for the customer. Therefore, Segments 9, 7, and 5 are the three targets, which have a better revenue-margin impact. If these three segments are not large enough, then Segments 4, 6, 8 can be addressed, and then the Segment 3.

How to use the tool

Use of this tool requires a competitive product analysis to build the first three groups of segments. A second activity involves the rating of the expected average revenue and margin with the customers introduced in the database. The segments will appear by sorting them. The targets are

35

approximated with micro-segments for size, sector, and location if strategic information is lacking in the database.

Strengths and limitations of the tool

The tool provides a way to define segments and targets. It allows the transition between the strategic segmentation and the operational choice of customers. It shows priorities by accounting for technical abilities and expectations for revenue and profit. However, the effort and time needed to fill the database with pertinent information is a limitation.

CHAPTER 3

WHAT MICRO-ENVIRON-MENTAL ANALYSES ARE NECESSARY

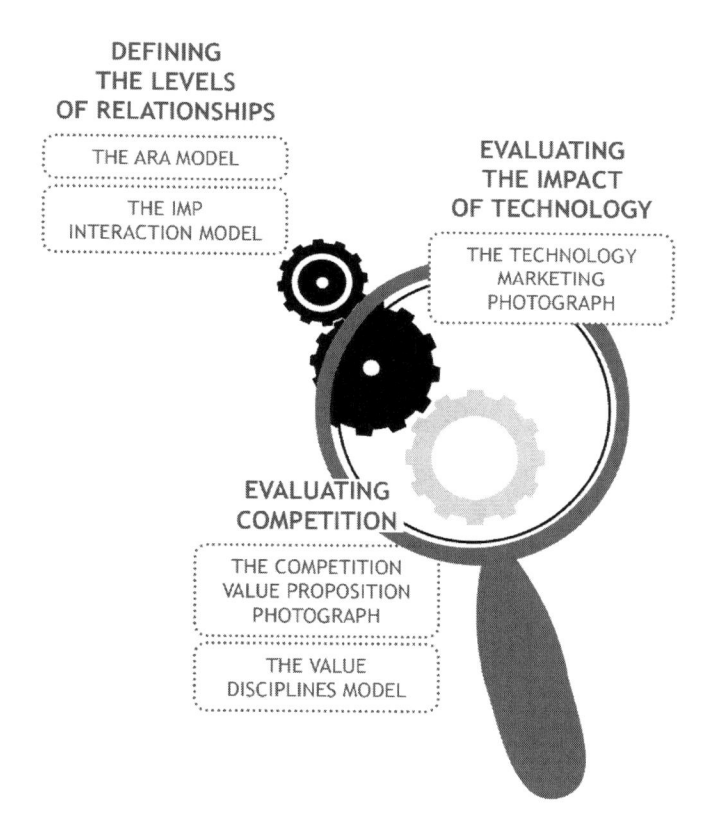

DEFINING THE LEVELS OF RELATIONSHIPS
- THE ARA MODEL
- THE IMP INTERACTION MODEL

EVALUATING THE IMPACT OF TECHNOLOGY
- THE TECHNOLOGY MARKETING PHOTOGRAPH

EVALUATING COMPETITION
- THE COMPETITION VALUE PROPOSITION PHOTOGRAPH
- THE VALUE DISCIPLINES MODEL

Micro-environmental analyses can be used evaluate company operations and deal levels. For example, a deal of one thousand screws between a Chinese manufacturer and an American manufacturer is underway. The deal is far more important if the screws are to be used on aircrafts motors than on toys. The complexity and impact of the value proposition seen by players is also very different. B2B marketing should include several micro-environmental analyses, including the following: a picture of the specific levels of relationships between customers and suppliers, the impact of technology, and a detailed understanding of competitors' value proposition. A series of five tools is proposed to conduct these analyses.

Defining the levels of relationships
- Tool 12: The ARA Model
- Tool 13: The IMP Interaction Model

Evaluating the impact of technology
- Tool 14: The Technology Marketing Photograph

Evaluating competition
- Tool 15: The Competition Value Proposition Photograph
- Tool 16: The Value Discipline Model

Tool 12: The ARA Model evaluates actors, activities, and resource interactions

The ARA Model (Brenann, Håkansson, & Johanson, 1992; Hakansson & Snehota, 2003) provides a three-layer visual of the interactions among B2B partners in the transaction: the actor bonds, the activity links, and the resource ties. The three types of interactions have interrelated effects. The interactions are generated by a network of actors, a variety of resources, and models of activities.

The *actor layer* refers to the nature of the relationships among individuals: levels of proximity, trust, influence, and commitment. These levels will trigger judgment on the feasibility of the deal and necessary adaptations, as well as the required learning and personal benefits for the each organizations.

The *activity layer* refers to the nature of specific activities generated by the deal at each phase: levels of integration, communication, and coordination. These activities exist across several functions of the enterprise; they are organized in processes so that the entire value chain can be mobilized including R&D, logistics, production, IT, HR, sales, service, and marketing.

The *resource layer* refers to the types of resources that partners decide to allocate and their availability, adequacy, and appropriateness.

Resources include manpower, expertise, money, equipment, goods, patents, infrastructure, and so on.

The three layers of ARA are interrelated: Activities require resources, which foster individual relationships, which subsequently impact activities. The whole interrelation system—actor bonds, resource ties, and activity links—moves and adapts together. The interactions are not symmetrical; they can be unequal. Similarly, they are not only limited to two actors; other parties may also be involved.

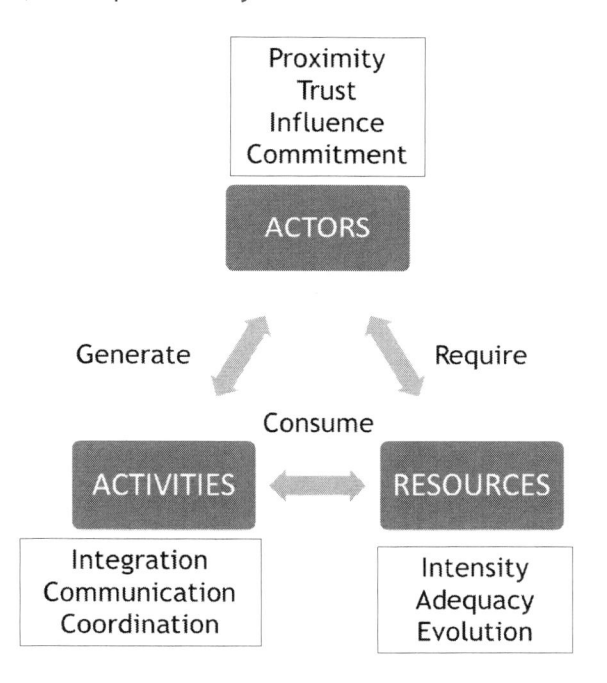

FIGURE 3.1 *The ARA Model.*

How to use the tool?

First, the interactions between the supplier and the customer are listed. For each interaction, the people involved are listed, as well as activity and the resources required. Then, specific factors are chosen to describe the interaction. The tool proposes 10 factors, but other ones can also be adopted depending on the field of business. Finally, decisions can emerge from this analysis regarding the nature of individuals' time and activities, and the required resources for each deal.

Strengths and limitations of the tool

This tool triggers a focus on three particular types of relationships, which allows the company to analyze the business from this three-way perspective. A limitation is that it is high-level view. The next step is the analysis of the detailed processes involved with each relationship. The tool IMP B2B Interrelation Model may help.

Tool 13: The IMP B2B Interaction Model synthesizes the interactions between customer and supplier

Different from the ARA model, IMP B2B model (Hakansson & Snehota, 2011) was developed by the Industrial Marketing and Purchase Group to represent the interrelationships between two partners. Individuals' relationships are separated, as with ARA, with a focus on the social relationships and their variations, which are based on personal experience and objectives. Opposite of individuals are the system and organization. Their interrelations are made up of product, information, and financial exchange, which are based on their structure and strategy. Additionally, the model incorporates two environmental layers. The larger one is the ecosystem, which includes the market and the positions of the two partners inside it. The second is the relational climate, which results from the ecosystem and the two partners' relationships. The climate is defined with levels of proximity, dependencies, and collaboration.

```
                           ECOSYSTEM
       Market                                    Positions
                        RELATIONAL CLIMATE
            ┌─────────────┐              ┌─────────────┐
            │  System &   │   Products   │  System &   │
            │ Organization│  Information │ Organization│
            │  Structure  │ Transactions │  Structure  │
            │  Strategy   │              │  Strategy   │
            ├─────────────┤   Relations  ├─────────────┤
            │ Individuals │  Adaptations │ Individuals │
            │  Experience │              │  Experience │
            │  Objectives │              │  Objectives │
            └─────────────┘              └─────────────┘
              Proximity Dependancies Collaboration
```

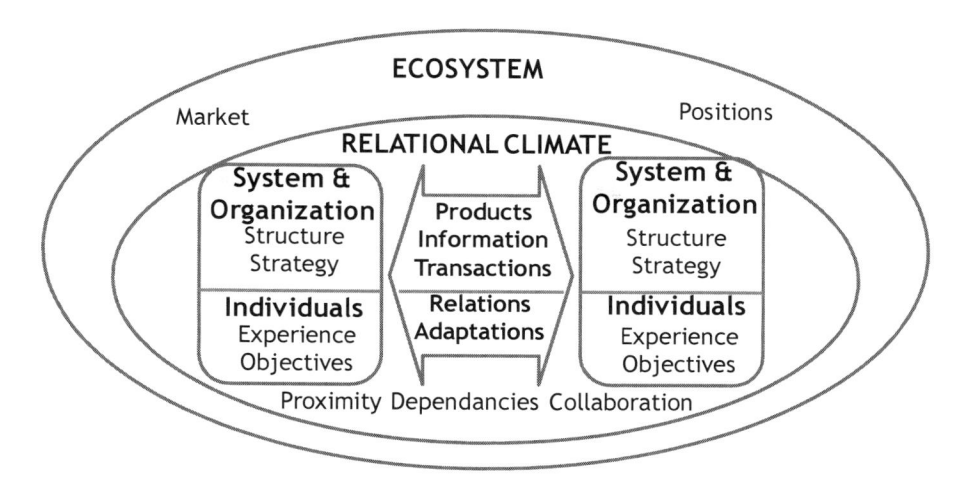

FIGURE 3.2 *The IMP B2B Interaction Model.*

How to use the tool?

In the first phase, the main relationships between supplier and customer are listed. For each relationship, information regarding products and transactions processed is described. Then, the implications for both sides in terms of strategy and structure are delineated. In a similar way, individual interactions are listed, including experience and personal objectives. Finally, global levels of proximity, dependence, and collaboration are evaluated. Decisions may be taken if such levels are not satisfactory.

Strengths and limitations of the tool

This tool is useful to underline the relationships among individuals, actors, and the system and organization; individuals are considered value-adding agents. It invites both sides to check if personal objectives are in line with organizational strategies amidst the numerous interrelationships. The tool helps to draws a parallel analysis of individual and organizational relationships, which provides a picture of climate—whether favorable or unfavorable. A limitation of the tool is that the relationships can be difficult to track and evaluate due to their volume and complexity.

Tool 14: The Technology Marketing Photograph guides the impact analysis

The Technology Marketing Photograph tool lists the technology factors that impact the marketing strategy. First, it contains the impact on the products—functions, performance, cost, and ergonomics. Second, it details the impact on the customer relations, and third, on new market accessibility. It lists the technology metrics used to assess the value of each. For example, precision is a metric of the GPS (global positioning system), or the consumption of an electric motor technology. It points out the technologies that disappear due to the appearance of a new technology, as well as the impact on other associated technologies. Finally, it shows which competitive company possesses the technology and a potential acquisition process, including partners and necessary lobbying.

TABLE 3.1 *The Technology Marketing Photograph*.

Technology name	
Impact of the technology	On the product or service functions
	On the product performances
	On the ergonomy
	On the costs
	On the customer relation
	On market accessibility
Technology metrics	
Substituted technologies	
Associated technologies and platform impact	
Competitors that have mastered the technology	
Technology acquisition model	
Suppliers and other possible partners	
Lobbying necessity	

How to use the tool?

Despite its apparent simplicity, this tool is not easy to use because it is difficult to anticipate the impact of technology with yearly precision. The buzz generated by the new technologies—enthusiasm followed by disillusion and forget—blurs visibility. The tool can be used with the Delphi Method. First, find experts in the technology. Second, choose different topics proposed by the tool and seek experts' opinions. Then, conduct a triangulation of responses (i.e., common responses are identified and a common vision is developed) and give the results to the experts. Next, administer the quiz again so that experts can provide their answers to the same questions. The second triangulation serves as the final result.

Strengths and limitations of the tool

This tool translates technology jargon and complex descriptions into a list of factors, helping to identify opportunities to use technology. A limitation of the tool is that it requires collaboration from experts and marketing managers in order to evaluate the product, market, and resources. Networking is a key marketing activity.

Tool 15: The Competition Value Proposition Photograph supports a comparison of offers and customer benefits

DEFINITIONS

Product value is customers' perceptions of the benefits of a product. *Customer value* is the future profit generated by a customer. The *benefit* is a generic positive impact on customers due to a purchase. An *advantage* is a contextual positive impact of one purchase to one customer.

The Competition Value Proposition Photograph aims at a thorough understanding of competitive offers and their benefits. The tool is divided into four parts. The first part describes the different factors linked to products and services, starting with the range and scope and ending with the services linked to products. The second lists the pricing tactics. The third and fourth parts detail the support to users and buyers. The description is not limited to a product feature and performance comparison, but rather, extends to other factors appreciated by buyers. The tool pushes to analyze what may influence buyers' value consideration and decisions. For some actors, such as distributors, factors such as the range perimeter are more important than the product features.

TABLE 3.2 *Description Criteria of Products And Services (Examples).*

PRODUCTS AND SERVICES	PRICING	CUSTOMER SUPPORT TO USER
•Height: segments covered	•Standard catalog price	•Garanties
•Depth: redundant products	•Free products or services	•Training
•Width: complementary products	•Commission	•Hotline
•Product features & options	•Pay-per-use pricing	•Consultancy
•Product performance	•Discounts to volume	•Information feedback
•Infrastructure support	•Discounts to annual purchase	•Product management
•Compatibilities	•Discount bracket	•Community of practice
•Customization	•Discounts on duration	•Facility
•Certifications	•Packages of several products	•Storage
SERVICES LINKED TO PRODUCTS	•Payment terms	**SUPPORT TO BUYER**
•Delivery	•Lease interest	•Project definition
•Installation	•Premium service price	•Project management
•Start-up	•Guaranties price	•Financing
•Integration and configuration		•Rental
•Online and on-site maintenance		•Fleet management
•Training		
•Guaranty of performance		

The pricing techniques are particularly rich in B2B. The calculation of discounts may vary according to many factors, which can be contractual or not. The competitive pricing analysis is often difficult due to the secrecy of negotiations. Users and buyer supports often involve major purchase decision criteria. The comparison of competitors' value proposition is efficient if the attributes of the offer are translated into generic benefits, and for each customer into its specific advantages. This tool combines the three lists. The marketing specifications, in particular, should describe the attributes and average benefits to the customers of the aimed segment.

TABLE 3.3 *Defining Advantage And Benefits From Features (Example).*

ATTRIBUTES	ADVANTAGES	BENEFITS
o Performance 　o Speed 　o Size 　o Weight 　o ... o Functions o Ergonomy o Design o Quality o Customization o Flexibility o Modules o Price o ...	o Image o Time o Security o Health o Comfort o Money o Cash o Revenue o Risk reduction o Customer satisfaction o Employee engagement o ...	o We save 1 hour a day o We save 2 euros per unit o It will be adapted to 45 employees o It will avoid $3,000 in recovery costs a year o Customer loyalty should increase by 2% o ...

How to use the tool?

The way to use the tool is to have three sources of information: (a) competitor and other publications, (b) customer interviews, and (c) feedback from the sales force. For each source of information, the questions for each item are asked. Results should be carefully separated by customer segments in order to understand preferences and differences.

Strengths and limitations of the tool

This tool offers a wider perspective on the performance of competitors than a pure product comparison. A limitation of the tool is that it is necessary to track competitive price. Also, a lot of customer support today is provided to buyers in a personal way, such as on password-protected websites. This can make it difficult to obtain the information.

Tool 16: The Value Disciplines Model compares company performance with competition

DEFINITIONS

Customer intimacy is the ability to know the customer organization and employees well enough to quickly, appropriately, and accurately respond to their needs. A Kano survey (Kano, Seraku, Takahashi, & Tsuji, 1984) is a questionnaire used to evaluate the importance, preference, indifference, or opposition to each feature of a product, service, or support.

The Value Disciplines Model of Treacy and Wiersema (1995) proposes three general factors for comparing the marketing performance of competitors. First, Product Leadership includes all efforts to differentiate the product, propose unique selling propositions, and master the technologies. The second discipline is Operational Excellence, which refers to the competency to perform activities in the supply chain, best cost of production and delivery, lean processes, and elimination of quality issues. The last factor is the Customer Intimacy, or proximity to the customer, which is visible through the number of contacts and by mutual understanding of the common value (Brock & Zhou, 2012). Intimacy with the customer helps to improve short-term responsiveness to customer events, as well as long-term adaptability to market changes.

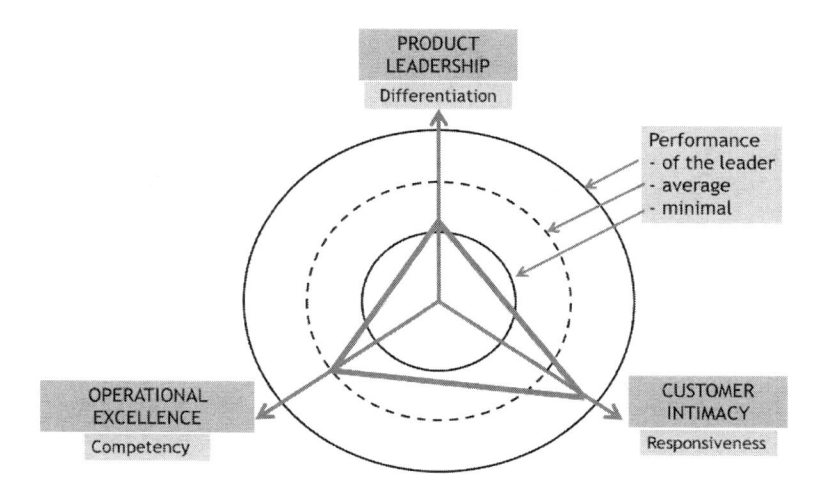

FIGURE 3.3 *The Value Disciplines Model.*

How to use the tool?

The model utilizes a two-step strategy. First, customer insights and preferences are evaluated using a list of items that define the three dimensions of the enterprise's field of business. This can be done with a Kano-type of survey. Then, customer preferences trigger the choice of discipline in which the company should be a leader. In the two other disciplines, performance needs to be above average.

Strengths and limitations of the tool

This tool serves as opportunity to compare competitors in a market with two additional criteria, beyond the product and service feature differences. With Operational Excellence, other dimensions—such as product quality, time to deliver, response time, mean time between failures (MTBF), mean time to repair (MTTR), customer satisfaction net promoter score (NPS), etc.—appear. With Customer Intimacy, performance includes tracking customer behavior, understanding needs, and including customers at each step of the new product process. Valuable customer intimacy translates into product modification and customization, one-to-one customer relationships, and partnerships that promote global solutions. The limitation of this tool is the ability to identify the criteria of each discipline and to measure competitors' performance within the proposed dimensions.

CHAPTER 4
HOW TO MAKE A MODEL OF B2B CUSTOMER BEHAVIOR

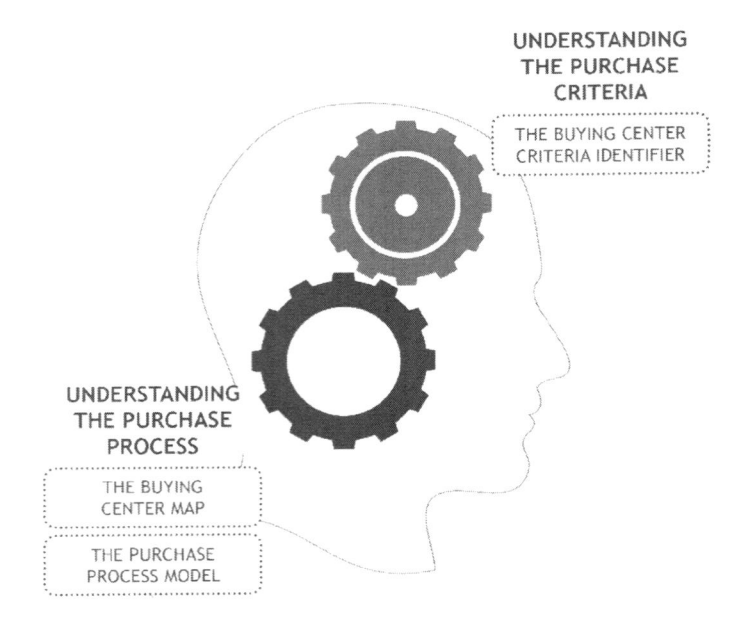

UNDERSTANDING THE PURCHASE CRITERIA
- THE BUYING CENTER CRITERIA IDENTIFIER

UNDERSTANDING THE PURCHASE PROCESS
- THE BUYING CENTER MAP
- THE PURCHASE PROCESS MODEL

The B2B customer is an organization, which most of time has appointed persons and assigned processes for purchase activities. Understanding customer behavior cannot be avoided, as it will determine all operational marketing and sales activities of the supplier.

What is specific to B2B?

B2B customer behavior can be similar to a B2C purchase for some low price, low volume, and non-critical products. In other cases, specific elements emerge and vary substantially, including the following:
- the number of people consulted by the purchase manager is higher,
- the number of people who consent to the agreement is higher,
- the procedure of purchase is written and controlled,

- all purchases are documented and registered, and
- the phases of the purchase are organized.

Thus, in order to model customer behavior, the decision criteria must be understood, then the purchase contributors and process. Three tools are proposed to model this behavior.

Understanding the purchase criteria
- Tool 17: The Buying Center Criteria Identifier

Understanding the purchase process
- Tool 18: The Buying Center Map
- Tool 19: The Purchase Process Model

Tool 17: The Buying Center Criteria Identifier lists customer motivations for decision-making

DEFINITIONS

The *buying center* is the group of individuals that contributes to the purchase process. The *total cost of ownership* (TOC) is the sum of the purchased products, services, consumables, and internal costs triggered by the purchase—such as training, reorganization, or insurance.

The Buying Center Criteria Identifier is a tool that has to be defined for each person in the buying center. It lists decision criteria across five categories (Blythe & Zimmerman, 2011). The buying center must be identified by the salesperson. The status of the buying center is determined with a consolidated picture of all its members. Five groups of criteria may exist, but vary according to the buyers' business field and context. The first list concerns the identity of the selling company, such as size and characteristics. The second focuses on the value proposition, including the product range width, which demonstrates the extent to which needs are covered. The third deals with the financial aspects of the proposition, including total cost of ownership. The fourth deals with customer relations. Finally, the last deals with delivery abilities, such as the area covered and deployment.

COMPANY:	PERSON:	

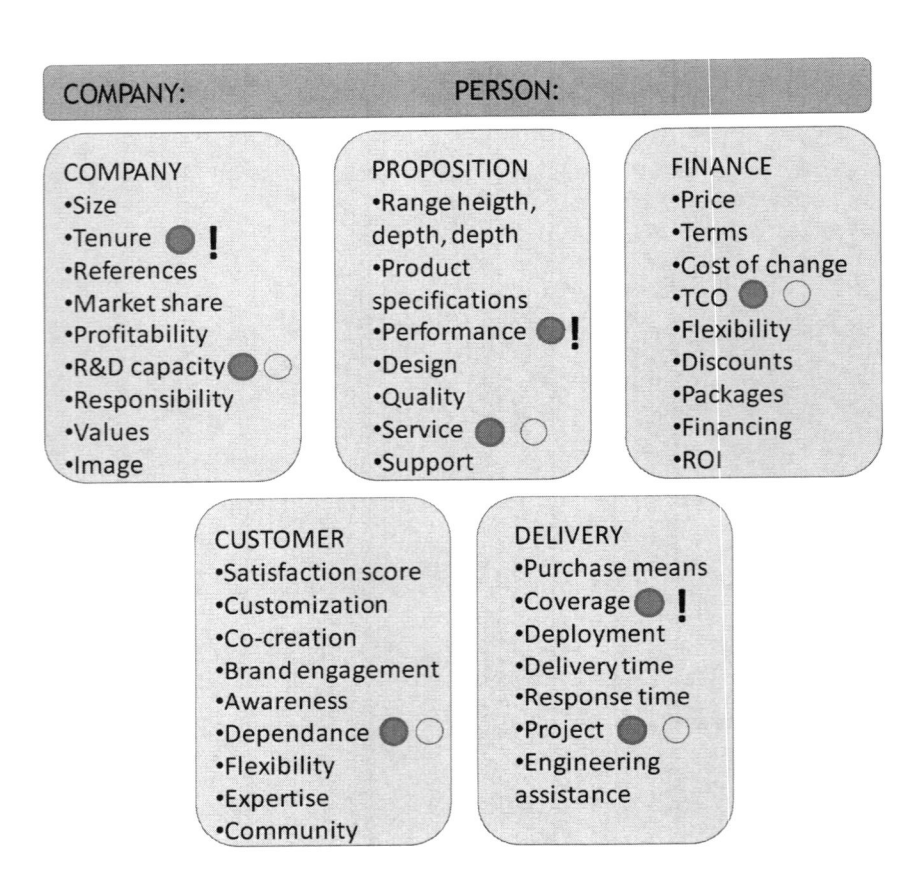

COMPANY
- Size
- Tenure ●!
- References
- Market share
- Profitability
- R&D capacity ●○
- Responsibility
- Values
- Image

PROPOSITION
- Range heigth, depth, depth
- Product specifications
- Performance ●!
- Design
- Quality
- Service ●○
- Support

FINANCE
- Price
- Terms
- Cost of change
- TCO ●○
- Flexibility
- Discounts
- Packages
- Financing
- ROI

CUSTOMER
- Satisfaction score
- Customization
- Co-creation
- Brand engagement
- Awareness
- Dependance ●○
- Flexibility
- Expertise
- Community

DELIVERY
- Purchase means
- Coverage ●!
- Deployment
- Delivery time
- Response time
- Project ●○
- Engineering assistance

FIGURE 4.1 *The Buying Center Criteria Identifier.* ● = Important; ○ Decision maker has a positive opinion of the supplier of this item; ! Decision maker has a negative opinion.

In the case in Figure 4.1, the person in the buying center is motivated by R&D capacity, performance, service, total cost of ownership, technical dependence, area coverage, and project management. The selling company has an issue with product performance and coverage.

How to use the tool?

The tool is used by conducting direct consultation with customers and the sales force. The first step is to identify the buying center, and then for each member, identify their criteria. If segmentation is based on the sales process, the results will be homogeneous inside the segments. If it has been made with other criteria, the results will be heterogeneous and data will be drawn from a larger sample.

Strengths and limitations of the tool

The criteria identifier is powerful to understand a business. It varies according to the segments and each customer. It is helpful at the global marketing level and at the local sales deal level. Ongoing evaluation is needed because members of the buying center constantly change their minds.

Tool 18: The Buying Center Map defines the multiple roles of the purchase process participants

DEFINITIONS

The buying center, also called also the *decision making unit* (DMU), is the group of persons who participate in the customer purchase process, whether internal or external to the company. The *initiator* is the person who requests the equipment and generates the purchase process. The *decision maker* is a person who must give his or her agreement to allow the purchase. The *influencer* influences the members of the buying center without being a decision maker. The *sherpa* is the person who shares contacts to help navigate inside the company. The *specifications* are the product abilities.

The Buying Center Map is an essential tool for sales people and marketing managers to understand who is involved in the deal. It details the different roles of the buying center members, while recognizing that most often an individual plays several roles. The roles include the initiator, who requests that a purchase be surveyed; the purchase manager, who is responsible for the purchase procedure and negotiation; the Sherpa, who provides the contacts; the influencer; the absolute influencer; and the decision maker. The decision makers are often groups of individuals; they generally sign an internal document to agree upon the purchase. The purchase manager is always in charge of the procedure and the negotiation, but is not always a decision maker. In addition to the roles, the criteria of choice and information need of members are included.

INDIVIDUALS / ROLES	INTERNAL					EXTERNAL	
	Purch.	R&D	Produc.	IT	CTO	IT Service	Supplier Partner
Initiator		X					
Resp. of procedure	X						
Negociator	X				X		
User		X	X				X
Sherpa	X						
Influencer		X	X	X		X	
Absolute influencer				X			
Decision maker		X	X	X	X		X
Criteria of choice	Credibili. price	functions ergonomy	Perform. connectivity	Compatib. integration	Parten. prix	language	functions ergonomy
Information need	References	Functional specifi.	Technical specifi.	Architechture	Transformation	Technical specif.	Functional specif.

FIGURE 4.2 *The Buying Center Map.*

Figure 4.2 is an example of a buying center map for PLM (Product Life Management), a software used by R&D, production, and two external companies. In this case, the purchase manager is responsible for the purchase procedure, the negotiation, and for acting as the sherpa. The manager's criteria are supplier credibility and price. The IT director and the chief technical officer are not users of the product, but have key roles. The former is looking for compatible software for his existing infrastructure, and for easy integration. He or she needs information on the architecture of the software. The latter is watching the price and the possible extension of partnership to other suppliers. He or she wants to know the details of the company transformation, which are needed prior to implementation. The R&D director needs detailed specifications of the product.

How to use the tool?

If their experience is extensive enough, the sales force is the population that should provide the information in the tool. Consultation with customers is the second, complementary method. After generating the content, the tool can be used to train the new sales people; to determine who will help them to answer to the buying center members; and to generate blueprints of customer relations, sales tools, and communication messages.

Strengths and limitations of the tool

This tool provides the salesperson with a comprehensive view of the deal, so that he or she can prepare the best tactics. It is valuable for marketing managers to decide who must be contacted and with what information. A limitation of the tool is that there are numerous roles that are constantly changing. In practice, the salesperson must identify the main players. The marketing managers focus on the most important roles and provide only the most pertinent information to sales personnel.

Tool 19: The Purchase Process Model describes the phases of the deal

DEFINITIONS

The *RFI* is the Request for Information. It is the first document of a tender and asks suppliers interested in a deal to contact the customer and complete the company information. The *RFQ* is the Request for Quotation or *RFP*, Request for Proposal. It is the second document of a tender and asks for a detailed offer and prices to respond to a specific need. The *POC*, Proof of Concept, is a test of the product in real life by the customer before purchasing.

The Purchase Process Model is applied to a deal analysis by the salesperson, and to a global sales phase analysis by marketing managers. It shows the participation of all buying center members in each phase of the deal. For example, the first phase is generally the need identification. The responsibility of the purchase manager is often to coordinate the phases, conduct consultation, publish RFI and RFP, organize decision meetings, process the ordering, check the delivery, and manage payment. The purchase manager often writes the specifications of the product or service with consultation from a number of people. He or she selects a few suppliers with the RFI, then publishes the RFQ to get proposals. The purchase manager will compare the offers, negotiate, choose, and eventually request a POC before purchasing. Later, the buyer may coordinate an evaluation of the product, service, and supplier after purchasing and using the product or service.

INDIVIDUALS / PHASES	INTERNAL					EXTERNAL	
	Purch	R&D	Produc.	IT	CTO	IT Service	Supplier Partner
Need identification	X	X		X			X
Specification	X	X	X	X		X	X
Search suppliers RFI	X	X					
Short list selection	X	X	X		X		
Tender RFQ	X						
Negotiation	X						
Choice	X	X	X	X	X		X
Test POC		X	X	X		X	X
Purchase	X						
Use		X	X	X		X	X
Evaluation	X	X	X	X		X	X

FIGURE 4.3 *The Purchase Process Model.*

Figure 4.3 uses the same example as the Buying Center Map. We can see that the choice was made in a meeting that included a supplier of the company who will also use the product. The salesperson will have to contact this supplier and provide him or her with information. In the same way, the POC will be critical and will involve the IT service company. The marketing manager will train the sales force in this process and communicate with customers, IT service companies, and specific suppliers.

How to use the tool?

Content for the tool is generated by consulting with sales personnel with extensive experience as well as customers. The two sources of data provide a better understanding of the process. The result is used in the training of the new sales force, and in the design of the blueprint for customer contacts, which can be electronic or physical.

Strengths and limitations of the tool

This tool models the purchase process and provides a general model for customers and suppliers. It allows for easy analysis of the progression of the deal, critical milestones, and participants' roles at each phase. Nonetheless, the process is not always clear, and can be designed by customers at the time of the deal. It can be an opportunity for the sales force to propose the process. It is necessary for the buyer to be in agreement regarding the general model of the purchase; however, other buying center members may view the process differently. Thus, the model may vary based on different viewpoints.

CHAPTER 5

HOW TO ANALYZE THE INTERNAL STATUS OF THE COMPANY AND SYNTHESIZE

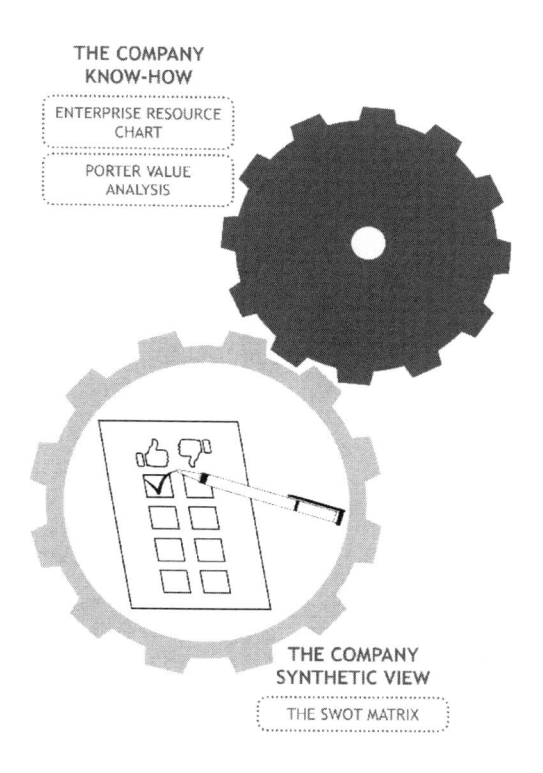

THE COMPANY KNOW-HOW
- ENTERPRISE RESOURCE CHART
- PORTER VALUE ANALYSIS

THE COMPANY SYNTHETIC VIEW
- THE SWOT MATRIX

Internal analysis of the company is essential to building the marketing strategy. The company know-how and abilities must be regularly evaluated. Any marketing program profits from the know-how of the company. Through internal analysis, the company can check the extent to which resources match the operational objectives.

What is specific to B2B?

Some activities are different in B2B than B2C. They can be underdeveloped, overdeveloped, or totally different. The following are examples of the differences:
- R&D activity is often more important,
- production includes more ability to customize,
- more technologies are utilized,
- the logistics are more complex,
- distribution includes multiple formats
- interrelationships with customers are more frequent, and
- mass communication is less important.

This chapter proposes three tools to identify the know-how and create a synthetic internal and external model of the company.

The company know-how
- Tool 20: The Enterprise Resource Chart
- Tool 21: The Porter Value Analysis

Synthetic model of the company
- Tool 22: The SWOT Matrix

Tool 20: The Enterprise Resource Chart lists the company's key abilities

DEFINITIONS

The *core competencies* of an enterprise are the technical knowledge bases needed to differentiate the business and employ the business model (Hamel & Prahalad, 1996). A *key performance indicator* (KPI) is a business metric used to evaluate activities that impact the success of the enterprise.

Internal analysis of the company includes defining its abilities and core competencies. The Enterprise Resource Chart guides this analysis by providing 10 resource items. Quantitative measurements are necessary as well as qualitative information. For example, an R&D resource is the number of patents in the intellectual property portfolio, as well as the types of technological problems solved by the patents. In B2B, the ability to conclude partnerships can be considered a strength, and it is critical to building a performing distribution network. The IT

infrastructure has become a key strategic asset to future projects. Multiple sources of revenue and profit also serve as a framework for the enterprise abilities.

Revenue	Revenue sources, growth, recurrence
Profit	EBIT, profit per revenue source, EBIT variation factors
Human Resource	Manpower, expertise, organization ability, learning capacity
Partners	Technological, product, service, marketing alliances
R & D	Patents, engineers, design equipment, budget
IT infrastructure	Servers or cloud, database, ERP & CRM performance
Manufacturing	Production means, productivity, quality, flexibility
Marketing	Image, awareness, communication know-how, budget
Distribution	Sales people, distribution abilities, coverage, market share
Logistics	Performance, delivery time, stocks levels, costs

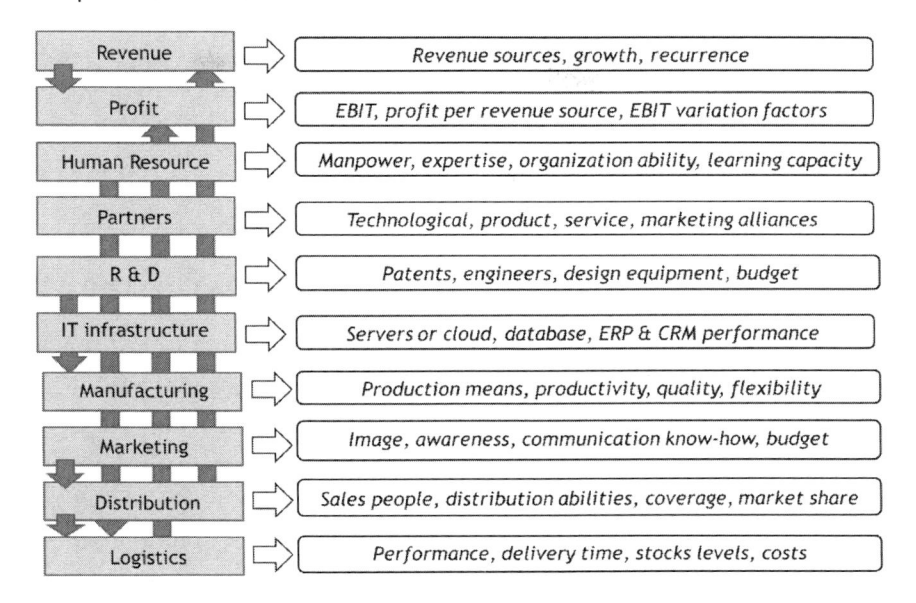

FIGURE 5.1 *The Enterprise Resource Chart.*

This resource analysis can be seen with different perspective. First as a budget capacity, including R&D budget, marketing budget, etc. Second, it can be seen in terms of competences—technological, sales, HR management, etc. The core competences include five to 10 competencies that differentiate the company from its competitors. Third, it can be seen as a capacity to partner when the competence exists but is not internal.

How to use the tool?

In a first phase, the 10 resources are globally evaluated; some of them can be non-relevant and suppressed, while others can be added according to the business field. Analysis should concentrate only on important resources, not resources that are easy to get or buy. In the second step, the KPIs of the resources are chosen. Then, internal documentary research and interviews are performed. Finally, the results are compared against a benchmark, usually a competitor or other companies successfully utilizing similar resources. For example, the quality of manufacturing can be compared to top players.

57

Strengths and limitations of the tool

This tool is helpful for displaying the enterprise know-how and defining its strengths. After utilizing this tools, programs can be identified to better manage risk. A limitation of the tool is the process, which requires extensive evaluation from a range of experts.

Tool 21: The Porter Value Chain helps to identify the added value of the enterprise

DEFINITIONS

The *value addition chain* is a chain of activities that a firm employs in a specific industry in order to deliver a valuable product or service to the market (Porter, 1985).

After using the Enterprise Resource Chart, the Porter Value Chain identifies the heart of activities—where added value is greatest. Activities that have poor value addition should either be improved or outsourced to a more efficient partner. The activities are separated into primary and support activities. Porter used one area for both marketing and sales. In many B2B companies, sales and marketing are preferably separated into two value blocks. The procurement and partnership area was added to this model because these activities are essential to B2B; online and onsite services and administrative finance and IT infrastructures were separated.

Support activities	Admin, finance, IT Infrastructure					
	Human resource					
	Product and technology developement					*Margin*
	Procurement & Partnership					
Primary activities	Inbound logistics	Production	Outbound logistics	Sales Marketing	Servicing Onsite Online	

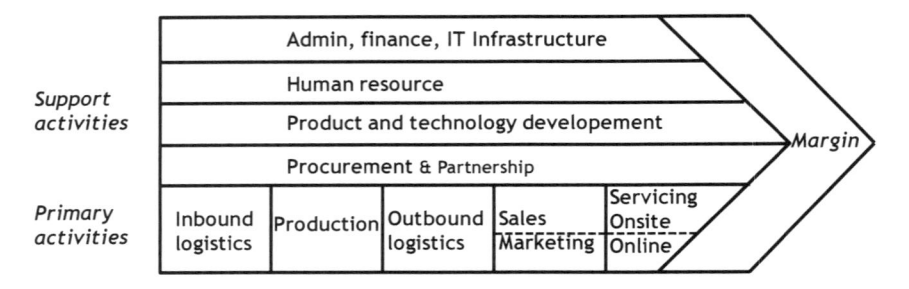

FIGURE 5.2 *The Porter Value Chain.*

The list of the activities can be completed; the position of the activities as support or primary should be listed according to the business field. In the engineering or construction business, companies are selling projects. They sell before producing, so *sales and marketing* and *outbound logistics* could be positioned before *production*.

How to use the tool?

The value chain is analyzed using research on the company processes and management. Use of the tool requires document analysis and interviews with company practitioners. A benchmark can be completed with companies performing similar activities. Once a picture of the company's best know-how is developed, it can be further defined for each business unit.

Strengths and limitations of the tool

The tool is easy to grasp, and is a powerful way to analyze the know-how of the enterprise. Conducting the exercise offers an in-depth view of added value compared to the competition and best-in-class companies. Benchmarks should be identified. For example, it may be more fruitful to analyze large distribution companies as a benchmark for value addition than the competition. A limitation of the tool is that it requires the mobilization of many expert resources.

Tool 22: The SWOT Matrix synthesizes the analyses and suggests strategic directions

The SWOT Matrix is the most popular decision tool used in companies (Hill & Westbrook, 1997). It synthesizes the different analyses and triggers strategies. The internal analysis is summarized in two parts: strengths and weaknesses. The external analysis is summarized in opportunities and threats. These four categories include many possible topics, both internally—R&D, product range, distribution, services, logistics, brand, etc.—and externally—competition, market, customer behavior, etc. The tool influences decisions based on the status of the

59

company. If the weaknesses and threats are important, the company has to protect its actual business and take actions to remove weaknesses and prevent threats. If the company weaknesses and threats are limited, the company can use its strengths and seize the opportunities.

	STRENGTHS	WEAKNESSES
Internal analysis		
External analysis	OPPORTUNITIES	THREATS
	Offensive Opportunities	Defensive Reactions

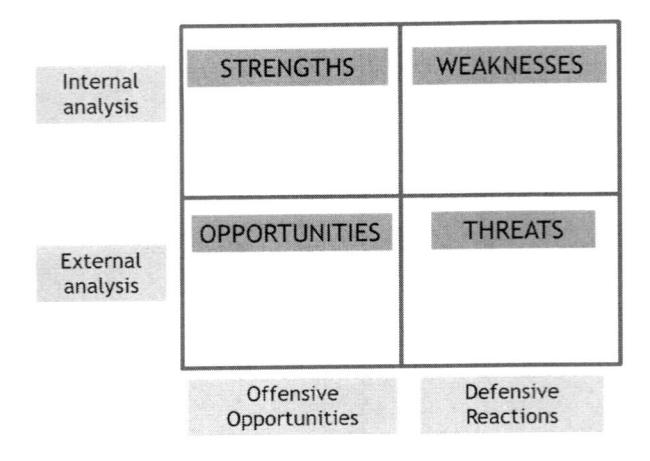

FIGURE 5.3 *The SWOT Matrix.*

How to use the tool?

In the first phase, the external environment is analyzed, and separated into threats and opportunities. In order to avoid confusion, the threats are potentially negative factors influencing the business from the outside; they should not be considered as opportunities that are possible extensions of the business. In order to limit the number of items, they can be rated by importance so that resources and programs focus on the main priorities.

Strengths and limitations of the tool

The SWOT Matrix is mostly used at the global level. The matrix contains all the points of the two analyzes. It is powerful, but may contain too many points. Limits are necessary in order to focus on the most important elements. In order to reach the final result, another way to use the SWOT Matrix is to repeat the exercise per topic; strengths, weaknesses, opportunities, and threats can be analyzed for technologies, the full range, a single product, the distribution, a segment, a country, etc. The final matrix should include the most important points from each SWOT analysis.

CHAPTER 6

HOW TO SELECT THE GLOBAL COMPANY STRATEGY

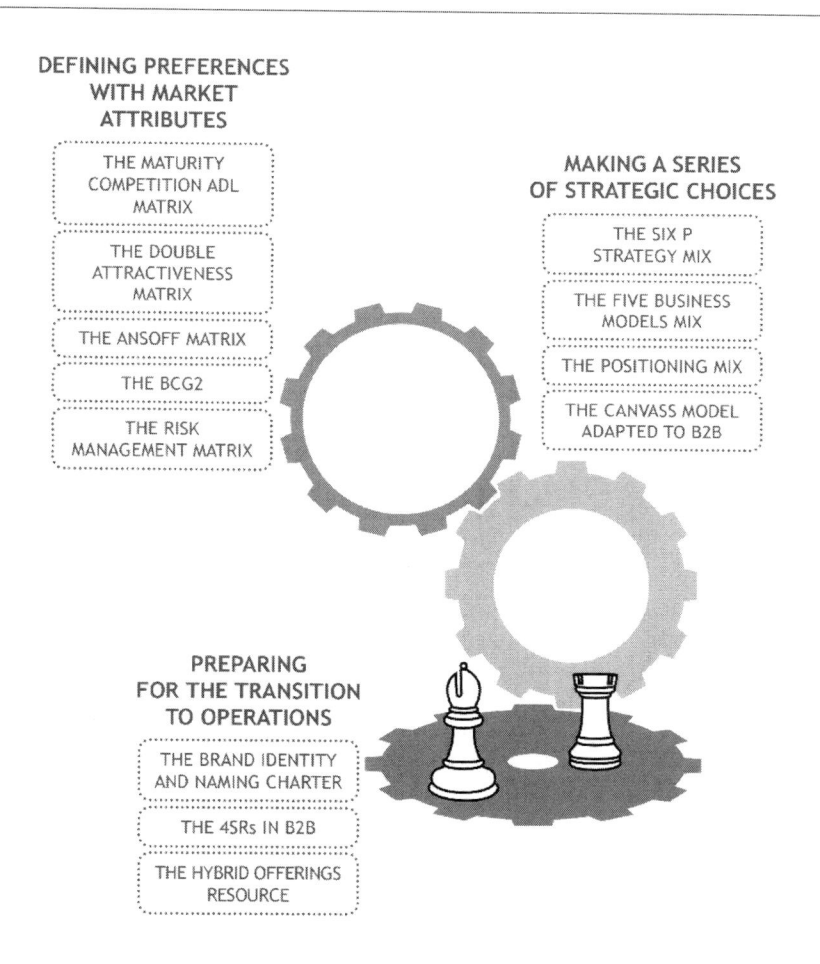

DEFINING PREFERENCES WITH MARKET ATTRIBUTES
- THE MATURITY COMPETITION ADL MATRIX
- THE DOUBLE ATTRACTIVENESS MATRIX
- THE ANSOFF MATRIX
- THE BCG2
- THE RISK MANAGEMENT MATRIX

MAKING A SERIES OF STRATEGIC CHOICES
- THE SIX P STRATEGY MIX
- THE FIVE BUSINESS MODELS MIX
- THE POSITIONING MIX
- THE CANVASS MODEL ADAPTED TO B2B

PREPARING FOR THE TRANSITION TO OPERATIONS
- THE BRAND IDENTITY AND NAMING CHARTER
- THE 4SRs IN B2B
- THE HYBRID OFFERINGS RESOURCE

Building a marketing strategy primarily involves defining the target market segments, the products and services, and the revenue and profit sources. Many tools have been proposed by research that can be applied to B2B as well as B2C marketing.

What is specific to B2B?

B2B activities offer more options. For example, technology is more prevalent, so tools are proposed to track the maturity level. Revenue often comes from a mix of products and services, so the tools must include multiple sources. Product and company positioning options are larger. The traditional 4Ps (Kotler, 1972; McCarthy, 1960) do not fully apply to business markets. For example, the term "place" is not applicable, as most of time the customer does not go to the supplier premises.

Strategic marketing includes two main activities: (a) defining preferences according to market attributes and making strategic choices, and (b) preparing the transition to operations. These activities are supported by using 12 tools.

Defining preferences with market attributes
- Tool 23: The Maturity-Competition ADL Matrix
- Tool 24: The Dual Attractiveness Matrix
- Tool 25: The Ansoff Matrix
- Tool 26: The BCG2
- Tool 27: The Risk Management Matrix

Making a series of strategic choices
- Tool 28: The Six P Strategy Mix
- Tool 29: The Five Business Models Mix
- Tool 30: The Positioning Mix
- Tool 31: The Canvass Model Adapted to B2B

Preparing for the transition to operations
- Tool 32: The Brand Identity and Naming Charter
- Tool 33: The 4Rs of B2B
- Tool 34: The Hybrid Offerings Resource and Competence Links

Tool 23: The Maturity-Competition ADL Matrix suggests when to invest or disinvest

DEFINITIONS

The *installed base* is the number of products in use by customers. A customer installed base is the number of products in use by a single customer.

The opportunity to invest in the existing business of an enterprise depends on specific criteria. The Maturity-Competition Matrix, or ADL Matrix (Armstrong, 1996), focuses on the maturity of the market (i.e., its potential growth, flatness or short-term decline, and its competitive position). When maturity is high, the tool suggests to invest if the competitive position is strong (harvest) and to disinvest if the position is weak. On the other hand, if the market is young, it proposes investing if the position is strong and either investing or stopping investment if the position is weak.

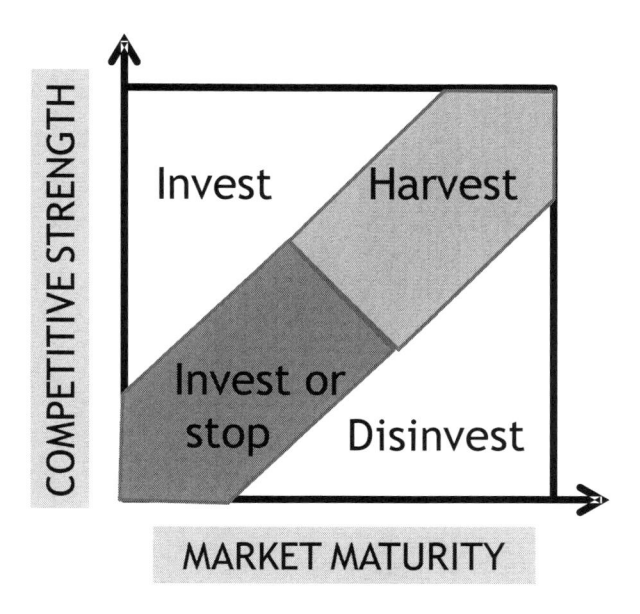

FIGURE 6.1 The Maturity-Competition Matrix.

In B2B, the long duration of market maturity has to be taken into account. The market take-off can last many years, and during this time, it should not be considered as flat. The growth may be pushed by other factors, such as regulation.

How to use the tool?

The competitive strengths and maturity levels need to be defined with descriptive factors specific to the business field. For example, market share, installed base, product differentiation, and prices can be used for competitive strengths. Size, number of users, growth, and so on, can be used to define maturity levels. Then, positioning is determined for the program of investment. The global picture provided by the tool allows for a comparison of the programs.

Strengths and limitations of the tool

This tool forces marketing managers to evaluate market evolution in relation to the competition in order to identify options for future decisions. It considers maturity and competitive strength to be uniform in the market. This may not be the case for enterprises that have a "sanctuary" location, where they have a strong market share and the market is mature, nor in the opposite location in which the market is late and the presence is poor. Thus, a matrix per area or segment may be necessary.

Tool 24: The Dual Attractiveness Matrix helps to optimize the customer-enterprise fit

The Dual Attractiveness Matrix examines the attractiveness of an activity from both the customer and enterprise perspective. For each factor, a specific list of evaluation metrics is made. Revenue, investment level, margin, generated profit, new technology learning, and so on, can help to measure the attractiveness to the enterprise. Intention to buy, potential satisfaction, and process cost reduction are among the motivations of the customer. The matrix shows that the investment can be made when attractiveness on both sides is high, and stopped when it is low on both sides. When only customer attractiveness is high, the company will lose money and another business model has to be invented to monetize customer interest. When only the enterprise attractiveness is high, the marketing manager has to change the value proposition so that the company becomes more attractive to customers.

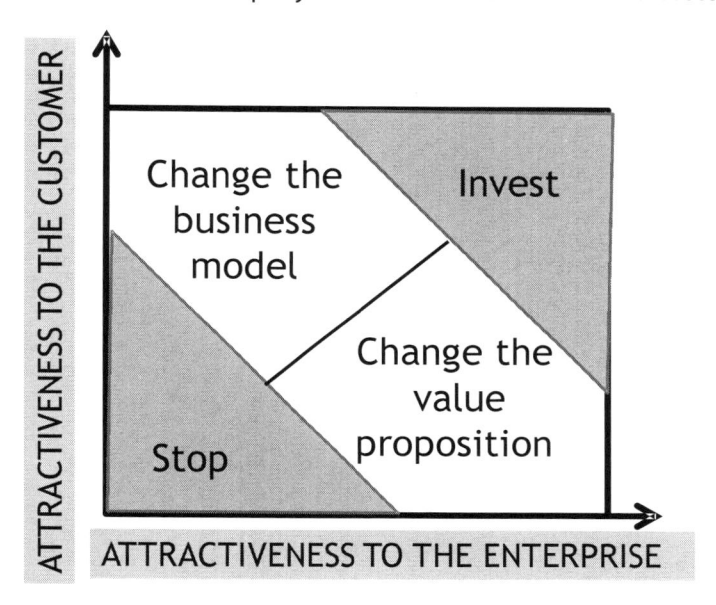

FIGURE 6.2 *The Dual Attractiveness Matrix.*

Change of value proposition is a common B2B marketing exercise because changing a business model is more difficult and also requires a change in organizational culture.

How to use the tool?

In the first phase, the indicators of attractiveness for both sides are defined and the company products are positioned in the matrix. Then, the new product programs are also positioned in the matrix. Next, detailed business models are generated for the top left programs and a change in value proposition is proposed for the bottom right programs. Finally, at the end, the matrix is repositioned.

Strengths and limitations of the tool

This tool can be used for the total business of the enterprise, or for a product line, product, or project. It can be used for the whole market, or a specific segment. It requires executives' agreement regarding the two types of attractiveness. A limitation of the tool is that the ability to measure attractiveness may be challenging due to the additional know-how required; insight on customer behavior may be needed to make precise sales forecasts, evaluate costs, predict profits.

Tool 25: The Ansoff Matrix helps measure new product risk levels

The Ansoff Matrix (Ansoff, 1987) is a tool that helps to measure the level of risk of strategic marketing activities. It uses two dimensions: (a) the target of existing or new customers, and (b) the new or existing products. If its activities are limited to existing products and customers (Area A), risk is short-term and limited. If the activities focus on new products to existing customers, the main risk is technical (Area B), as the customer needs and profiles are well-known. If the activities are centered on new customers with existing products (Area C), the risk concerns marketing and sales investments. Finally, if the marketing is centered on new customers and new products (Area D), the risk is at the maximum level. Such risks should be reconsidered.

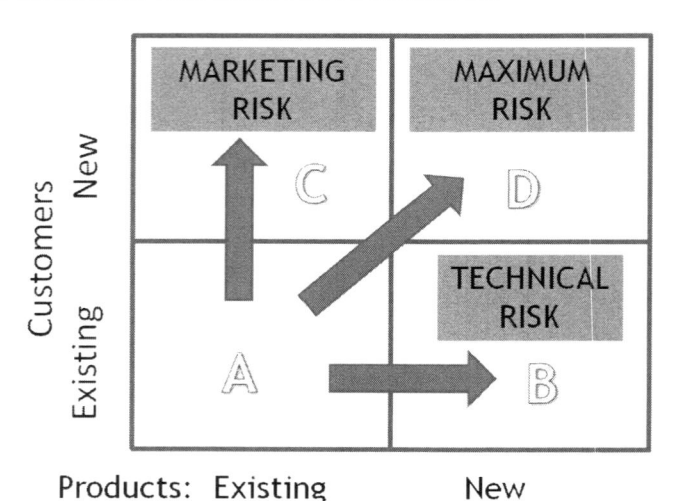

FIGURE 6.3 *The Ansoff Matrix.*

How to use the tool?

In the first step, the total market is evaluated for each area of the matrix. Then, each company program needs to be agreed upon with criteria that allow for measuring revenue. This includes a knowledge of customers in the borders of the existing market. For example, for low-end customers, buying capacity is at the limit—above or below target customers. Lastly, the evaluation of the risk is made for each program.

Strengths and limitations of the tool

The tool is very simple and any activity can be seen within the two dimensions. The tool aids in designing company strategy by helping the company to question the type and level of risk it wants to take. A mix of A-B-C activities in the four types ensures revenue and profit (in Square A), technical progress (in Square B), and marketing and sales progress (in Square C). The tool considers existing customers to be static, and existing products are profitable when customers are stable. This may be a limitation in some industries in which adapting to existing customers is a permanent but necessary risk that could be lowered by obtaining new customers; change of product is necessary in order to lower risk. For example, changing from a large- to medium-sized company could be a risk reduction.

Tool 26: The BCG2 Matrix helps to manage differentiation

DEFINITIONS

Differentiation is the way in which a company makes a different value proposition to customers compared to the competition. Differentiation factors are more numerous in B2B marketing. They include not only the performance and features of products, but also their applications, customization, and ergonomics. For instance, the same professional high performance glue for metal can be differentiated when adapted for use with different types of metal. User support, quality of sales, and technical relations are differentiators. The method of deployment for a solution can also make a difference.

The BCG2 Matrix of the Boston Consulting Group (Armstrong, 1994) uses two product variables: (a) competitive advantage, and (b) differentiation opportunity. The tool helps to choose the level of specialization and the market covered. Determining the strength of each variable will aid in adopting different policies. A strong competitive advantage with weak differentiation opportunity corresponds with a volume and cost strategy. By contrast, a strong competitive advantage with strong differentiation opportunities triggers specializations in all the different segments. A weak competitive advantage with strong differentiation opportunities can limit strategy to niche markets. If successful, this strategy would allow movement to more segments—toward the specialization cell. The same position with weak differentiation opportunities represents a dilemma status(i.e.,predictable_abandonment).

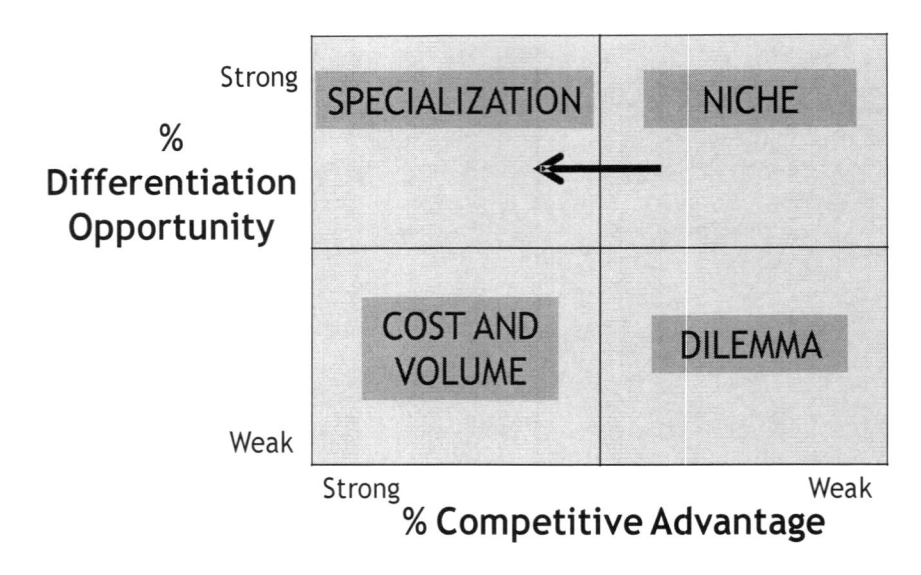

FIGURE 6.4 *The BCG2 Matrix.*

This tool provides a picture of differentiation abilities as well as the pathway from niche to specialization when the cost strategy is not profitable. For example, a color producer with many different applications could choose to focus or refocus on specific segments—print, textile, packaging, construction, etc.—before extending specialization to all segments.

How to use the tool?

First, a list of factors is built to describe the competitive advantages and the differentiation opportunity levels. Then, the existing value proposition and new programs are positioned in the matrix. Finally, the strategy of differentiation is debated for each program.

Strengths and limitations of the tool

The tool helps to define differentiation opportunities, but is limited to two variables. The BCG2 matrix suggests decisions that do not consider other variables such as market barriers, local legislation, or compulsory customization. Also, markets with small quantities are not sensitive to volume. Industries that have local customized markets cannot choose the cost and volume strategy. This tool is valuable when these other variables have lower impact on product strategy.

Tool 27: The Risk Management Matrix proposes a risk typology and tactics

DEFINITIONS

Intelligence is a program of business field analysis. It concerns competition, technology, partnerships, and so on.

The Risk Management Matrix is used to decide when it is necessary to allocate resources to address a foreseen risk. It proposes two criteria: (a) probability of the risk, and (b) importance of the risk. B2B strategy and marketing activities are more involved than in B2C because the complexity and origins of the risk are greater—including technology risk, product development risk, distribution risk, sustainable development risk, and regulation risk. This tool suggests that when both the probability and importance of the risk are low, the risk should be ignored. When the importance is high and the probability is low, risk should be anticipated. For example, a company begins lobbying to test the chance of a new technology before product development. If the importance is low, but the probability high, the company should adapt. This means that it must make incremental changes so that regularly encountered risks no longer hinder its processes. For example, regular turnover of the sales force may be cured by a permanent trainee school. Product misuse should be avoided by better ergonomics. The last type of risk occurs in cases when the importance is high and the probability is also high. In such instances, the company is in crisis and urgent action is needed: Company strategy and operations must be transformed. In B2B, the end of a patent—which attracts competitors to the market—is a typical case in which companies must generate important transformation programs to survive.

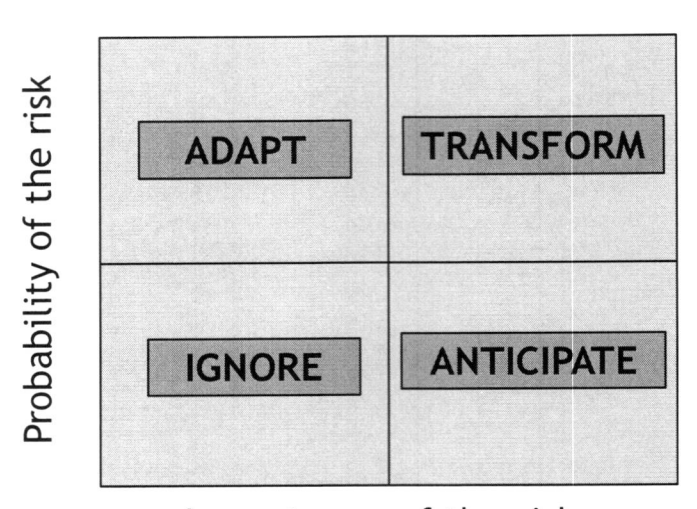

FIGURE 6.4 *The Risk Management Matrix.*

How to use the tool?

The list of possible risks is generated in the first phase, including physical, chemical, R&D, systemic, political, economical, customer, etc. The SPECTRED tool can be used for the external risks and the Value Chain tool for the internal risks. Then, risks are evaluated across the two dimensions using the company and competition experience, and interviews with experts. In the last phase, decisions are planned to change (or not change) programs.

Strengths and limitations of the tool

The risk Management Matrix is useful for identifying any type of risk. It serves as a practical way to decide immediate actions, make simple preparations, or refrain from actions associated with a particular risk. As the tool is focused on universal risk, it may be difficult to address specific questions such as the following: Do we know all of the risk? Do we accurately measure their importance? Do we accurately measure the probability of risk? Utilizing the tool may require having a large research program concerning competition, regulation, distribution, technologies, etc.

Tool 28: The Six P Strategy Mix proposes an array of strategy combinations

DEFINITIONS

Penetration is a strategy used to capture the maximum market share. *Coverage* is the market space in which the enterprise is able to sell to and provide services to customers. *Horizontal integration* is the strategy of buying competitors and capturing their market share. *Vertical integration* is the strategy of buying suppliers or customers to capture their profits or secure the relationship. *Skimming* is a strategy used by market leaders to keep high prices and maximize profit per customer.

The five frequently proposed growth strategies are as follows: (a) low price penetration, (b) high price skimming, (c) vertical integration, (d) horizontal integration, and (e) diversification. In B2B, these strategies can succeed by following specific factors. Technology is often most important. Customer need coverage and solution performance are also important factors due to the complexity of needs. The Six P Strategy Mix suggests six possible strategies and indicates that some combinations may generate synergies, while other combinations may be not possible.

TABLE 6.1 *The Six P Strategy.*

SIX P STRATEGIES	DESCRIPTION
Pull strategy • Customer-focused	The maximum customer needs are addressed with a large range width. Often chosen by distributors, this strategy maximizes the revenue per customer.
Push strategy • Technology-focused	The offerings are limited to products and services benefiting from mastered technologies, so that they are always on the cutting edge and ahead of competition. All segments where the technology applies are targeted.
Profit strategy • EBIT-focused • Possible vertical integration	The proposition is limited to profitable products and services, at the expense of revenue. Height and width are limited inside the market, but the range can be extended with acquisition upwards to components or downwards to more global solutions, as long as the EBIT is reached.
Performance strategy • Market driver-focused	The proposition is focused on a value to the customer, defined with a customer satisfaction driver, which corresponds to particular resources or know-how of the supplier. The range height and width are extended as long as the performance is met.
Price strategy • Market share strategy	The offerings are aggressively low priced in order to eliminate competition and increase market share. This strategy may be durable as long as it does not generate loss.
Place strategy • Coverage focused • Possible horizontal integration	This strategy looks for the largest market geographical coverage. It allows volume benefits and can include acquisitions of competitors in horizontal integration.

The penetration strategy corresponds with the price strategy, and the profit strategy corresponds with the skimming strategy. Horizontal integration is one possible place strategy. Vertical integration is one possible profit strategy. Pull and performance strategies are more present in B2B than in B2C. Push is a typical B2B distributor strategy.

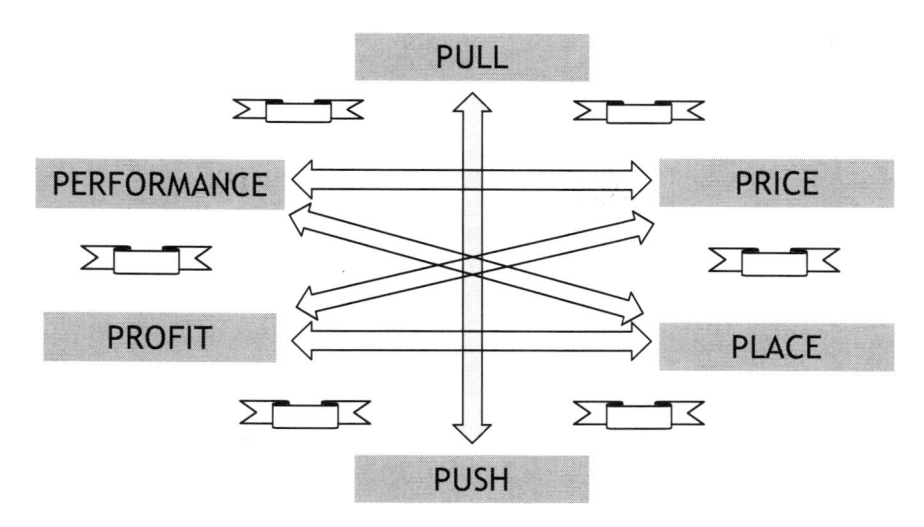

FIGURE 6.5 *The Six P Strategy - Compatibilities and Oppositions.*

In Figure 6.5, the banners between two strategies indicate that a synergy may exist between them. For example, a low price strategy is compatible with a place expansion. The arrows indicate that opposition may exist. For example, a pull strategy looks for maximum sales per customer, with variable sources of products. It is not compatible with a push strategy, which focuses on some technologies. A place strategy attempts to extend territories, which triggers a risk for performance, particularly in the service level.

How to use the tool?

In the first phase, evaluate the six P strategies in terms of investment, revenue, and market share. Then, underline the compatibilities and oppositions. Finally, build scenarios in which strategies are mixed, and finally, identify the P-strategy mix to implement.

Strengths and limitations of the tool

This tool shows many strategy possibilities, and allows companies to generate a robust mix of P strategies. It can be used to create several scenarios in order to identify options. The spectrum of knowledge to build the strategies is very large. It includes customer needs (pull), market size and elasticity (price), product profitability (profit), customer satisfaction drivers (performance), technology potential (push), and geographical market expansion possibilities (place). Use of the tool requires considerable effort in order to conduct a global evaluation.

Tool 29: The Five Business Models Mix helps to identify scenarios for the creation of revenue and profit

DEFINITIONS

An enterprise's *business model* is the plan for the creation of revenue and profit. There are typically five types of models (Lecocq, Demil, & Warnier, 2006). The *producer business model* is a model in which the enterprise creates and produces a product or service. The *distribution business model* is a model focused on finding and selling to customers. The *value-added reseller* (VAR) is a model in which the enterprise buys products and services, finds customers, adds services (i.e., customization), and sells a solution. The *license business model* is a model in which supplier authorizes the use of an asset, such as software, a patent, or a trademark. The *mutualization business model* is a model in which the enterprise gives back its profit to shareholders or associated members.

The Five Business Models Mix tool portrays the enterprise as a mix of business models. Each part generates a type of revenue and profit and contributes to the overall business model. Each actor may add several activities, creating a mixed business model (Coombes & Nicholson, 2013).

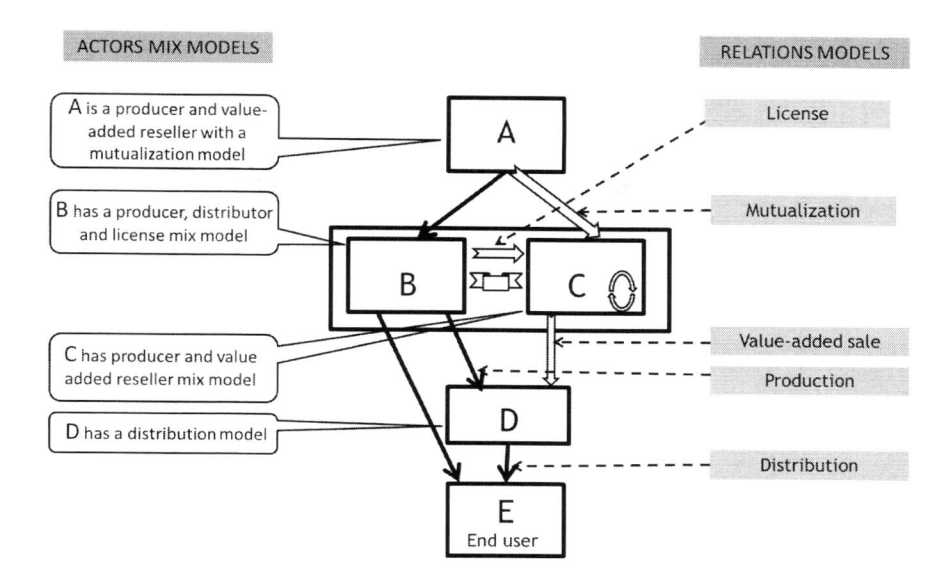

FIGURE 6.6 *The Five Business Models Mix (Example for Four Actors).*

In Figure 6.6, A gives its profit to B and C, which are its shareholders. It produces products for B, but customizes them for C. B has licensed to C the right to use a specific customized product. B can also sell to a distributor (D) or directly to end users (E). These rich relationships generate the five types of relationships and actors within mixed business models.

How to use the tool?

First, all of the possible activities corresponding to each of the five business models are brainstormed. For example, the production model can be transformed into a rental model including licensing to a subcontractor. It can be extended to direct sale, or sale with customization. Then, the revenue, profit, and investment are projected for each of the different scenarios. Finally, the best mix is identified and implemented.

Strengths and limitations of the tool

This tool serves as a very rich means of thinking "outside the box" and imagining new relationships, as well as new types of revenue and profit. A limitation of the tool is that it requires market and customer behavior knowledge in order to properly simulate the different scenarios.

Tool 30: The Positioning Mix illustrates brand and value proposition identity

DEFINITIONS

Positioning is the level at which customer needs are addressed. Positioning synthesizes the brand image, which should be memorable to the customer. It also serves to differentiate from competition. Both the level of addressing need and differentiation can occur in multiple ways. B2B positioning affords more choices than the typical bimodal axes in B2C (i.e., cheap/premium, utilitarian/luxurious, and entry-level/high-end). A *meta-message* is a piece of abstract information requiring interpretation, such as cues or propositions about the relationship between two communicators (Bateson, 1956), which would be two businesses in B2B. *Market drivers* are key motivators influencing customer purchases.

B2B positioning provides a mix of options based on the targeted customer segments and the strategy. Eight categories are proposed in the Positioning Mix tool. The basic position is the most common among B2B companies, and it is based on performance, quality, satisfaction, and price. This position sets forth a promise that is almost impossible to uphold. The leadership position includes slogans about the providers' success. The expertise position focuses on know-how. The segment position focuses on a limited group of customers. The benefit positioning focuses on always resonating with customers. The width position emphasizes the ability to meet a large need with range and coverage. The proximity position and values position represent meta-messages, which can be misinterpreted if not communicated effectively. It is preferable to make the positioning as clear as possible. Figure 6.7 contains 38 messages, though it is not exhaustive.

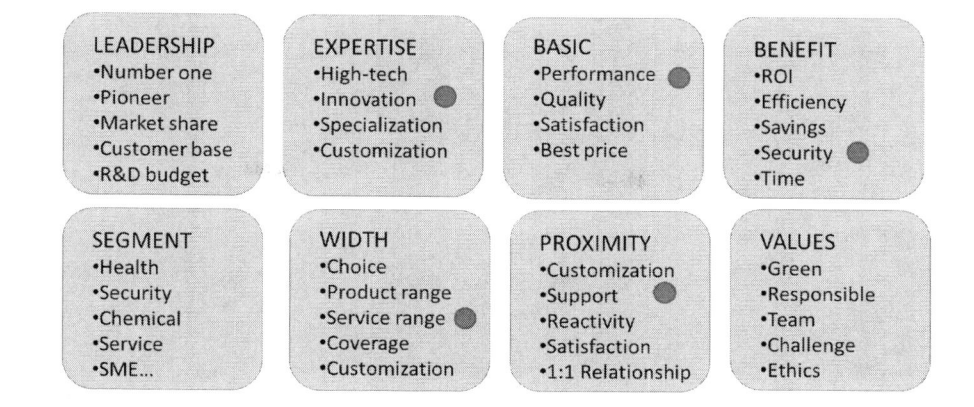

LEADERSHIP	EXPERTISE	BASIC	BENEFIT
•Number one •Pioneer •Market share •Customer base •R&D budget	•High-tech •Innovation ● •Specialization •Customization	•Performance ● •Quality •Satisfaction •Best price	•ROI •Efficiency •Savings •Security ● •Time

SEGMENT	WIDTH	PROXIMITY	VALUES
•Health •Security •Chemical •Service •SME...	•Choice •Product range •Service range ● •Coverage •Customization	•Customization •Support ● •Reactivity •Satisfaction •1:1 Relationship	•Green •Responsible •Team •Challenge •Ethics

FIGURE 6.7 *The Positioning Mix (Example)*.

B2B companies may have a positioning that is limited to the message in the tagline that appears below the company brand name. They should be enriched with few messages, which together create a clear positioning. In the example in Figure 6.7, the dots show the company positioning. The company offers security benefits based on performance and innovation, as well as service and support.

How to use the tool?

First, a customer survey is used to assess the market drivers per segment. Then, positioning is determined at the company level; at best it includes a mix of the most promising drivers, which helps the company to reach strategic targets, such as revenue and profit. Then, positioning is determined each time a new product is launched. This should be compatible with the company positioning. For example, if innovation and customer cost savings are the company positioning, then, for a new product, the same drivers apply and specific drivers can be added, such as customization and high volume efficiency.

Strengths and limitations of the tool

The tool is flexible and helps to develop a progressive definition of the positioning. It helps to build a comprehensive image instead of a short slogan. A limitation is the budget for communication in B2B, so the positioning is mainly known by customers via the sales force. The marketing team should be in charge of training regarding the company positioning.

Tool 31: The Canvass Model Adapted to B2B synthesizes strategies

DEFINITIONS

Positioning is the level at which customer needs are addressed. The *business model* is the strategic plan for operations, including sources of revenue, the intended customer base, products, alliances, and financing details. The *blueprint* is the customer relations pathway before and after sales. An *influencer* is a person who influences the behavior of members of the buying center. A *prescriber* is a person who suggests to the buyer a specific product. The *direct distribution* is made up of the manufacturer's employees. The *indirect distribution* is made of external distributors.

The Canvass model (Osterwalder & Pigneur, 2010) is a figure that points out the key elements of a business model and interrelationships. It starts with the brand positioning and the value proposition. The latter includes the products, services, and any free support. Moving down the model, the offer is sold by the distribution network, which can be direct or indirect. The brand and distribution network create customer relations and relations with influencers (i.e., certifiers and prescribers). Customers include buyers, users, and decision makers. Both customers and influencers are in contact with competitors. Moving up the model, the value proposition triggers the need for competencies and operations, which require costly resources. When know-how and resources are missing, partnerships can be formed or concluded. Revenue and costs generate profit. Bidirectional relationships exist between allied partners and company operations and competencies: They cross-fertilize each other. In the same way, customers influence their experience with the brand and with the distribution network.

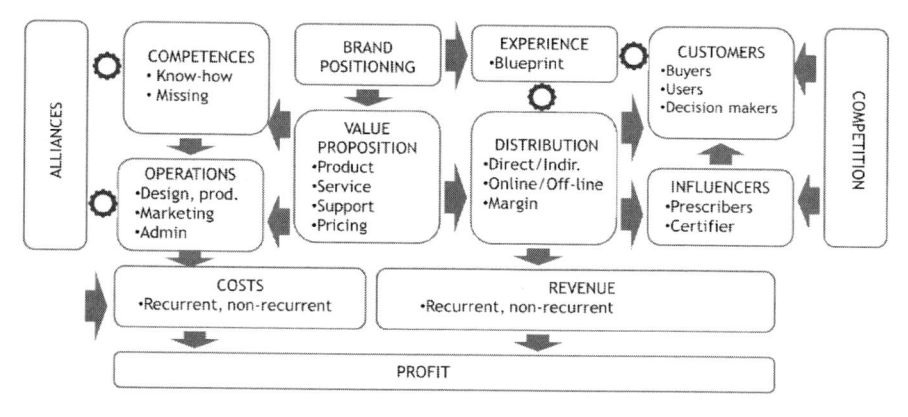

FIGURE 6.8 *The Canvass Model Adapted to B2B.*

How to use the tool?

The Canvass Model represents a synthesis of the company business model. It is generated after surveys and decisions about all the elements. When it is built, marketing managers check the comprehensiveness and global coherence of the items. Then, they can challenge the model by changing or adapting elements. The model can produce several scenarios.

Strengths and limitations of the tool

The tool can be used in a dynamic way: One or several key points are changed and other points are re-evaluated. For example, if the customer relationship is modified with new Internet 2.0 tools, the Canvass Model suggests evaluating proposed changes to distribution, value proposition, revenue, competition, etc. The tool offers flexible options for integrating multiple business models. A limitation of the tool is that it requires a large number of validations: market size, R&D, production and marketing competencies, partnerships, and profits.

Tool 32: The Brand Identity and Naming Charter helps visualize the positioning strategy

DEFINITIONS

The *Brand Identity Charter* is a document that provides the rules for usage of all of the brand identity attributes, including graphical elements like the logo and colors, and verbal elements such as the baseline and positioning. The *Naming Charter* is a document which describes the convention of the creation of names of products and ranges.

The positioning is visible in the value proposition, the distribution model, the customer experience, and the communication. The Brand Identity and Naming Charter promotes development inside and outside of the company. The identity part conveys the company's global attributes. The other parts of the tool translate company identity into operational applications. Using the charter, marketing managers can identify the product range, major benefits, as well as communication rules; R&D can use the product design principles; and sales can use the arguments.

IDENTITY
Who we are?
What is our business field?
What is our offer?
What is our expertise?
POSITIONING
Who are our customers?
What customer value do we deliver?
Major benefits of our products and services
What relationship do we propose?
What are our team values?
Our mission statement
Baseline

COMPANY NAMING
The name indicates the business field and limited effort is required to remember it
Subsidiary names remind customers of the group name
PRODUCT NAMING CONVENTION
Principles of self-explanatory names
Family naming
Product and services naming
Options and module naming
Localization naming
ADDRESS NAMING
Website URL naming
E-mail address naming and signature

FIGURE 6.9 *The Brand Identity and Naming Charter (Part 1).*

GRAPHIC DESIGN
Principles of design
Logo look
Logo defined as a symbol of the positioning
Color code for print and electronic matters
Typography choice
Logo attached to text rules
Guidelines for screen designs
Guidelines for product design
Guidelines for documents
Guidelines for other matters

SALES ARGUMENTS
Benefits linked to features
COMMUNICATION APPLICATIONS
Business cards
Brochures
Word, PowerPoint
Screens examples for PC, tablets, mobile
Email ads
Banners
Exhibition stands
PRODUCT DESIGN
Visual examples
Ergonomics principles
Interface

FIGURE 6.10 *The Brand Identity and Naming Charter (Part 2).*

Management and key employees create the brand charter in order to formulate the strategy and utilize a communication agency to help structure the identity and produce the tools.

How to use the tool

Once the tool is produced, it is easy to use with the rules described in the charter. In order to maximize comprehensibility, users can discuss problems using the visual materials and verbal conversations. In practice, a responsible person should be available to support employees and partners who need help with interpretations. An update of the charter is necessary when the strategy changes. In practice, brand communication efforts will depend on the importance and complexity of the purchase (Brown, Zablah, Bellenger, & Donthu, 2012).

Strengths and limitations of the tool

The brand charter is not popular in B2B and its use is often limited to graphic design for logos. Nevertheless, the tool can be used to understand the common strategy and has day-to-day applications. Using the tool can help to improve sales arguments, company presentations, product look and feel, and communication materials, all of which can subsequently become easier to produce. Limitations of the charter include the level of detail required to complete it as well as the discipline required to adequately apply the rules.

Tool 33: The B2B Marketing 4SRs defines B2B operations

DEFINITIONS

A *solution* is a global value proposition that ensures a result or benefit to the customer over a certain period of time. It may include products, chargeable services, or free support.

The 4SRs is a radical tool to examine the operational marketing direction from a B2B perspective. The famous 4Ps of Kotler (Kotler, 1972) is a mnemonic for these marketing activities, which include Product, Price, Place, and Promotion. Other Ps have been added, such as Planet and People to remind companies of sustainable development requirements. Concerning *Product*, if we take the B2B point of view, the customer's motivation is to get a permanent *solution* that delivers a result and includes the product, service, and support over a period of time. So the word "solution" is better suited. The *Price* dimension is always key, but is a relative purchase criterion in B2B, as the buyer is looking for a beneficial *return* to the company—cost reduction, employee satisfaction, quality improvement, etc. *Place* refers to supplier geographic locations where the B2C customer can go and buy a product. In B2B, the buyer is visited by the salesperson or buys on the Internet or by phone, and cares less about the supplier's physical location. B2B marketing activities involve *reaching* the customer with lead generation, and attracting multiple people who participate in the decision over the negotiation period, an ability which is sometimes compared to *seduction*. Despite the fact that the B2B sales cycle is limited to business matters, it involves face-to-face meetings, considerable efforts to convince the other party, and a final agreement between the two partners. *Promotion* in B2B refers to communication programs, discounts programs, selling packages (e.g., five for the price of four), and so on. In B2B, *support* and the *relationship* to the buyer or user are most important aspects; they include analysis of customer issues, product customization, permanent technical support, and a quality sales relationship over the customer lifespan. Communications budgets are typically only 1 to 2% of the revenue because expenditures for the sales force can reach over 20%. For this tool, *Planet* and *People* have been renamed *sustainability* and *responsibility*.

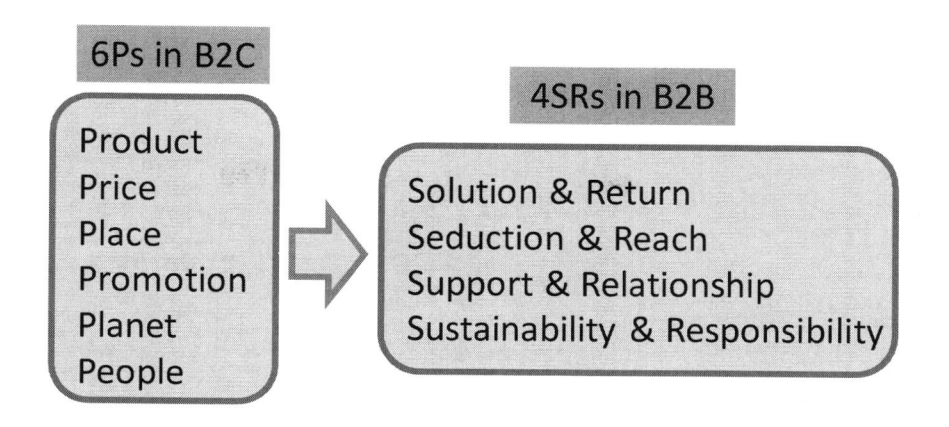

6Ps in B2C
- Product
- Price
- Place
- Promotion
- Planet
- People

4SRs in B2B
- Solution & Return
- Seduction & Reach
- Support & Relationship
- Sustainability & Responsibility

FIGURE 6.11 *The B2B Marketing 4SR.*

How to use the tool?

This tool helps to generate a marketing plan by following the eight steps mentioned. The first activity is to define the customer solution per segment and its return on investment. This corresponds with strategic activity. Then, the operations to generate initial customer acquisition are identified (i.e., seduction and reach). Then, the after-sale activities are identified (i.e., support and relationship). The last elements—sustainability and responsibility—cover all three activities and are taken into account at any step in the marketing processes.

Strengths and limitations of the tool

The 4SR tool gives accurate dimensions to the B2B operational activities. It requires important customer insight to be successful. Defining a product is easier than finding a solution; fixing a price is easier than generating a customer return. Specifying a customer support and long-term relationship involves understanding actors' needs and communication preferences.

Tool 34: The Hybrid Offerings Model shows the resources and competencies required by products sold with services

DEFINITIONS

Hybrid offerings include both products and services. *Start-up* is the service needed to help the customer start using the product. *Deployment* is the service including delivery, integration, and start-up. The *supply chain* includes manufacturing and deployment.

B2B companies that offer products almost always sell associated services in order to ensure that the customer can use and benefit from products as promised. Services are key to customer loyalty and suppliers' profitability and thus, hybrid offerings are very common in B2B. The Hybrid Offerings Model was derived from Ulaga and Reinartz's (2011) model. It demonstrates the mix of competencies needed and the links with resources. The resources are doubled, since there are two activities, product and services. The ability to manage both with efficiency requires specific competencies (Gebauer, Paiola, & Saccani, 2013). The tool displays the three important benefits to suppliers.

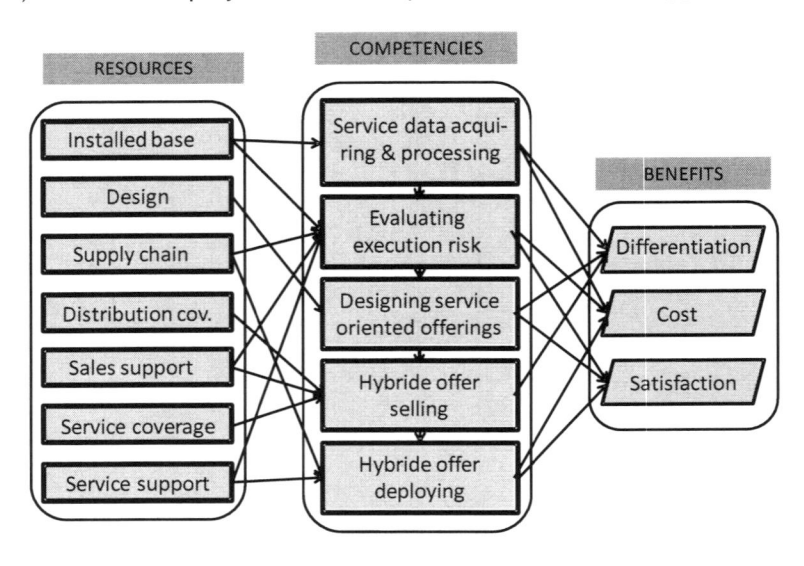

FIGURE 6.12 *Hybrid Offerings Model.*

For example, selling hybrid offerings is often a difficult endeavor for account managers used to selling only products or only services. Designing products that are easy to service (e.g., online) is also a particular competency.

How to use the tool

This tool helps to analyze the necessary resources and required competencies for offering particular products and services. The tool shows a minimum of seven resources, which may be completed according to the business field and company status. Then, the specific competencies required for hybrid business offerings are listed, along with their benefits. The five competencies and three benefits identified by the tool can also be revisited. The company can then identify its fit for hybrid business. For example, if its CRM database is scattered among many distributors and deals need coordination, processing and analysis can be difficult. In such instances, the fit to the model will not be perfect and a transformation will be needed in order to build a high quality common database accessible to distributors.

Strengths and limitations of the tool

This tool helps to track strengths and weaknesses linked to hybrid offerings and to identify areas for improvement. A limitation is that it may require particular expertise in order to recognize the benefit opportunities, resources, and specific competencies needed.

CHAPTER 7
HOW TO INITIATE NEW PRODUCT OR SERVICE GENERATION

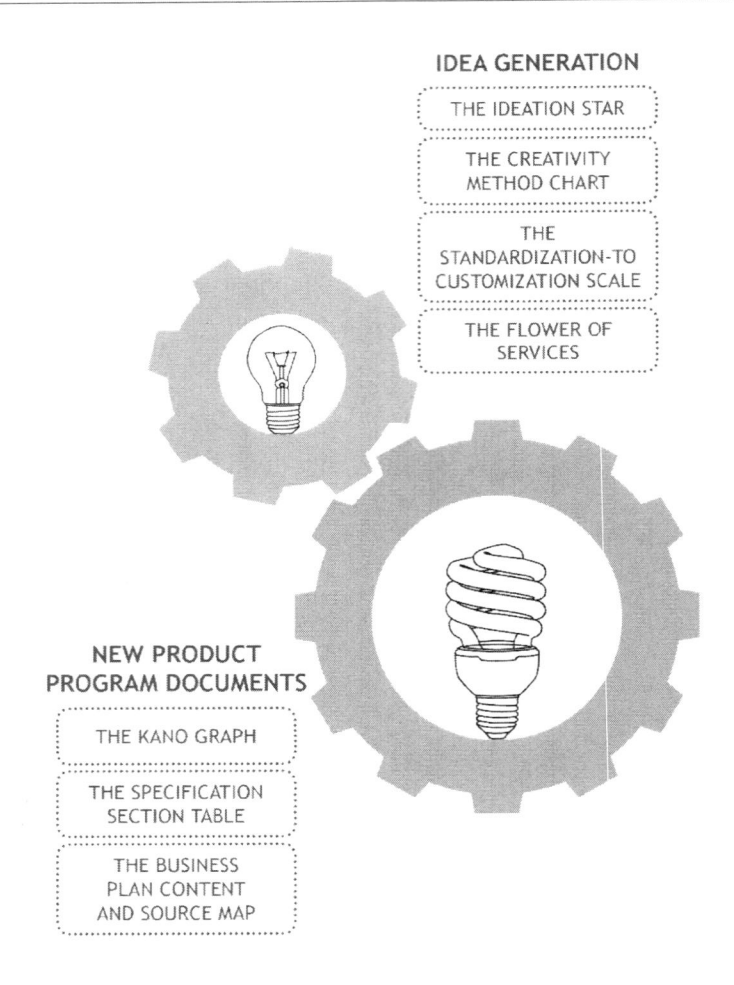

IDEA GENERATION
- THE IDEATION STAR
- THE CREATIVITY METHOD CHART
- THE STANDARDIZATION-TO CUSTOMIZATION SCALE
- THE FLOWER OF SERVICES

NEW PRODUCT PROGRAM DOCUMENTS
- THE KANO GRAPH
- THE SPECIFICATION SECTION TABLE
- THE BUSINESS PLAN CONTENT AND SOURCE MAP

Strategic marketing managers are the leaders in generating new products and service programs. This activity requires rigorous research, consultation, imagination, analyses, and so on, before program documents are generated and presented in order to get a launch agreement.

What is specific to B2B?

In B2B, new product programs may require more R&D resources. Products are often more complex. There is also a greater number of people proposing ideas for improvement. Innovation is not limited to products, but can also include distribution, business models, and customer relations. Product customization is more frequent and can itself be a form of innovation.

This chapter proposes seven tools to help make decisions related to idea generation and the generation of documents for new product programs.

Ideas generation
- Tool 35: The Ideation Star
- Tool 36: The Creativity Methods Hit Chart
- Tool 37: The Standardization-to Customization Scale
- Tool 38: The Flower of Services

New product program documents
- Tool 39: The Kano Graph
- Tool 40: The Specification Sections Table
- Tool 41: The Business Plan Content and Source Map

Tool 35: The Ideation Star defines multiple activities to generate product ideas and their impact

DEFINITIONS

Pull innovation is innovation based on customer needs. *Push Innovation* is innovation based on technology. *Open innovation* is innovation based on alliances. *Incremental innovation* involves minor product improvements. *Radical Innovation* generates major customer behavior changes. *Ideation* is the process of idea generation. *Crowdsourcing* is a method for sourcing information or ideas from a large number of people using collaborative Internet tools.

87

The ideation is the sum of several marketing activities. The Ideation Star outlines seven sources of ideas, and for each of them, the needed marketing posture and type of innovation employed. For example, the customer is a major source of ideas, which requires marketing investigation and generates pull innovation. Creativity is a current B2B ideation method; it requires marketing imagination and the ability to animate heterogeneous groups with specific methods. Creativity often triggers radical innovation.

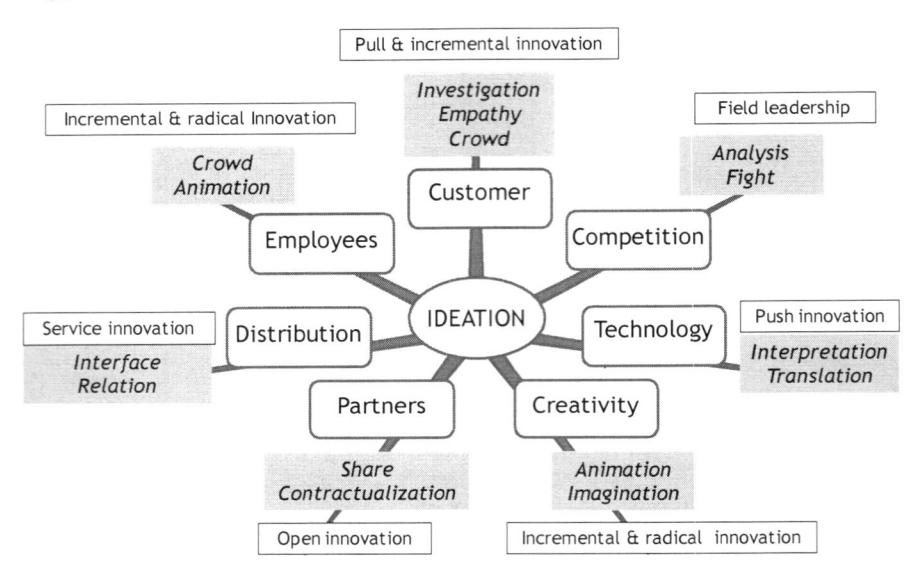

FIGURE 7.1 *The Ideation Star*.

The heart of the star is the ideation activity. The first level from the heart represents the sources of ideas and the second represents the relevant marketing competencies. The last level represents the types of innovation generated by the sources.

How to use the tool?

First, the business field actors and the objectives of the innovation serve as spontaneous sources of innovation. Second, this list is examined in order to see if additional sources from the tool are necessary. Third, the protocol of idea generation is set up—interviews, crowd funding, creativity methods, etc. Then, the marketing department should see if it has the ability and posture to implement the new methods or if it has to find a partner supplier. Finally, all of the ideas are put together and can be sorted using other tools.

Strengths and limitations of the tool

This tool allows companies to choose from many sources and shows the impact on innovation. Analyzing the competition and fighting it with better performance is far from sharing know-how and contracting with partners or interpreting new technologies. The tool draws attention to the impact of different sources in terms of global strategy. In practice, a mix of sources is preferable, but should be in line with the objectives of the company management. For example, a need for diversification will be better served by sources such as creativity and distribution. In this instance, partners, customers, and competition would become secondary priorities.

Tool 36: The Creativity Method Chart proposes seven successful ideation methods

DEFINITIONS

Brainstorming is a creativity method based on a set of rules for idea generation (e.g., no censorship, no judgment, listening, respect others' ideas) and spontaneity. The other creativity methods use additional artifacts.

Creativity is one of B2B marketing's key abilities and an important source of incremental as well as radical innovation. The generation of creative techniques requires structured sessions as well as unfocused brainstorms. The organization should provide a road map for creating ideas and present the constraints and evaluation criteria. Sessions can include small multidisciplinary groups or larger online groups using collaborative tools. The sessions should start by introducing the organization, followed by a spontaneous brainstorm. Then, more focused methods should be utilized. We propose seven methods which are complementary and well-suited to B2B for idea generation pertaining to new products, services, partnerships, processes, customer relationships, etc.

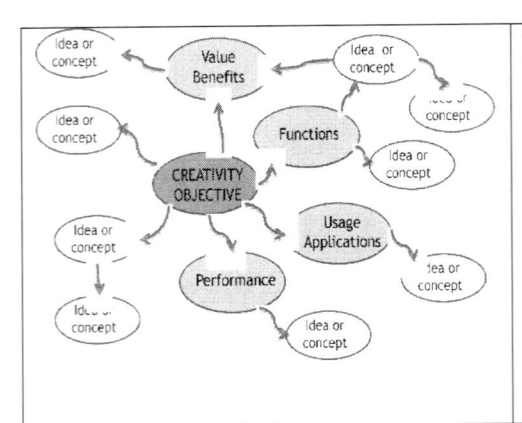

The Mental Map

This method invites one to start with the creativity objective description and define the "root" areas of ideas coming from it. Each area triggers ideas, which then trigger other ideas, and so on. The initial ideas may be forced when the intention is to cover specific areas. For example, areas functions, value, usage, and performance may be included in the initial map. The method provides participants with a useful representation of areas on which to work.

FIGURE 7.2 *The Mental Map Creativity Method.*

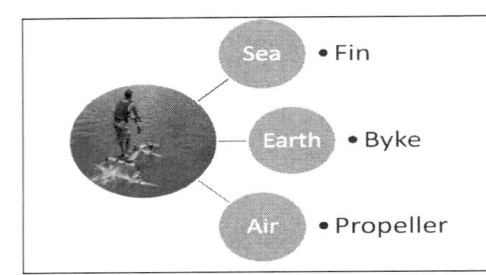

The Analogy

The analogy helps locate proximal or distal areas that have common points with the objective. The ideas generated are concepts derived from "outside the box." For example, a machine used to walk on water takes transportation ideas from sea to earth and air, which engenders new divergent concepts.

FIGURE 7.3 *The Analogy Creativity Method.*

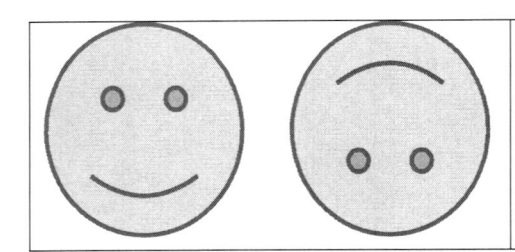

The Inversion

This method invites one to develop ideas to solve the opposite of the given objective. An example is finding the worst machine to automatically load boxes in a truck. Each idea is then analyzed and reversed. This activity is both concrete and fun.

FIGURE 7.4 *The Inversion Creativity Method.*

The Deformation

This method starts with the present products or services and modifies them in size, look, duration, modules, ergonomics, organization, contacts, time, etc. The progression can move to different directions. This method is easy to use after the mental map, which proposes the areas of deformation.

FIGURE 7.5 *The Deformation Creativity Method.*

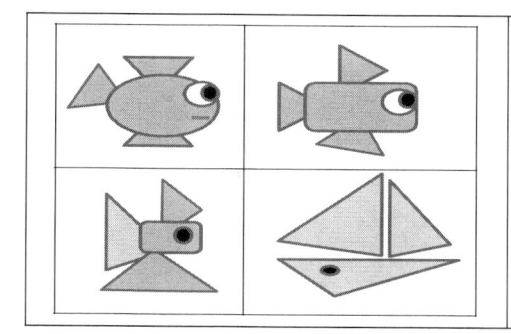

The Expectation–Element Matrix

This method requires a previous market survey of customer expectations and element of offerings. It develops a search of ideas for each couple expectation-offerings element in the matrix. For example, an expectation of performance is reconsidered with each feature.

EXPECTATIONS	Benefits	Usage	Functions	Performance
Module 1				
Module 2				
Module 3				
Feature 1				
Feature 2				
Feature 3				

FIGURE 7.6 *The Expectation-Element Matrix Creativity Method.*

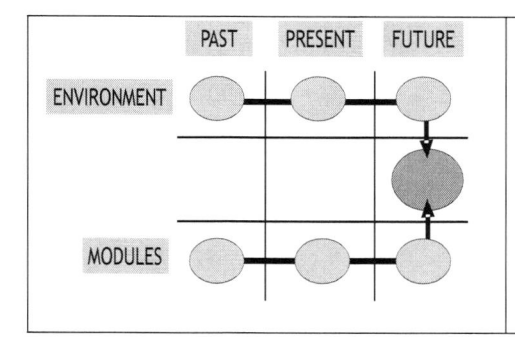

The Nine Windows

The Nine Windows requires technology and an environmental survey. This activity invites one to describe the elements or subsystems of past products and imagine them in the future. The same exercise is completed for the components of the environment or global system. The future product is then created from the mix of both evaluations.

FIGURE 7.7 *The Nine Windows Creativity Method.*

The Trends
The Trend method suggests that one list the areas that influence the product—such as usage, technology, material, textures, media, constraints—and for each of area, to describe the possible trends. In the second phase, they provide the layout for idea generation.

FIGURE 7.8 *The Trends Creativity Method.*

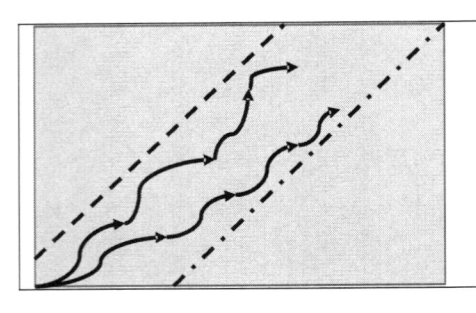

How to use the tool

Though brainstorming is typically the most utilized method, a structured pathway of methods is preferable because it gives more oriented ideas toward the objective. The Mental Map is frequently chosen to start after the brainstorm. Some methods require preparation, a survey, or consultation. The path of methods is made up of two criteria: (a) the expected divergence from the current situation, and (b) level of conceptual or concrete solution. The order depends on the group population and whether they like to begin with a smooth or strong divergence. For example, the Matrix, Inversion, Trends, and Nine Windows are less divergent than the Analogy and Deformation. Before they are filtered, ideas are revisited, grouped, and reinforced.

Strengths and limitations of the tool

These methods are very productive and dozens of ideas can be formulated in just a few hours. Carefully choosing participants and methods can help to better focus on the objective than brainstorming. A limitation, however, is the expectations generated by the process. Many ideas are produced; some of them should be implemented in order to gain credibility and encourage more sessions.

Tool 37: The Standardization-to-Customization Scale helps to decide the level of local adaptation

DEFINITIONS

Localization is the adaptation of products, services and support to local context.

As soon as B2B companies wish to extend their sales abroad or extend to specific customer bases, they need to decide the level of adaptation required for their products or services in order to meet the local conditions and specific customer needs. The Standardization-Adaptation Scale developed by Tamer-Carvusgil for foreign countries (Tamer-Carvusgil, Knight, & Riesenberger, 2014) can be adapted to B2B as well as for customers with a specific need. The tool evaluates the factors that trigger localization based on the local conditions or customers, and assesses the impact and benefits of such factors. The factors include the market, customer requirements, pricing, industry similarity or difference between countries, regulation, and cultural and political stance toward foreign companies. The seven levels move from zero localization, as in many raw material industries, to 100% adaptation to the area, with a product or service dedicated to one market—like joint-ventures built with local companies—and full customization. The benefits of standardization need to be calculated, such as cost reduction due to increased volume, and compared to the benefits of adaptation, such as better market reach and customer need fulfillment.

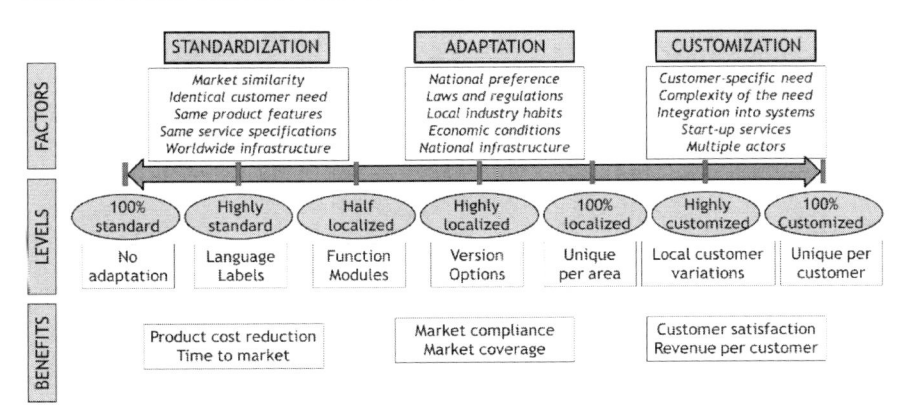

FIGURE 7.9 *The Standardization-Adaptation Scale.*

The variations of adaptation may be limited to language and compliance with local regulations, or may include completely different specifications and pricing structures. Each market has local requirements and specific customization needs, which are often visible in individual sales with customers.

How to use the tool?

In the first phase, the seven levels are analyzed and translated into specification sheets. The place and people in charge of the adaptations and customization need to be decided, from the production site to the customer site. The corresponding investments, revenues, and costs are then evaluated. The tool shows where to eliminate options if they do not produce enough revenue or profit. The remaining scenarios are checked against the company positioning, which they must support. Finally, the company competencies are checked. In particular, distribution should be able to cope with adaptations.

Strengths and limitations of the tool

The cost of market customization may be so high compared to the expected profit that many B2B companies refrain from coverage in certain countries. Local components, minimal value addition, or manufacturing challenges can all discourage localization. The tool's seven levels suggest finding compromise with mid-level adaptation and customizations to capture some of the local market.

Tool 38: The Flower of Services identifies the firm's service differentiation strategy

Services are very expensive to set up and maintain. The Flower of Services (Lovelock & Wirtz, 2010) helps to visualize—in an attractive way—the services delivered by the firm. In B2C, the tool distinguishes the core business from the facilitating or enhancing services in the petals—information, consultation, order taking, hospitality, safekeeping, billing, payment, and exceptions. In B2C, services are separated into five categories. The first includes services that belong to the core business of the company. A company's core services may be engineering, renting, or financing large projects. The second category is the group of facilitating services, which are proposed by companies in the business field in order to aid the core business. Such services can include e-procurement, payment facility, delivery, and so on. Both groups are positioned in the heart of the flower. The petals are the most visible part and include the enhancing, supplementary services, which aid in differentiation and complement performance. As an addition to the Lovelock model, services can be divided into (a) unique services of the firm, (b) services in common with the competition, and (c) services offered by competition which the firm lacks.

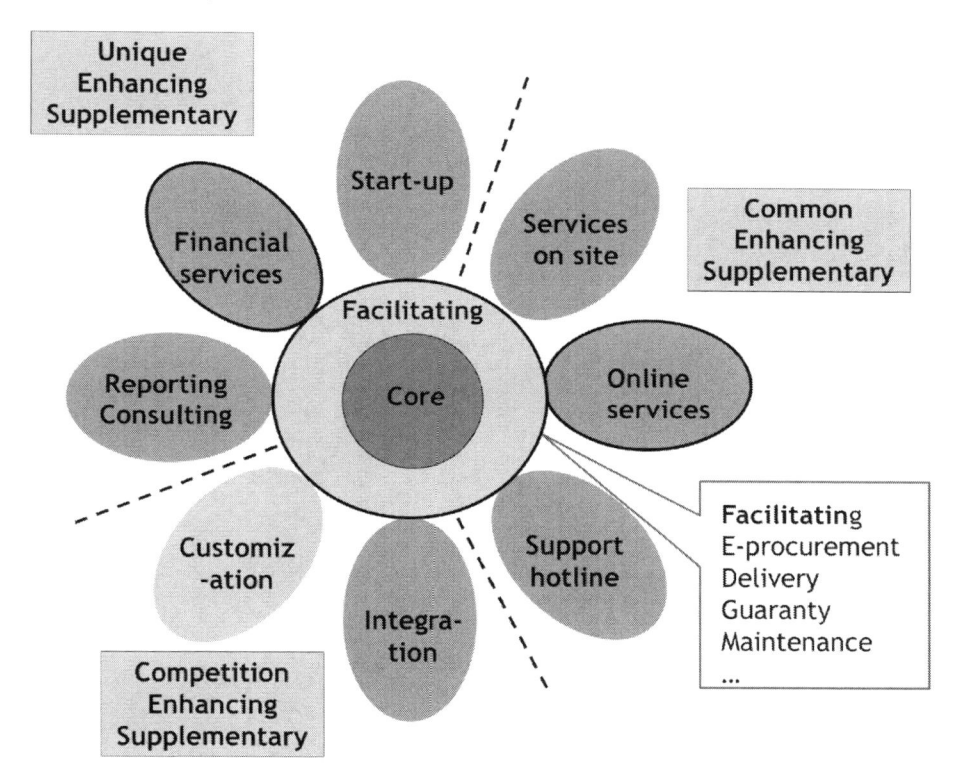

FIGURE 7.10 *THE Flower of Services.*

The flower may also show who is providing the service in the value chain. In Figure 7.10, the manufacturer delivers the financial and online services (circled ellipses), and the distributor the others. In this example, the distributor/manufacturer is performing consulting and start-up services, but the competition only customizes solutions at a high level. The firm should consider if this approach is appropriate.

A second way to present the Flower of Services is to use the Cova categories based on the Service Dominant Logic (Cova & Salle, 2008). This theory (Vargo & Lusch, 2004) suggests that the service to organizations corresponds better to their strategies than sold products. The firm wants to be able to decide its solution, use products, have a positive experience, change solutions to adapt to the environment, and build expertise. Product purchase is less flexible. The service categories of this tool also underline which customer needs are addressed by different networks, which can help decision-making and usage experience.

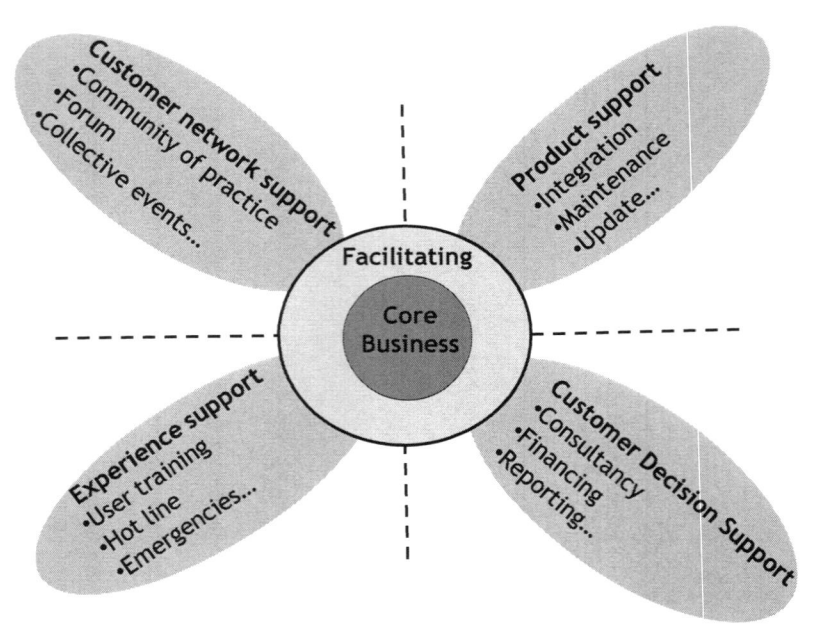

FIGURE 7.10 *The Flower of Services (Example 2)*.

How to use the tool?

This tool helps to first define the core activities and translate them into a service offer. Then, all services in the market that facilitate sales are identified. Next, all other services in the market that generate revenue (or not) are listed. Then, the tool suggests brainstorming areas of services; ideas for services should also be listed. The full picture includes a view of new revenue and differentiation. This tool triggers market surveys to measure the potential of services.

Strengths and limitations of the tool

The image provided by the tool gives an immediate grasp of the competitive position of the service. It is important to constantly evaluate the mix of services. Services can be tested or proposed in a limited area, or with a limited or invisible customer base. A limitation of the tool is that it requires an evaluation of competitors' services, which may not be visible, only accessible to a limited number of customers, or fully customized. Several flowers may be necessary per segment or even per customer.

Tool 39: The Kano Graph qualifies innovations using customer responses

In B2B, innovations may have both positive and negative effects for clients. The Kano Graph (Kano, Seraku, Takahashi, & Tsuji, 1984) is a tool that helps one anticipate customer responses. It uses a specific customer survey questionnaire including the following questions: (a) "If the innovation is present, do you like it, expect it, are neutral, live with it, or dislike it?", and (b) "If the innovation is not present, do you like it, expect it, are neutral, live with it, or dislike it?" The figure allows the splitting of the responses into six categories. The "Must Have" innovation is compulsory. *Delight* represents high degree of satisfaction and attractiveness, whereas *reverse* is undesirable and unwanted (i.e., should be reversed). *More is better* is linear, occurring when satisfaction is proportional to the presence of the product. *Neutral* indicates no impact and, therefore, is typically not useful. In the figure, *questionable* answers are illogical and, thus, eliminated.

CUSTOMER RESPONSES		If the innovation is not present, you...				
		Like	Expect	Are neutral	Live with	Dislike
If the innovation is present,	Like	Q	D	D	D	MB
	Expect	R	N	N	N	MH
	Are neutral	R	N	N	N	MH
	Live with	R	N	N	N	MH
	Dislike	R	R	R	R	Q

MH Must have, MB More is better, D Delight, R Reverse, N Neutral, Q Questionable

FIGURE 7.12 *The Kano Questionnaire Report.*

The five types of customer responses provide the most important customer reactions, which subsequently inform product innovation. Using the Kano graph, the positioning of the different innovations can be determined.

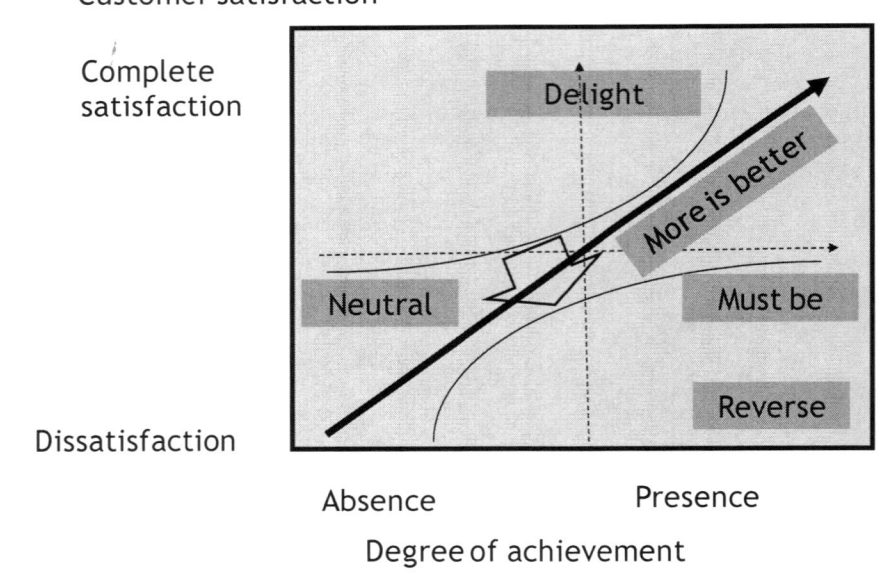

FIGURE 7.13 *The Kano Graph.*

In the graph, one line represents "delight" innovations and another "must be" innovations. With additional users, the initial innovators/customers move to other newer products, and the status of delight moves toward must be.

How to use the tool

In practice, the market survey is processed with the questionnaire and the analysis is performed by segment. The innovations are sorted and compared with a graph per target. Must be innovations will be adopted, while reverse and neutral innovations will be eliminated. Additional factors, such as the profitability or the fit with the distribution, will be taken into account to determine the more is better and delight factors.

Strengths and limitations of the tool

This tool is powerful in its ability to classify the innovation attractiveness and measure its possible negative impact on specific segments. Users who wish to have easy solutions do not expect the same innovations as those who have sophisticated applications. The tool helps to avoid the unnecessary development of innovations with reverse impact. A limitation lies in the ability to garner customers' clear perceptions and reactions to the innovation.

Tool 40: The Specification Section Table lists the content of new product or service specifications

DEFINITIONS

The *product marketing specification* is a document that describes what the product should do for customers, including the benefits, usage, functions, performance, and features. It is written by the marketing team. The *product technical specifications* is a document that describes how the product is made, including its components, architecture, and system. It is written by the project manager.

Marketing writes the specification of the product or service and delivers it to R&D after the executive committee agrees to start the project. It describes the elements necessary to the team to design, produce, and deliver the product or service. Further, it details the "What it can do" for the customer, and not the "How it is done," which the R&D team will decide.

TABLE 7.1 The Specification Section Table (Example).

Content	Description
Context	Synthesis of facts and surveys that justify the project
Strategy	Reminder of company strategy and existing range. New product or service targets, positioning, value addition, business model.
Functions	Product and service intention, functions, destination, and expected results.
Features	Features, performance, and technical elements linked to a customer benefit.
Value	Benefits generated by the product or service, which justify the purchase: time, cost reduction, operational performance, image, satisfaction, quality, etc.
Usage	Targeted customers' expected experience with the product or service.
System	Associated products, services, and infrastructure. Compatibilities. Integration services.
Customization	Product personalization level. Made by a system, the customer, distributor, manufacturer, etc.
Environment	Accessibility, space, equipment, persons, information, security
Support	Free services; hot line, forum, community of practice, training, consultancy, information, usage dashboard, recovery, etc.
Price	Price list and average discount per segment, distribution model.
Evaluation	Performance, quality, durability, look, compliance, ease of use, error level, service competence, response time, recovery time, courtesy, etc.
Responsibility	Environmental and social impact improvement or maximum accepted.
Distribution	Distribution profile. Technical, sales and marketing necessary abilities.
Finance	Financial business plan with quantities, manufacturing, service and distribution revenue, cost, margin, profit, ROI.
Annexes	Market survey results, competitive analysis, product range SWOT, etc.

The content sections are built according to the business field. In particular, raw materials, ingredients, modules, finished goods, and services have specific or well-developed chapters.

How to use the tool

The specification is constructed after many internal and external consultations and surveys. Some content is included inside the company's product creation procedures. The chapters are large enough to avoid misunderstanding at the time of the product design and launch. The specifications are sufficiently challenging to bear significant additional customer value and avoid easy duplication by competitors. Nevertheless, they should not be discouraging to the R&D team.

Strengths and limitations of the tool

The tool suggests that the specifications contain sections. The parts need to be customized utilizing the company's know-how, as should the content of the chapters. As long as the specifications clearly demonstrate that the business model and the value of products or services are fixed, they can be considered a flexible starting point for R&D, which can propose other ways to meet required objectives. Alternative functions to what is described in the document with partnerships and open innovation are examples.

Tool 41: The Business Plan Content and Source Map defines the twelve chapters and nine sources to build a new product business plan

DEFINITIONS

The *blue team* is a process of presenting a project to a person in order to get feedback. A *benchmark* is a comparison of a practice with a non-competitor organization. The *business plan* is a document that helps to make decisions about launching a business project and whether to stop or move forward when reaching major milestones. *Triangulation* is the use of several survey methods to answer a research question.

The production of a business plan is a compulsory B2B marketing activity that facilitates decision-making about new products and services. Products and services are designed at the beginning of a project and updated at the end of each phase if the initial hypotheses have changed. The chapters within a business plan cover the areas necessary for decision-making. In addition to the chapters seen in the Canvass Model Tool, the business plan details the supply chain, profitability, key actors, and a schedule. A project SWOT analysis can provide decision-makers important information about value addition.

TABLE 7.2 *The Business Plan Content Map (Example).*

MARKET • Need, value • Segments, target	VALUE PROPOSITION • Product • Service, support	TECHNOLOGY • Performance • Availibility
PARTNERSHIPS • R&D, production • Sales, marketing	DISTRIBUTION • Sales network • Customer experience	SUPPLY CHAIN • Production, delivery • Customization
REVENUE • Recurrent • Non-recurrent	RESOURCES • Recurrent • Non recurrent	PROFITABILITY • ROI, statements • Financing
KEY ACTORS • Managers • Sponsors	SCHEDULE • Milestones • Dashboard	SWOT • Evolution • Recovery plan

The content of the business plan will be adapted to the audience and the project. Eventually an annex of information will be added, which proofs or details the content.

TABLE 7.3 *The Business Plan Sources Map (Example).*

CUSTOM SURVEYS • Customers, actors • Products, technical	DATA BASES • Firm populations • Business field	SOCIAL NETWORKS • Groups, forums • Deals
COMPETITION • Exhibition, web • Marketplace	EMPLOYEES • Sales force deals CRM • Finance, R&D...	OPEN SOURCES • Surveys • Public statistics
EXPERTS • Blogs, white papers • Conferences	BENCHMARKS • Similar issues • Best practices	BLUETEAM • Business plan expert • Business angels

How to use the tool

The areas requiring consultation with decision makers are listed. Decision makers define the content of the business plan and the sources. Sources are typically very extensive and often unstable. The risk is the potential to get overwhelmed with too much contradictory information in some chapters and not enough in others. Thus, triangulation of several sources is necessary. A balance should be found between collecting more survey data and conserving time.

Strengths and limitations of the tool

This tool helps to enhance the completeness, coherence, and precision of the business plan. Decision makers judge these attributes before concluding whether or not to move forward with the project. Despite the use of surveys and quality of information, areas of the content will still be based on uncertain factors. This limitation should be made clear so that the risk is understood and accepted collectively.

CHAPTER 8
HOW TO PRICE A PRODUCT

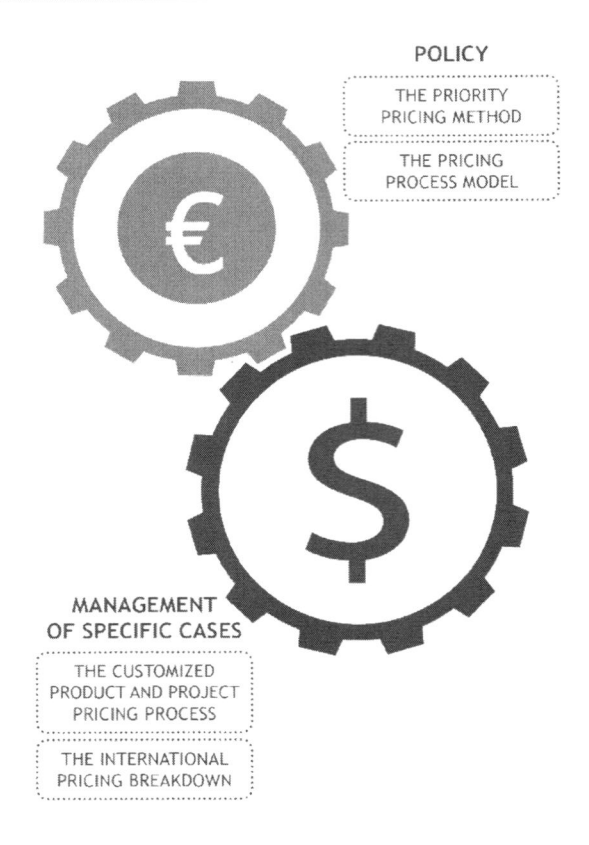

POLICY
- THE PRIORITY PRICING METHOD
- THE PRICING PROCESS MODEL

MANAGEMENT OF SPECIFIC CASES
- THE CUSTOMIZED PRODUCT AND PROJECT PRICING PROCESS
- THE INTERNATIONAL PRICING BREAKDOWN

Pricing is both a strategic and an operational marketing activity. When the targeted segments and the value proposition are defined, the products and services are priced to customers and distributors. When they are sold, many prices are lowered for distributors and customers according to operational tactics.

What is specific to B2B?

In B2B, most of time prices are negotiated at all levels of the business field, from producer to distributor and to end user. The variations in price are a consequence of many factors, from quantities purchased to special contractual clauses. The price is often non-visible and part of a global solution to customers through customized services. In some businesses, because the engineering costs of the products are particularly difficult to evaluate, pricing is conducted in way that ensures profitability. The pricing activity includes a global policy, an organized process, and rules for managing specific cases. Four tools are proposed to support pricing.

Policy
- Tool 42: The Priority Pricing Method
- Tool 43: The Pricing Process Model

Management of specific cases
- Tool 44: The Customized Product and Project Pricing Process
- Tool 45: The International Pricing Breakdown

Tool 42: The Priority Pricing Method leads to a compromise

DEFINITIONS

The *list price* is the public price or catalog price. The *achieved price* is the list price minus all various discounts. The *brand premium* is the bonus or penalty to customers' product price perception based on trust of the brand. The total cost of ownership (TOC), includes all customer costs generated by the purchase, such as products, services, supplies, process adaptations, and people training, up to the time of the purchase.

B2B product and services pricing is a regular and sophisticated exercise. Prices are fixed at each deal—adjusted according to list price and targeted average achieved prices—and benefit from a lot of flexibility. This implies both global and local approaches. The Priority Pricing Method aids in making pricing policy decisions from different strategic priority perspective and then arriving at a compromise based on the list and achieved price. The competition approach involves fixing a list price based on comparisons with the competition. In the context of a war on price, the discount will determine the percentage of deals won. Price has to be flexible in order to adapt to local competitive pressures. The perception approach involves fixing the list price according to the average value given by customers in market surveys. This approach accelerates the deal with limited customer surprise. Another approach, the elasticity approach, focuses on the market share priority. In this case, the targeted market share gives a price target. The customer EBIT (earnings before interest and tax, commonly the profit) approach takes into account 2 years of customer profit generated by the deal. The EBIT is calculated as the customer cost reductions minus TCO, plus the brand premium.

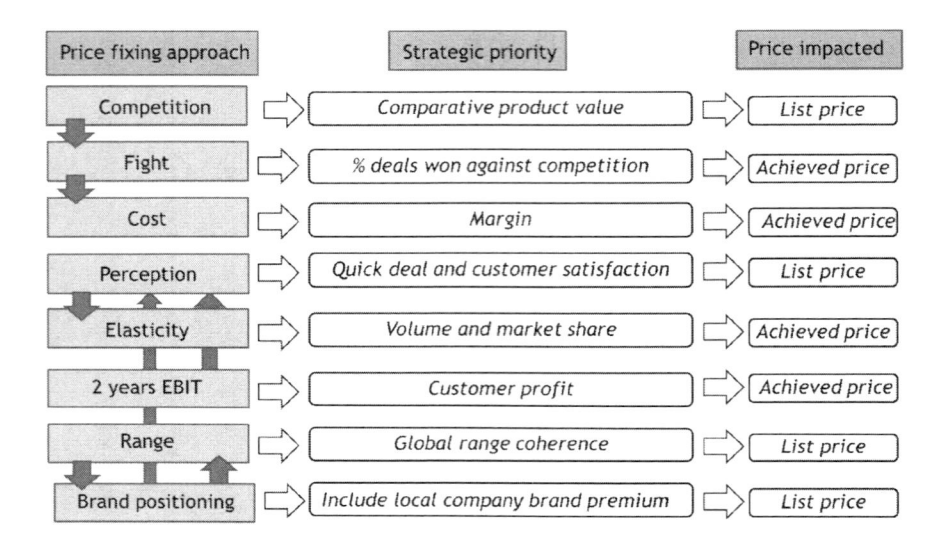

Price fixing approach	Strategic priority	Price impacted
Competition	Comparative product value	List price
Fight	% deals won against competition	Achieved price
Cost	Margin	Achieved price
Perception	Quick deal and customer satisfaction	List price
Elasticity	Volume and market share	Achieved price
2 years EBIT	Customer profit	Achieved price
Range	Global range coherence	List price
Brand positioning	Include local company brand premium	List price

FIGURE 8.1 *The Priority Pricing Method.*

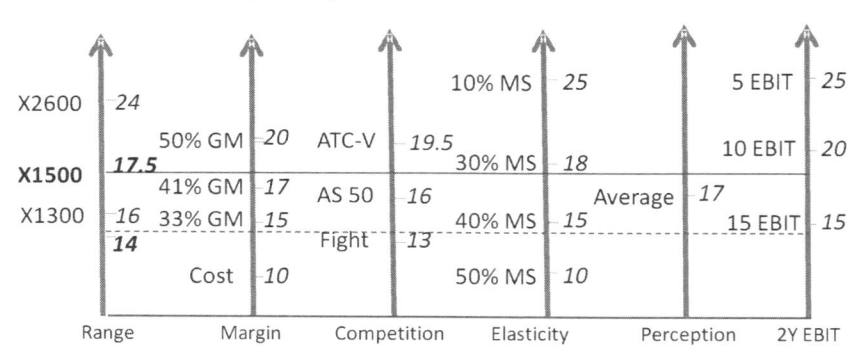

FIGURE 8.2 *Example of a Compromise Issued With the Priority Pricing Method.*

Priorities can be shifted so that a compromise can be reached. The list price is a compromise made by marketing managers, and the discount is a compromise made by the salesperson, branch manager, director, VP, or president based on its criticality.

106

How to use the tool?

In the example in Figure 8.2, the price of the X1500 has to be fixed. In terms of price list, it must be placed between the higher performing X2600 and lower performing X1300, and between the competition products ATC-V and AS50, but not too far from the average customer perception (i.e., $17k). In terms of achieved price, the margin must be over 15% on average; in the case of a price war, the sales force must be able to win a reasonable percentage of deals at $13k, knowing that the X1500 is higher performing than the AS50, and the target market share is 40%. These conditions lead to a list price of $17.5k and maximum discount to $14k. The $1k brand premium is particularly visible for customers who have a basic need (i.e., there is no difference between AS50 and X1500). The lowest discounted price is $1k higher than competition because trust in the company is more important.

Strengths and limitations of the tool

This tool helps to take the main priorities into account, agree upon the degree of importance, and find a valuable compromise. Based on the business field, some approaches may or may not be pertinent. This tool may require a market survey to assess customer perceptions, TCO, and benefits, as well as an evaluation of elasticity. A limitation of the tool is that it requires a competition price list and an analysis of discount local policy, as well as knowledge of product cost. Two pricing methods are not mentioned in the tool: (a) the *yield pricing*, which manages the price according to the demand fluctuations, and (b) the *Blue Ocean pricing*, which changes the business field habits and codes and creates a totally new value proposition (Cham Kim & Mauborgne, 2004).

Tool 43: The Pricing Process Model identifies seven steps for establishing B2B pricing

DEFINITIONS

The *floor price* is the minimum possible price offered by a supplier; the *ceiling price* is the maximum possible price that will still win a deal.

B2B product pricing is generally a complex process, where the marketing managers propose a global policy and the sales managers decide the final price per customer. In between, a cascade of pricing needs to be determined for each intermediary. The Pricing Process Model tool suggests computing the end user total price, including the TCO. The average distributor price is also computed, with a min-max price bracket evaluation. Different pricing methods are used, including the following: (a) sales potential sensitivity, (b) comparison with the competition, (c) incremental price, and (d) customer price acceptance compared to savings. This triggers a price compromise, for which the consistency is validated using the existing range of pricing. Finally, changes are implemented and monitored, including pricing to intermediaries.

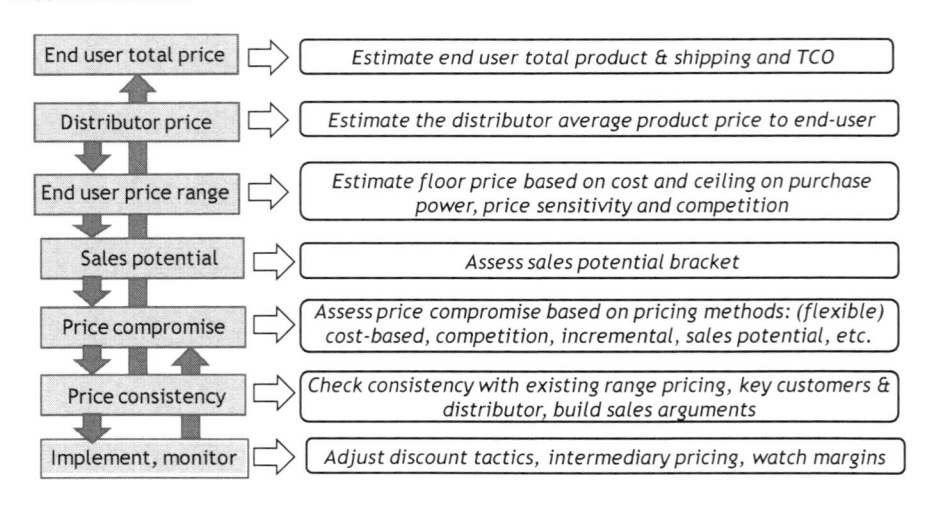

End user total price	Estimate end user total product & shipping and TCO
Distributor price	Estimate the distributor average product price to end-user
End user price range	Estimate floor price based on cost and ceiling on purchase power, price sensitivity and competition
Sales potential	Assess sales potential bracket
Price compromise	Assess price compromise based on pricing methods: (flexible) cost-based, competition, incremental, sales potential, etc.
Price consistency	Check consistency with existing range pricing, key customers & distributor, build sales arguments
Implement, monitor	Adjust discount tactics, intermediary pricing, watch margins

FIGURE 8.3 *The Pricing Process Model.*

Pricing requires a permanent intelligence organization to track competition tactics and customer preferences for purchases. The pricing process should be ongoing and constantly adjusted.

How to use the tool?

The order of actions and the arrows in the tool represent the steps to be taken. The end user total price is estimated, followed by the dealer price, which is found through consultation with the dealer. Then, the price range bracket and min-max potential of sale and profit are defined. This triggers the compromise debate. After discussion, checks and monitoring can help to fine tune the list and discount price.

Strengths and limitations of the tool

The process steps and milestones help to avoid over or under discounting, as well as improvisation, which is frequent during hot deals emergencies. Starting with end user ensures adaptation to the market, the price compromise gives realism to business, and price consistency checks promote feasibility. A limitation of the tool is that it requires considerable information to utilize it correctly—including estimations, different assessments methods, and field checks—not just adjustments to discounts.

Tool 44: The Customized Product and Project Pricing Process helps to avoid the six risks of complex deals

DEFINITIONS

The *tender office*, or bid desk, is in charge of tracking the tender publications, contacting all concerned managers to get their replies, and writing the responses. The *pricing committee* permanently tracks the lost or won deals with their precise conditions, and proposes price tactics to the account manager.

In B2B, custom-made products are a way to increase revenue and are frequently proposed. Unique projects co-created with the customer are also typical in fields like construction, software, consulting, and communication. The customer process includes calls for tenders, which help to identify customers' needs and develop contractual clauses. This triggers more risk than the sale of standard products from a catalog, which often has lower prices and contains the supplier's terms and conditions. The Customized Product and Project Pricing Process tool provides an example of pricing that overcomes six different risks.

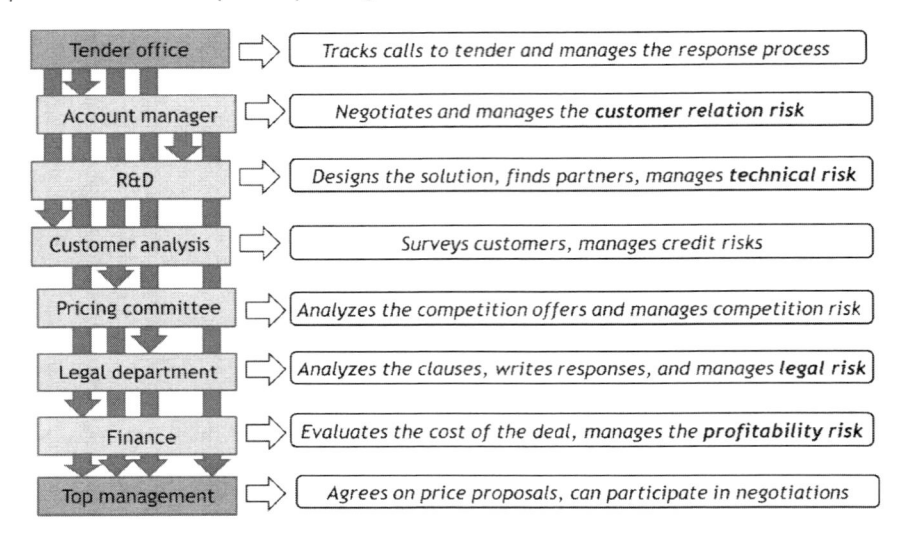

Tender office	Tracks calls to tender and manages the response process
Account manager	Negotiates and manages the **customer relation risk**
R&D	Designs the solution, finds partners, manages **technical risk**
Customer analysis	Surveys customers, manages credit risks
Pricing committee	Analyzes the competition offers and manages competition risk
Legal department	Analyzes the clauses, writes responses, and manages **legal risk**
Finance	Evaluates the cost of the deal, manages the **profitability risk**
Top management	Agrees on price proposals, can participate in negotiations

FIGURE 8.4 *The Customized Product and Project Pricing Process (Example).*

How to use the tool

In the first step, the risks of the deal are listed. The process is designed accordingly. In the example in Figure 8.4, an organization with the right expertise is responsible for each risk—relational, technical, legal, competitive, customer profile, and profitability. Other risks can be added, such as supply chain, service level, and partnership. The process is designed by marketing and is intended to include all entities.

Strengths and limitations of the tool

Frequent and predictable risks must be managed with a specific and official process. The application of the tool prevents the risk of complex deals. The limitation, however, comes first from expertise availability.

In particular, highly unpredictable risks require emergency organizations and procedures. In such circumstances, marketing and account managers must be able to mobilize management.

Tool 45: The International Pricing Breakdown lists the cost factors for foreign operations

B2B companies that intend to expand their operations abroad need to evaluate all of the elements that will impact their product cost. The International Pricing Breakdown highlights the main internal and external costs to take into consideration. It helps to check the consistency of the end user price compared to local competition. External international marketing costs are numerous and highly variable per country, including the following: custom, VAT policy, customer adaptation, shipping, etc. Internal costs may be at the same level of home operations or higher.

EXTERNAL COST

MARKET NEED	COMPETI-TION	CUSTOMER COST	LANDED COST	IMPORTER'S COST
Expectations Adaptations Price elasticity Currency	Strategy Coverage Offerings Prices	Documentations Financing Shipping Insurance	Customs Tariffs Warehouse Transportation	VAT Intermediaries Distributor Inventory

INTERNAL COST

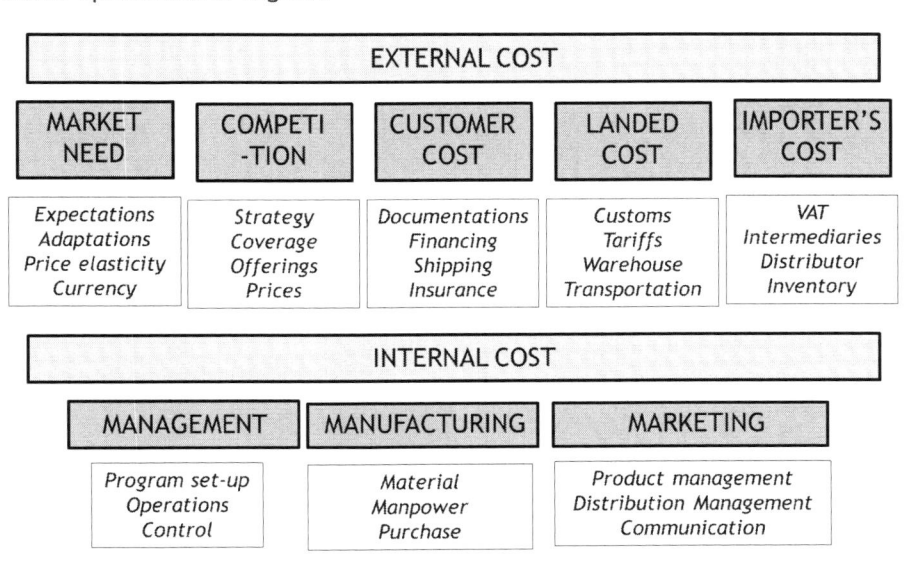

MANAGEMENT	MANUFACTURING	MARKETING
Program set-up Operations Control	Material Manpower Purchase	Product management Distribution Management Communication

FIGURE 8.5 *International Pricing Breakdown.*

For example, for a German company there is no difference in cost when selling to Austria compared to Bavaria, Germany. By contrast, the same company may have additional management, manufacturing, and marketing costs when selling to China. The factors impacting the end user cost determine the go/no-go decision. Local agents should have considerable knowledge of the local factors and should help in choosing the country penetration strategy.

How to use the tool?

The tool is defined for each country. Internal and external cost factors must be estimated and calculated. The total cost is the addition of both costs; it is not fixed, but varies according to management, distribution, transportation, market penetration, etc. When the total cost has been calculated, multiple scenarios can be drawn up to improve it.

Strengths and limitations of the tool

Thorough analysis of the cost breakdown is key prior to initiating any foreign marketing program. This tool proposes over 20 costs that can be adapted and completed per country. Cost calculations need to be regularly repeated and adapted based on regulations, competition, currency, and local economic factors. Internal factors can be consolidated and improved based on experience and the number of countries.

CHAPTER 9
HOW TO SUPPORT THE NEW PRODUCT GENERATION PROCESS

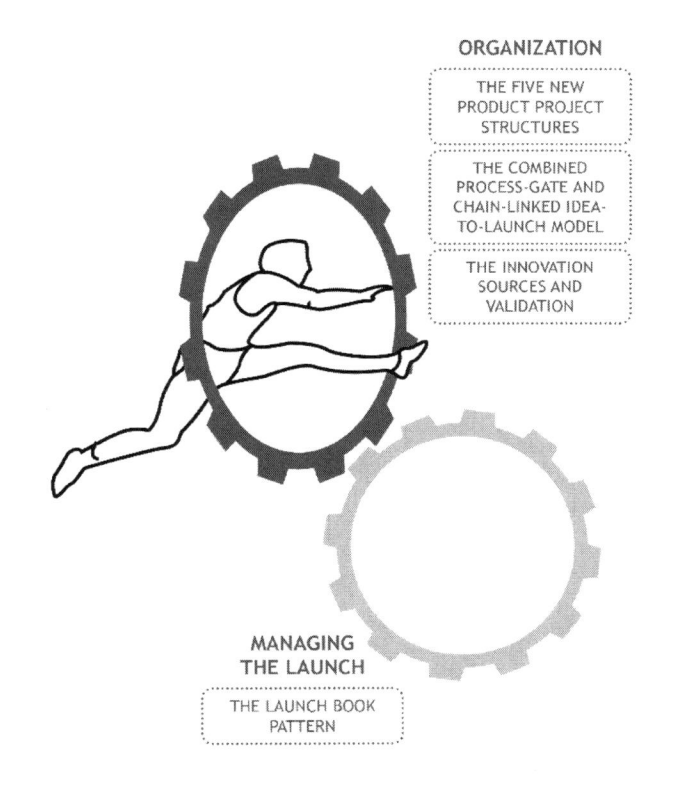

ORGANIZATION
- THE FIVE NEW PRODUCT PROJECT STRUCTURES
- THE COMBINED PROCESS-GATE AND CHAIN-LINKED IDEA-TO-LAUNCH MODEL
- THE INNOVATION SOURCES AND VALIDATION

MANAGING THE LAUNCH
- THE LAUNCH BOOK PATTERN

The role of marketing managers is to kick off the new product programs with the generation of product specifications and a business plan. During the product generation process, managers watch how the R&D department responds to the specifications and prepares for launch.

What is specific to B2B?

In B2B, the technical difficulties of creating a product are more pronounced. The R&D investment and time to market are not easy to evaluate, and can be twice as long as the initial prediction. The desired performance and price by marketing are typically not easy to achieve. Thus, communication between marketing and project managers should be tight throughout the program. A specific monitoring organization should be put in place.

The marketing activities surrounding the product generation process concern organization and validation. Four tools are proposed.

The organization
- Tool 46: The Five New Product Project Structure
- Tool 47: The Combined Process-Gate and Chain-Linked Idea-to-Launch Model
- Tool 48: The Innovation Source-Validation Frame

Managing the launch
- Tool 49: The Launch Book Pattern

Tool 46: The Five New Product Project Structure Models help to optimize organizational efficiency

DEFINITIONS

Virtual organizations are structures that work from a distance. *Adjacent individuals or organizations* are external persons or organizations connected via collaborative Internet tools.

New product initiatives have considerable organizational differences between business fields, company cultures, and project profiles. According to the existing professional expertise, the project positioning inside the company strategy and processes, and the necessity for tight versus light coordination, five structures can be selected. In the *functional structure*, the marketing manager or project Leader serves as a co-coordinator. When the specifications are agreed upon, the co-coordinator moves from one department (e.g., mechanics, electronics, software, quality) to the next. S/he must wait until that each department has finished its task before moving to the next one. In the *matrix structure*, an official project leader manages the team allocated by different departments. The project leader has the same level of authority as the department directors. In the *team structure*, the department directors lose their authority as long as the team exists, and the project leader is free to hire external contributors. In the *independent structure*, the project team is built separately from the company, with its own staff and has no link with the R&D and marketing people. In the last structure, the *virtual structure*, the project leader is working with volunteers from the community, most of time with collaborative tools. Adjacent partners can be invited to join the project at any time and may not always be visible.

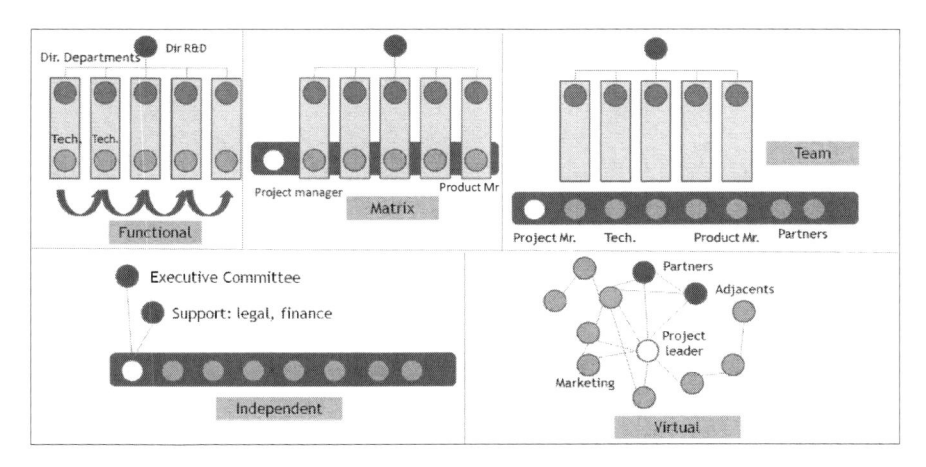

FIGURE 9.1 *The Five New Product Project Structure Models.*

Light projects with low budget can survive with the functional structure. Frequent projects benefit from matrix support. For important projects with significant budget, a team structure is often chosen. When the project is too radical and not adopted by the company culture and processes, an independent structure is preferable. Lastly, when multiple companies are involved with few contractual constraints, the virtual organization is chosen.

How to use the tool?

This tool is used to identify alternative choices. New product programs can be analyzed in terms of level of need for expertise, importance, fit with existing R&D processes, coordination among departments, and need for control. Based on these factors, the structure most conducive to product generation can be selected.

Strengths and limitations of the tool

Many projects do not survive because there is limited attention to structures. This tool is detrimental for adopting the right structure based on the project profile. A limitation is that five models may not be enough; structures can be mixed and adapted for large organizations, and can be changed during the life of the project.

Tool 47: The Combined Process-Gate and Chain-Linked Idea-to-Launch Model helps to develop control over new product projects

The process-gate model (Cooper, 2008) proposes five project steps and five "gates," considered as validation milestones. The preliminary step is to develop a permanent idea sourcing system, which ends with a screening process gate. The second step is to get a scope of all the areas impacted by the idea—IP, R&D, partnership, market acceptance. The second gate ensures that the idea is still consistent with the strategy and represents a clear marketing concept. The third step defines the precise business case, and ends with the gate feasibility, which covers market fit, distribution fit, and technical fit. The next step is the development of a product; it ends with the review of the product prototype. Then, the test activities give the customer and market feedback; this step ends with a second validation of revenue and profits. The next step is production, followed by the launch and optimization, which profit from initial sales data and best practices to improve the product and boost sales. Each stages ends with a gate. The Chain-Linked Model (Kline & Rosenberg, 1986) also incorporates retro-actions between steps. This can be particularly useful to ensure flexibility, especially given the uncertainty regarding the efficiency of gates when there are time pressures. Certain circumstances, such as long project duration, may trigger a repeat of the gate validations.

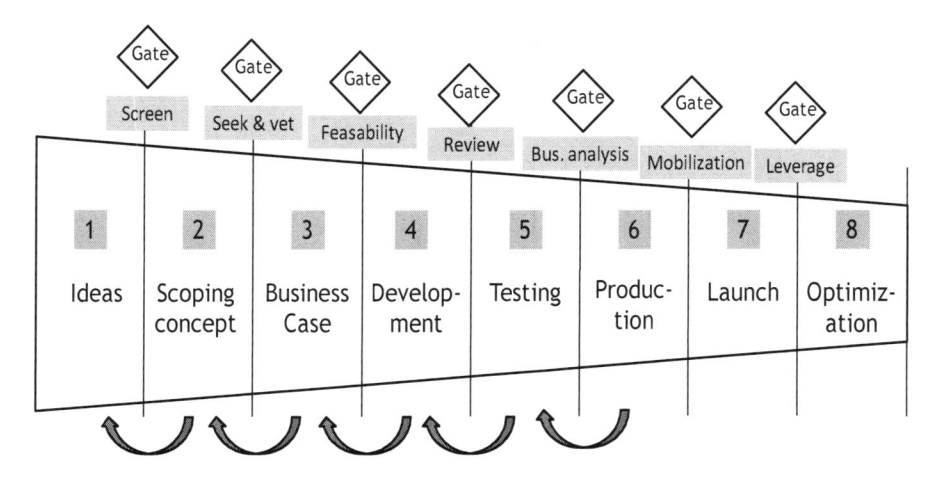

FIGURE 9.2 *The Combined Process-Gate and Chain-Linked Model.*

How to use the tool?

This tool helps to first decide what steps should be defined for a new product program. Eight steps are suggested. Then, the gates are selected. Lastly, acceptable retro-actions should be included. The tool elicits particularly rich debate between R&D and marketing managers.

Strengths and limitations of the tool

The model has clear and documented idea-to-launch phases. It is linear and requires important gate controls. Project governance needs to divide the responsibilities between project managers and gatekeepers, while at the same time remain flexible and forceful. The gates should not exclude parallel activities or spiral rethinking if new events trigger the need to reconsider previous conclusions. For example, an open innovation program may ease or accelerate a project at the development phase, but alliances should not exclude gates. Thus, a limitation of the tool is that while not forbidden, backward movement is costly and limited. According to some modern management styles, the absence of gates and backward movement in the spiral is considered to enhance expediency (Ernst & Young, 2015); however, they can increase risk considerably.

Tool 48: The Innovation Sources and Validation Tool ensures the efficiency of innovation contributors

The contributors to innovation are more and more numerous. Many of them are valuable sources of ideas, and at the same time, can contribute to the validation as consultants. The Innovation Sources and Validation Tool provides a simple way to list who can be instrumental, and decide the best period to incorporate their help during the product process. The tool proposes a generic example. In this case example, the generation of ideas is very large in the business; the marketing managers use creative methods to survey customers, analyze competition, consult with the sales force, and create crowdsourcing activities with employees. At the concept phase, customers are consulted, regulations are analyzed, and partners are identified to participate in the process. At the feasibility phase, R&D proposes innovations and consults with well-chosen, strategic subcontractors. During the development phase, customers test prototypes and distributors are also consulted for their feedback on the performance of the business model. Distribution also contributes to sales innovation at the launch time. Finally, the marketing organization looks for optimization opportunities during the post-launch period.

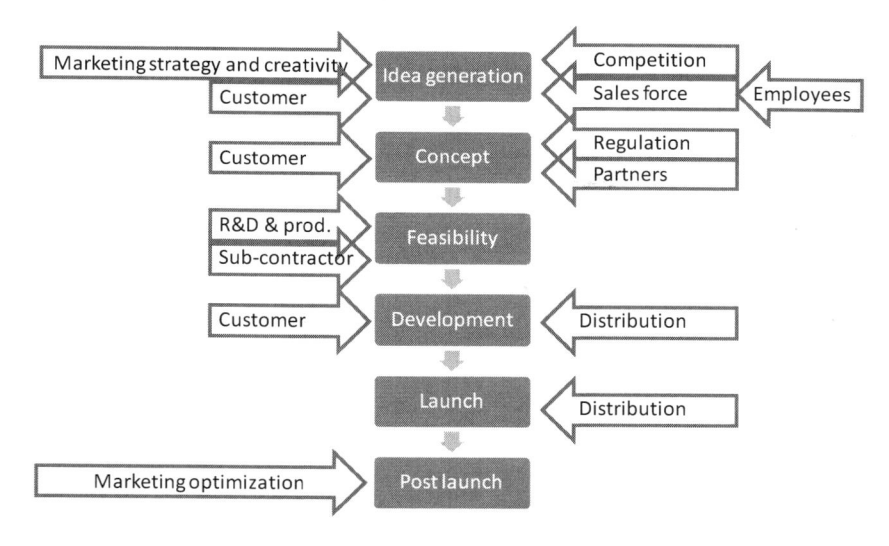

FIGURE 9.3 *The Innovation Sources and Validation Tool (Example).*

How to use the tool?

This tool helps to decide who will validate the project at each step. The evaluation of the risk probability and type will define the process. For example, an anticipated ergonomic risk, such as a misunderstood product interface, triggers a customer validation at the end of the development phase. More validations reduce the risk of project failure, but increase the time to market. Agreeing upon the global program of validations at the start will allow for the appropriate allocation of resources. In practice, consultation with well-chosen people is time-consuming and often omitted.

Strengths and limitations of the tool

This tool optimizes the contributions of all actors to the innovation and improves quality. It allows actors to be efficient at the right time. The tool suggests using a number of contributors. A limitation of the tool is the time and resources needed for marketing and accommodating consultants. This issue can be addressed by mastering remote 2.0 communication tools.

Tool 49: The Launch Book Pattern gives the need-to-know elements to ensure new product launch success

Launches are a major operational marketing activity. When the product certifications are difficult and expensive in different countries, or the technical or marketing support is important, they can last several years and require a large budget. Preparation is therefore a key factor to success in aligning the project manager and the distribution channels activities to the customer segments. The Launch Book Pattern provides a detailed sample plan for the marketing manager in charge. It includes the strategic information about the new product, as well as the proposition of the distribution model, support to sales force, and communication.

REVENUE TARGETS AND STRATEGY
- Revenue per source over next 3 years
- Launch budget
- Strategic positioning and message
- Major benefits, unique selling proposition

VALUE PROPOSITION
- Detailed specifications of product
- Product customization
- Distribution price list
- End user price list, packages
- Discount policy
- Changes to sales contract
- Product range positioning
- Competition comparison

TARGETED SEGMENTS
- Customer profile
- Existing solution issues and need
- Existing experience
- Life cycle

DISTRIBUTION
- Sales force profile needed
- Off-line, online, direct, indirect distribution model
- Customer support needed
- Marketing abilities needed
- Distribution management incentive
- Sales force commissioning
- Incentives and contests for distributor

FIGURE 9.4 *The Launch Book Pattern (Part 1).*

SUPPORT TO SALES FORCE
- Launch events
- Lead generation program
- Training schedule
- Sales training documents and tools
- Sales tools
- First success stories & references
- Certification quizzes
- Price list
- Sales contracts
- Customer lists
- Prospect lists
- CRM adaptations
- ERP adaptations
- Databases use
- Commissions
- Special launch offer
- Special sales contest

WEBSITE ADAPTATIONS
- Product presentation pages
- Demonstration tools
- Benefit valuation tool
- Business cases
- Testimonials
- Help me choose tool
- FAQ, help desks, product document downloads
- Forum
- Expert blog

COMMUNICATION TOWARDS PARTNERS
- Regulators lobbying
- Certifications & labels processes
- Lead providers
- Influencers
- Co-marketing programs

FIGURE 9.5 *The Launch Book Pattern (Part 2)*.

LEAD GENERATION SCHEDULE
- Lead quantity target
- Lead-to-sale transformation rate target
- Scenarios of customer blueprint
- Multichannel online media
- Message designs for media
- Off-line, exhibition presence
- Adwords
- Social network presence
- Newsletter announcement information
- Leads processing

CORPORATE COMMUNICATION
- Public relations
- Shareholders communication
- Business field and public actors communication

INTERNAL COMMUNICATION
- Internal newsletter
- Project leader testimonial blog
- Special processes linked to the new product

FIGURE 9.6 *The Launch Book Pattern (Part 3)*.

A lot of content is derived from the initial market surveys to generate the specifications. Other information comes from the distribution knowhow and benchmark.

How to use the tool

The content of the launch book can be decided with the consultation of distributors, who will contribute by preparing workshops. Each distributor will customize the book to make their own plan. In practice, the book is generated and completed in parallel with the launch preparation actions in a schedule. The launch activities are organized with concurrent meetings managed by the marketing managers and include all departments concerned: service, support, project leader, administration, supply chain, communication, and training.

Strengths and limitations of the tool

The tool acts as a guide to marketing managers in charge of the launch, as well at the group level and distributor's level. It helps define the essence of the product and details best practices to help ensure its success. The limitation, however, is the time pressure, since compiling the book requires consultation and collaboration with the field, which often comes with delays.

CHAPTER 10

HOW TO MANAGE THE PRODUCT PORTFOLIO

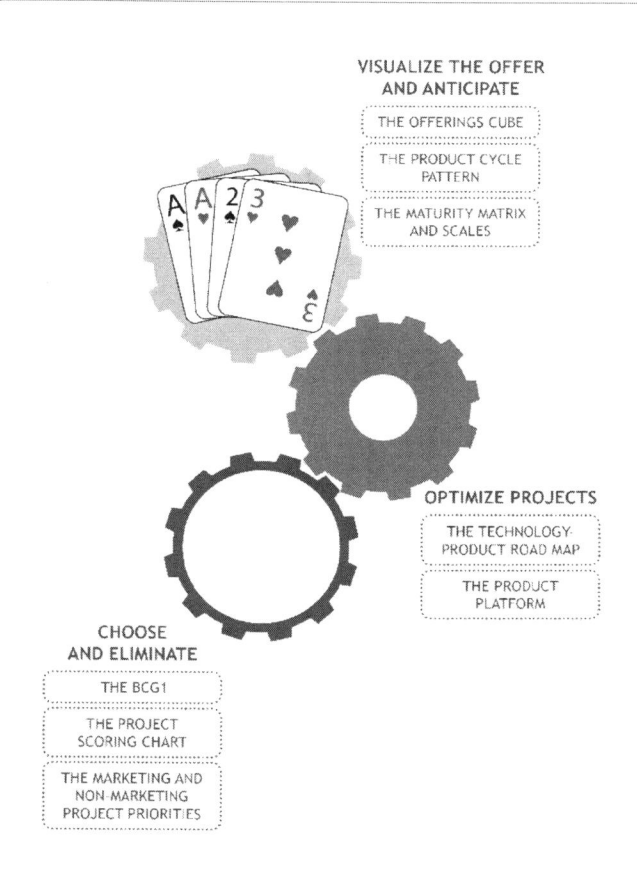

VISUALIZE THE OFFER AND ANTICIPATE
- THE OFFERINGS CUBE
- THE PRODUCT CYCLE PATTERN
- THE MATURITY MATRIX AND SCALES

OPTIMIZE PROJECTS
- THE TECHNOLOGY-PRODUCT ROAD MAP
- THE PRODUCT PLATFORM

CHOOSE AND ELIMINATE
- THE BCG1
- THE PROJECT SCORING CHART
- THE MARKETING AND NON-MARKETING PROJECT PRIORITIES

This chapter introduces the cycle of decisions, which is necessary to manage a global portfolio of B2B products and services. Tools are provided to address each step of decision-making process.

Managing a value proposition portfolio is an ongoing activity in marketing. It includes a series of interrelated tasks, which can be supported by specific tools. The idea is to start with a global evaluation of the existing product lines. It will be facilitated with the tool, Cube, which positions each product and shows relevant synergies. Then, a projection of sales is made using the tool, Product Life Pattern. This provides a dynamic vision of the business. The search to optimize technology opportunities can be made with the Technology-Product Map and the Product Platform tools. The next step is to choose projects, which can be done using the BCG, and Project Scoring Chart. The decision to drop products from the offer can also be made using the BCG1. After completing this process, it starts again, and remains ongoing.

What is specific to B2B?

In B2B, the cost of a sales representative and the cost of product development are so high that the product's global range must be carefully chosen. Optimizations and synergies in the technologies, in the distribution, and in the sales visits are searched for and identified. Compared to B2C, the number of product projects is also more important in terms of making incremental improvements; assessing options, services, and support; and developing new generations of a product. All of these elements must be justified under a specific global line management. Eight tools support the management of the portfolio.

Visualize the offer and anticipate
- Tool 50: The Offerings Cube
- Tool 51: The Product Cycle Pattern
- Tool 52: The Maturity Matrix and Scales

Optimize projects
- Tool 53: The Technology-Product Road Map
- Tool 54: The Product Platform

Choose and eliminate
- Tool 55: The BCG1
- Tool 56: The Project Scoring Chart
- Tool 57: The Marketing and Non-Marketing Priorities

Tool 50: The Offerings Cube visualizes the company ranges

DEFINITIONS

Offerings width is the number of complementary products or services sold to the same segment. *Offerings height* is the number of segments covered. *Offerings depth* is the number of redundant products that answer to the same customer need. *Sales synergy* is potential savings due to the sale of several products at the same sales meeting with customers. *Product synergy* is potential savings due to common efforts in R&D. *Purchase synergy* is potential savings in purchase activities.

A company's offerings can be conceptualized using the Offerings Cube. The width, which represents the number of product lines sold to a same segment, varies per segment. The height corresponds to the different segments addressed. The depth shows the redundancies, which are common in B2B marketing with mergers and acquisitions. The surfaces of the squares correspond to lines of revenue. In the graphic, thick lines represent sales synergies. The cube can be used to visualize the company's existing offerings, which can help to analyze synergies and redundancies. For instance, are the redundancies B3.1 and B3.2 intentional or did they result from historical factors? Was it decided to only offer the C2 product line to the mid-segment or are there opportunities to add product lines and create C1 or C3? Should a decision be made about the A range, which has a poor success and is limited to Segments 1 and 2?

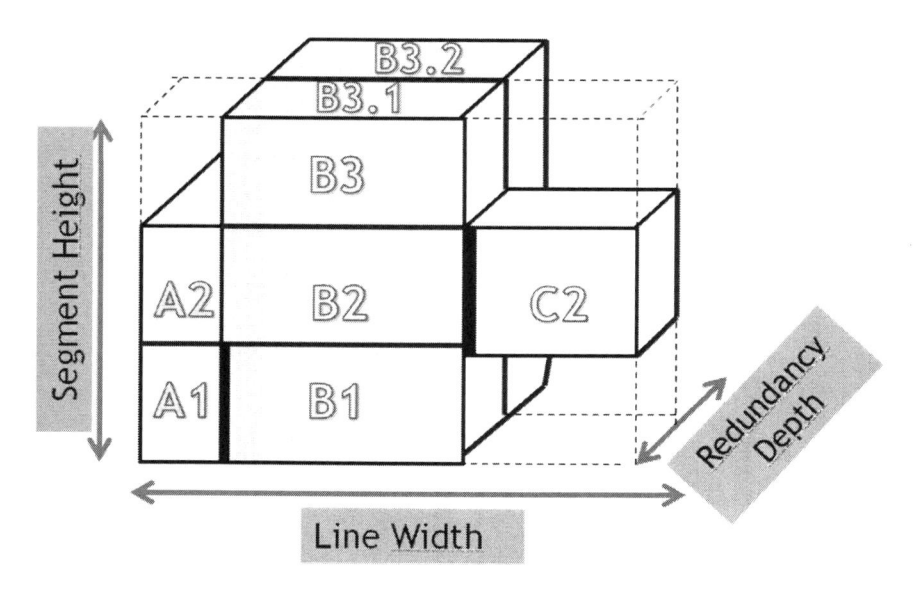

FIGURE 10.1 *The Offerings Cube.*

If there are too many products, they are structured in ranges to keep the Cube readable. Synergies between product lines are a key factor in B2B marketing. Product synergies come from the company perspective, with criteria such as the same technology for product lines, the same infrastructure to support such product lines, and the same production model.

Sales synergies come from the customer perspective, where the criteria would be the same buyer, the same prospect, the same buying process, and the same business field. From the first point of view, the synergy will reduce the design and production costs; from the second point of view, synergy will reduce the selling and marketing costs. Purchase synergies reduce the number of suppliers, the purchase process time, and the cost.

How to use the tool?

When the global strategy is defined—for example by utilizing the 6P Mix—the height of the offerings is decided (i.e., the targeted segments). For each segment, the width is decided (i.e., the types of need covered by several products). Then, the depth is decided for each product. Manufacturers may limit R&D costs by reducing width and avoiding depth in a push strategy; B2B distributors who want to offer choice may do the opposite in a pull strategy.

Benefits and limits of the tool

The Offerings Cube allows for an easy understanding of the ranges. It helps to extend the ranges in order to increase revenue, and at the same time identify synergies. The chosen number of products is a compromise: Too many reduces efficiency for manufacturers and distributors, too few limits revenue. The tool is relevant with a minimum of products and segments.

Tool 51: The Product Cycle Pattern anticipates sales and marketing actions

DEFINITIONS

The *product cycle* is represented by a curve with the number of sales over the life of the product, including the second-end market and recycling of material.

The Product Cycle Pattern is a model that can be used to represent the evolution of product revenue. It helps to carefully manage the take-off phase as well as decline. The curves reflect the different phases, from launch to withdrawal from the sales catalogue, and can be used to identify patterns in product revenue simulation. It is very useful to track curves for past products as well as investments in communication and distribution. A Gauss curve is traditionally used, with the succession of product generations.

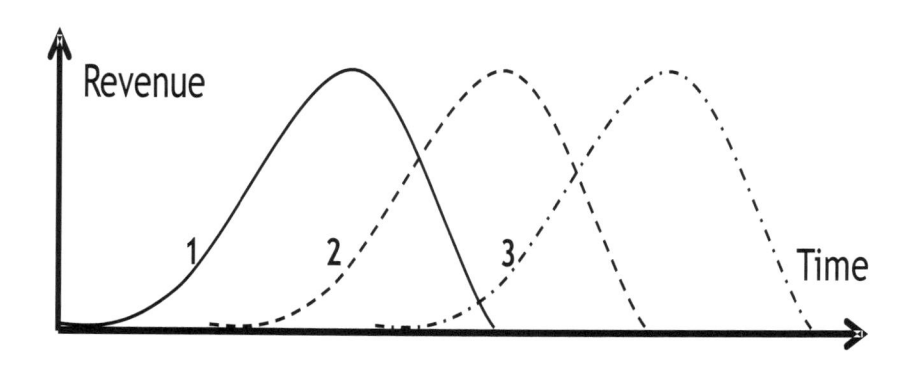

FIGURE 10.2 *The Gauss-Type Pattern of Product Cycle.*

In fact, the Gauss pattern corresponds closely to reality. Each industry has patterns and depending on the type of innovation, patterns are different for take-off, plateau, and decline. Three patterns are presented in Figure 10.2. Pattern 1 in the graphic represents incremental innovation, where the manufacturer replaces an old product with a new one to its usual customers—for example, an improved diesel motor in the trucking industry. Limited customer learning is necessary. Pattern 2 shows a radical innovation, with a common B2B slow take-off: Buyers are resistant to the company learning transformation and limit their risk. Pattern 3 represents cycle, where innovation is limited and sales are correlated with the economic environment typically in the raw material field.

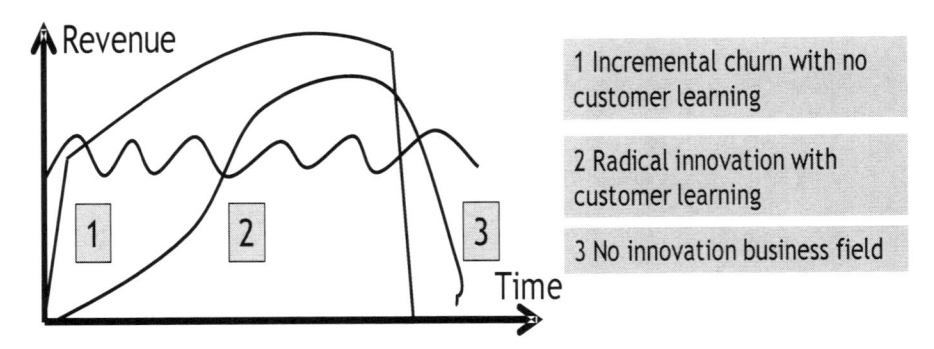

FIGURE 10.3 *Three Patterns of Product Cycle.*

1 Incremental churn with no customer learning

2 Radical innovation with customer learning

3 No innovation business field

The Product Cycle Pattern includes a series of marketing actions to make decisions based on product phases. Table 10.1 provides an example.

TABLE 10.1 *Example of Marketing Actions per Product Phase.*

Marketing phases	Introduction	Growth	Maturity	Decline
Target	Early adopters	All market	All market	Business critical
Product line	Limited	Larger	Large and customized	Lower priced
Relation	Tight relations and support	Diversified relations	Free services increase	Minimum support
Communication	To lead users and opinion leaders	To prospects and customers	To installed base and competitors' base	No communication

The product cycle is not limited to the period from launch to withdrawal. Today, it includes the secondhand market and recycling. B2B markets are particularly concerned with these activities; they are highly interested in recycling materials from their respective industry as well as from other industries. This is represented by the circular economy, in which industries remain in close proximity, and the waste of one production serves as the raw material for the next.

How to use the tool?

The tool should be used as soon as the product design and production is decided. It includes the volume of sales forecast and the marketing strategy at each phase. Adaptations may be necessary based on the business field, other products in the range, the second-hand market, competition, etc. Targeted customers and marketing budgets are anticipated for each phase. The tool is updated at the end of each phase of the product cycle.

Strengths and limitations of the tool

This tool is useful in fast-moving industries with regular launches and multiple products that need monitoring. It can be used also when products last a long time and generate services over the life cycle. The tool can be used to simulate sales in non-disruptive environments; however, it does not provide a means of anticipating changes due to competition, regulation, or distribution.

Tool 52: The Maturity Matrix and Scales help decide investment effort

The Maturity Matrix displays the different positions of a new product according to the market and technical maturity. The matrix is divided into five areas (see Figure 10.4). In the bottom left area, both maturities are low: Neither the customer nor the technology is ready. It is too early and highly risky to invest, except for companies that accept research and marketing expenditures for a long period of time. The two triangles are areas where the investment is important either in (a) marketing to educate the customer, or in (b) technology progress. In the top right area, the product arrives too late: The technology is mature and available to anyone and the market is already saturated; thus, price is driving customer choice. The middle area is the ideal position. There, the investment in technology and marketing is moderate, yet there are still opportunities for differentiation.

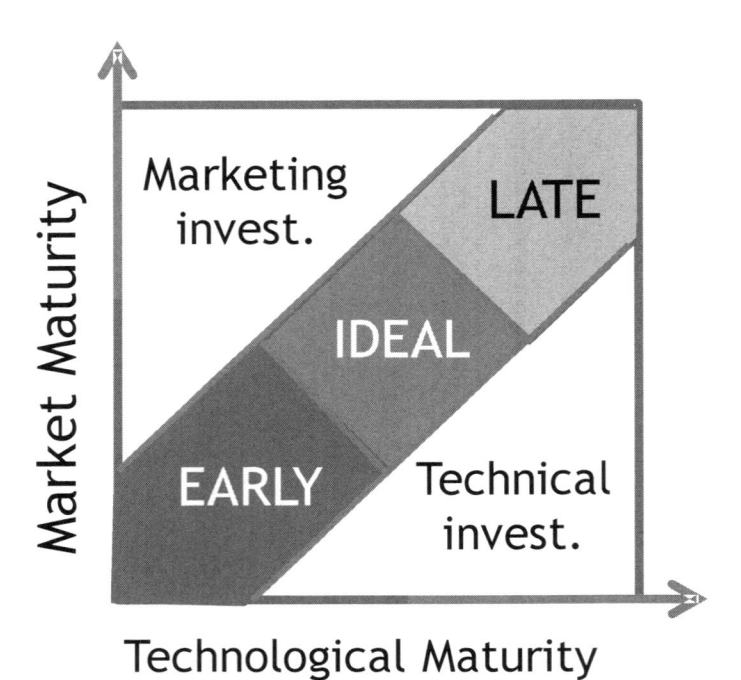

FIGURE 10.4 *The Maturity Matrix.*

This tool can aid managers in making an evaluation of the risks associated with new products using two complementary perspectives—market maturity and technology maturity. As an example, before extending a product line with higher performance, it is important to analyze the maturity of the technology as well as customer acceptance. Batteries in the car industry are an example whereby neither the technology nor the market were mature. Different maturity indices exist, such as the NASA index or Technology Readiness Index (TRI), which help to make this evaluation (Parasuraman, 2000). Figure 10.5 provides scales of market maturities (top to bottom on the left) and technology maturities (top to bottom on the right) based on six levels.

The Market Maturity Scale	The Technology Maturity Scale
Launch	Manufacturing
Business plan	Industrial Scenario
Market Appraisal	Technology Feasibiity
Test with Customers	Product Experimentation
Tartetted Analysis	Technology Exploration
Market investigation	Emerging concept

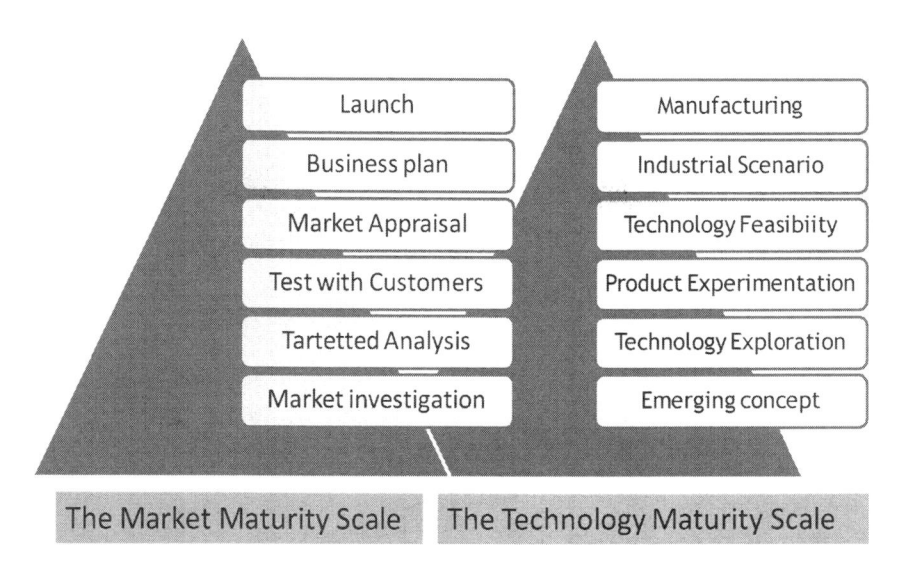

FIGURE 10.5 *The Market and Technology Maturity Scales.*

How to use the tool?

The first step is to adapt the two scales to the business field. Additional levels can be added or substituted. Then, the markets and technology to analyze are chosen. Research is conducted to establish the levels, including document search, interviews with experts, community participation, surveys, and other methods. Triangulation of multiple sources is recommended to ensure that the conclusions drawn are robust.

Strengths and limitations of the tool

This tool pushes marketing and R&D managers to work together in order to manage company risks across two dimensions. It is applicable when the market needs communication investments to take off, or when the technology requires adaptations to fit the market. Using this tool requires an ability to evaluate what investments are needed based on the maturities. Practice is needed to develop this ability.

Tool 53: The Technology-Product Road Map optimizes technology opportunities

The Technology-Product Road Map presents the links between the technologies mastered by an enterprise and its product lines. Technologies and their successive versions are presented at the top of the figure. The bottom shows the product line evolution. In the example, the technology T1.1 has evolved to T1.2, which created an opportunity to move product P1.1 to P1.2. Mastering the technology T2.1 provided the means to create a new high-end product, P2.1. Whereas the product P1.3 was not created from technology progress, technology advancement in T2.1 to T2.2 resulted in the evolution of products—P2.1 to P2.2 and P1.3 to P1.4. This was possible with a common platform for both the P2.2 and P1.4 products.

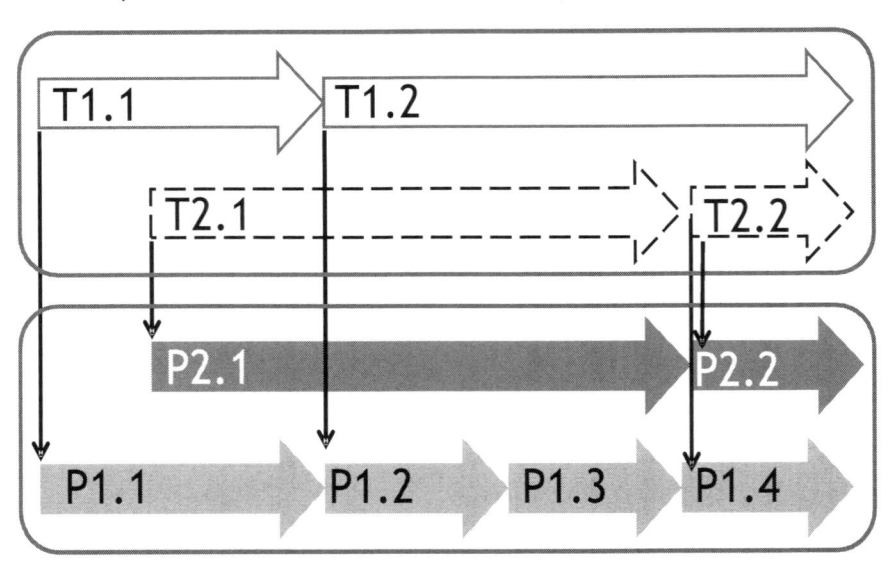

FIGURE 10.6 *Technology-Product Road Map.*

The technologies that can generate product evolutions should be carefully listed. Technologies for product performance—such as ergonomics, production process improvements, new environments, and accessories—could also be included. The pace of new product creation tends to accelerate, resulting in profits from small incremental evolutions or important radical evolutions.

In order to better understand the marketing potential of new technologies, each one is associated with specific performance criteria. For example, GPS technology performance can be measured in precision. Plasma technology for screens can be measured in pixel number per surface area and color resolution. Thus, when possible, the progress of any technology should be translated into performance metrics. Figure 10.7 adds a scale of metrics. It clearly shows how technology T2.1, with a metric of 950 (in units of technology performance), progressed to 1250 in T2.2, which was beneficial to P1.2. Similarly, T1.1 was released with a performance at 1550 and improved to 1750 by T1.2, which was beneficial to both P2.2 and P1.4. This shows that the two products, P2.2 and P1.4, do not differ on these metrics, calling into question the differentiation of the products.

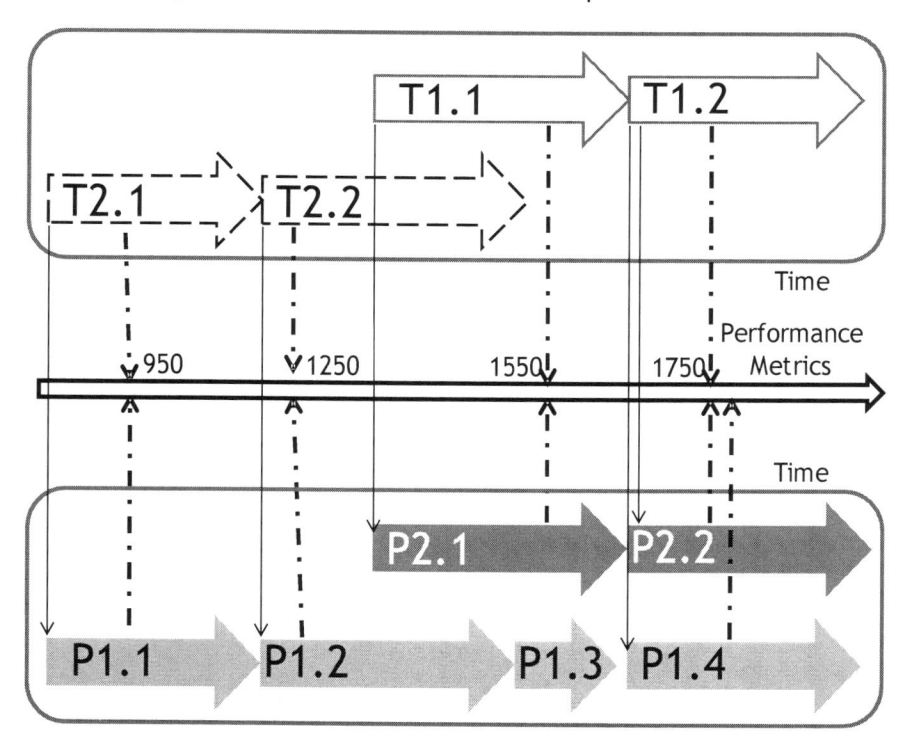

FIGURE 10.7 *The Technology Product Road Map and Metrics.*

How to use the tool?

The technologies mastered by R&D or technological partners are listed, and their performance is translated into metrics. Then the evolution of the performance is forecasted. Consultations with experts can help to anticipate the evolution of technologies that are currently outside the business field, but may be helpful in the future. This allows marketing to define the product road map and write specifications.

Strengths and limitations of the tool

This tool is powerful for technology-dependent business fields. It gives a common representation and synchronizes the range evolution associated with each new technology acquisition. A requirement of the tool is that it requires marketing managers and R&D or innovation managers to work closely together. Managers should agree on a schedule of technology releases as well as the metrics for measuring the benefits of technologies.

Tool 54: The Product Platforms Tool optimizes R&D expenditures

DEFINITIONS

A *product platform* is the architecture of a product, which can be used for several products. A *technology platform* is a group of technologies built for a series of products.

A product platform displays elements to aid in building a series of products or services with limited investment. The elements can be parts, software, infrastructure, modules of space, human interface, etc. Each element has its own technological evolution, but maintains its connection to the platform. Changing one or several elements may trigger the generation of a new product, a new version, or a new accessory. Platforms are a basic way to multiply incremental innovations and create a range from a first product. Product platforms may be based on a stable technology platform, which is used for several ranges over a long period.

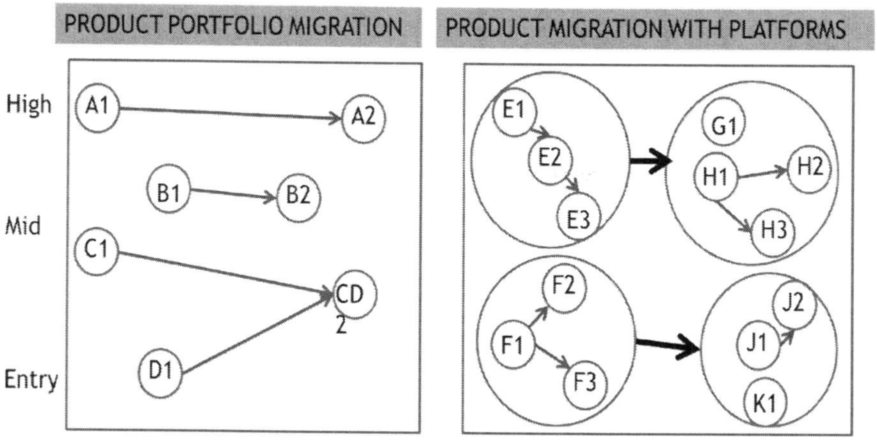

FIGURE 10.8 *The Product Portfolio Migration With Platforms.*

How to use the tool?

Using this tool begins with the generation of possible platforms with R&D managers. Then, the different opportunities associated with each platform are analyzed. Opportunities include the reduction of cost and time for development, as well as multiple product versions and customization. However, each platform triggers additional costs and constraints to allow product range generation. The last phase is to decide which platform to adopt.

Strengths and limitations of the tool

The Product Platform is a time- and R&D cost-saving tool, but not a low cost product producer. Utilization of the tool requires strong discipline from both marketing and R&D managers. Product platforms serve as a foundation and should be respected in order to promote future development. In particular, platforms propose interfaces to connect modules and options. If marketing managers introduce specifications that are not compatible with them, or if engineers do not follow the specifications, then the platform disappears. For example, an attempt to reduce the cost by suppressing the platform's interfaces may kill the product evolutions which come from interfacing modules.

Tool 55: The BCG1 Matrix manages product entry and exit

DEFINITIONS

The *market* of a product or service is the total revenue of all the products of the same type sold in 1 year in a specific area.

This definition involves defining the market, including identifying customers and the scope of products, as well as knowing actual sales. In some industries with local and international producers and distributors, the parameters are blurred and thus, evaluating the market size and share is difficult. For instance, the market size and share of a producer of sand extracted from a river in North Dakota might be difficult to measure. The Boston Consulting Group (Hambrick, MacMillian, & Day, 1982) tried to overcome the issue of determining market share by using the relative market share to the closest competitor. We could extend this concept to a reasonable number of competitors who are frequently fighting for the company product line.

This tool has been one of the most utilized for the past 50 years. It helps users to decide which product lines or business units to develop, to keep, or to eliminate. The tool is a matrix based on two criteria: (a) the relative market share, and (b) the market growth of each line. In the matrix, the product lines are shown with circles, which are proportional in size to the cash generated from each. The relative market share is the ratio market share of the product line or the market share of the closest competitor. The "Stars" product line in the matrix requires investments and promises future revenue. "Cash Cows" generate profit with limited revenue increase. "Question Marks" belong to growing market, but have low market share. They require radical investment decisions: either increase investment so that product can become a leader or quit. For "Dogs," abandonment must be scheduled.

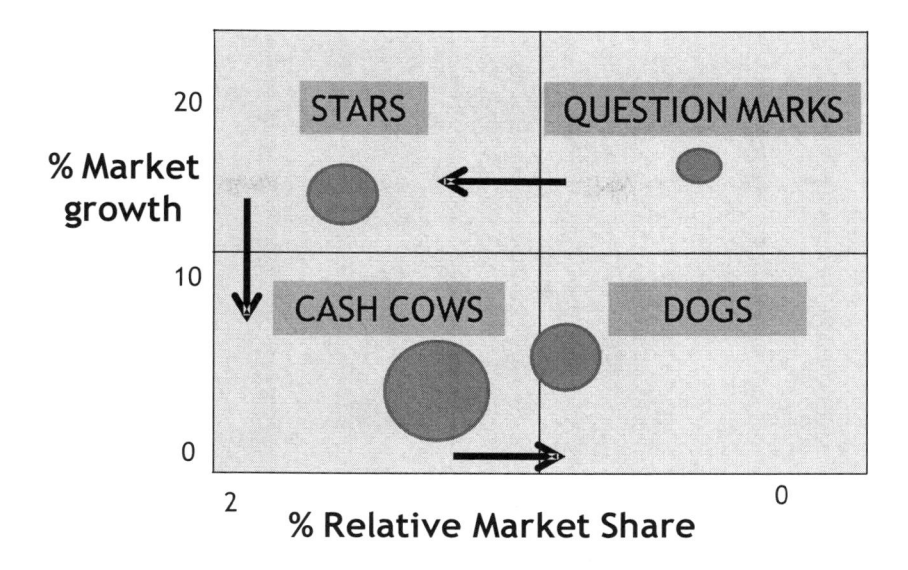

```
20 ─┤    STARS          QUESTION MARKS
% Market
growth
10 ─┤    CASH COWS         DOGS

 0 ─┘
     2                        0
         % Relative Market Share
```

FIGURE 10.9 *The BCG1 Matrix.*

The benefit of this tool is that it can help global product management to try to maintain a balance among product lines. Question Marks are turned into Stars and Stars into Cash Cows, which eventually become Dogs. Maintaining balance among product lines limits the need for investments and loans. For example, the price of sodium hydroxide (caustic soda used in many chemical industries), is linked to volume: The market share and market growth determine a company's competitiveness as well as product line decisions.

How to use the tool?

The first step is to evaluate the market size, growth, and shares. It is necessary to use multiple methods, including customer surveys, sales distributions, analysis of the competition, and interviews with experts, among others. Then, the company and competitor products are positioned, and conclusions are drawn.

Strengths and limitations of the tool

The tool gives four categories of products, which suggest strategic decisions. The market size and market shares of competitors must be known to apply this tool. Second, profitability should be linked to the market share. Industries such as semiconductors and industrial chemicals follow this pattern. Luxury industries might not be concerned with market share to the same degree. Lastly, the BCG1 matrix ignores the possible synergies among product lines. For instance, a Star together with a Question Mark could be a successful cross-sell opportunity. On the other hand, the BCG1 could also miss financial dependencies among product lines. For instance, Cows may finance Stars. Companies that manage their financial lines separately may not follow the rationale behind the BCG1.

Tool 56: The Project Scoring Tool defines criteria and helps prioritize project decisions

DEFINITIONS

The *customer base* is the total customers who have bought products or services and keep regular relationships. An *offensive project* intends to extend the customer base. A *defensive project* intends to keep the customer base.

B2B companies do not lack new product ideas; rather, most of time they are overwhelmed with projects. The Project Scoring Tool helps users to decide which project is most suitable according to the type of innovation. When the innovation is incremental—limited to improvements of existing products or services—the existing distribution, customer segments, R&D, and supply chain are considered adequate. The criteria for decision-making are revenue, margin, investment, and character of the project (offensive or defensive). The last point is linked to the existing range position. If the range is weak or the environment is a threat, defensive projects that improve the line are favored. If the range is strong, offensive projects that extend the line are favored. Table 10.2 is an example of three projects: (a) new product, (b) new application of an existing product, or (c) new accessory in a weak environmental position. The score of the new product in the offensive/defensive position is high because it would replace a declining product. The three projects receive a mark according to their output in margin, revenue, and investment requirements. In the example below, Project B is chosen because it fits better into the offensive/defensive strategy and brings more revenue, despite a heavy investment (1/10) and lower margin than Project A.

TABLE 10.2 *Project Scoring Tool for Incremental Decisions.*

Project	A	B	C
Type	New application	New product	Accessory
Offensive / defensive	4	9	2
Revenue	4	9	2
Margin	9	6	4
Investment	5	1	8
Score	22	25	16

Other criteria can be utilized to adapt this tool to a particular business field. The maximum score is 10, which may also vary based on the strategy employed.

When the innovation is radical, criteria are more fundamental and are concerned with the global fit of the product into company assets. In addition to revenue, margin, and investment, the customer base, distribution network, and R&D capacity are also watched. The customer fit includes the ability to sell the innovation to the existing customer base as well as the known prospect base size. The R&D fit concerns the compatibility with the technology portfolio, technology access, royalty opportunities, and research means. The criteria are weighed based on the company strategy. Additionally, uncertainty is an important aspect of the evaluation in radical innovation. The example in the Table 10.3 shows a more interesting project (Project E compared to Project D), with more margin (8/10 vs. 6/10) and lower investment (7/10 vs. 3/10), but more uncertainty (23% vs. 15%) and a need to change the customer segment (6/10 vs. 9/10).

TABLE 10.3 *Project Scoring Tool for Radical Decisions.*

Criteria	Weight	Score	Uncertainty	Score	Uncertainty
Customer base fit	15%	9	10%	6	20%
Distribution fit	15%	7	15%	6	25%
R&D and partners fit	20%	6	10%	9	20%
Revenue	20%	8	15%	7	25%
Margin	20%	6	25%	8	25%
Investment	10%	3	30%	7	30%
Score	100%	39	15.7%	43	23%

Other factors should also be considered in radical innovation, including the following: strategic learning opportunities in R&D, distribution, customer relations, and availability of a project leader within the company or a sponsor outside of the company.

How to use the tool

The first step is to agree upon the type of innovation—radical or incremental—and then define the criteria to be taken into account. Objective criteria are essential; nonetheless, some criteria may not be measurable. Then, the knowledge and estimation effort is needed to complete the chart. Conclusions are drawn using a transversal team, reflecting the expertise of multiple disciplines.

Strengths and limitations of the tool

This tool is an excellent way to harmonize the executive committees and to select the best projects. Scores are prepared and estimated by marketing and R&D, and are then selected by the executive committee. The committee should reach agreement on the scores after debate, if needed, and should also consult with R&D and customer relations internal or external experts.

Tool 57: The Marketing and Non-Marketing Project Priorities Tool takes into account qualitative factors to decide priorities

DEFINITIONS

The *voice of the customer* refers to customers' frustrations, wishes, dreams, and fears. *Strategic learning* is the acquisition of knowledge or know-how that is perceived as vital for the future. *Technology access* is the process of acquiring technology and related knowledge.

New product and service projects are numerous and continually challenge B2B companies. The prioritization of projects is therefore necessary; however, many factors exist that are difficult to evaluate and not present in the scoring exercise. These elements may influence decision makers in a non-explicit way. The Marketing and Non-Marketing Project Priorities tool thus provides 14 typical qualitative factors in order to promote open discussion inside executive committees. It differentiates among various marketing factors in terms of how they fit the customer voice, as well as the will to test a new business model. The ability to quantify the market is another example that may not typically be debated that poses a real issue for radical innovation. The sensitivity to go to incremental-only innovation is another example. The non-marketing factors in this case include the fit to the existing technology portfolio and the presence of a champion who may manage the project.

Marketing Priorities
- Voice of Customer Fit
- Business Model Test
- Offensive / Defensive
- Incremental / Radical
- Differentiation
- Market Size vs. Risk
- Quantifiable Market

Non-Marketing Priorities
- Portfolio Fit
- People Attraction
- Strategic Learning
- Champion Presence
- Technology Access
- Patent Opportunities
- Royalty Opportunities

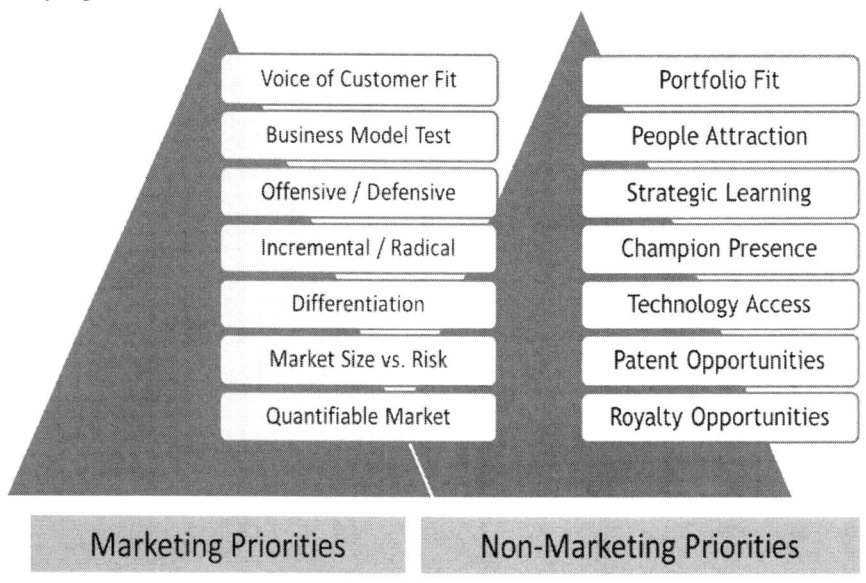

FIGURE 10.10 *Marketing and Non-Marketing Project Priorities Tool (Example)*.

How to use the tool

The tool can be used as a complementary agenda to the presentation of a new product project. The content can be adapted to the case by requesting decision makers' comments prior to the meeting. The factors can then be debated so that all elements and preferences are assessed.

Strengths and limitations of the tool

The tool allows one to explicate all of the project decision-making factors at hand. For example, an R&D vice president can make it clear that he or she is only interested in a project because of its strategic learning consequences. Conversely, he or she may be against a project, doubting the market quantification. A limitation, however, is the tool's very ability to detect all of the factors necessary for a sound decision and hence, people's ability to debate them.

CHAPTER 11

HOW TO SELECT AND SUPPORT THE DISTRIBUTION MODEL

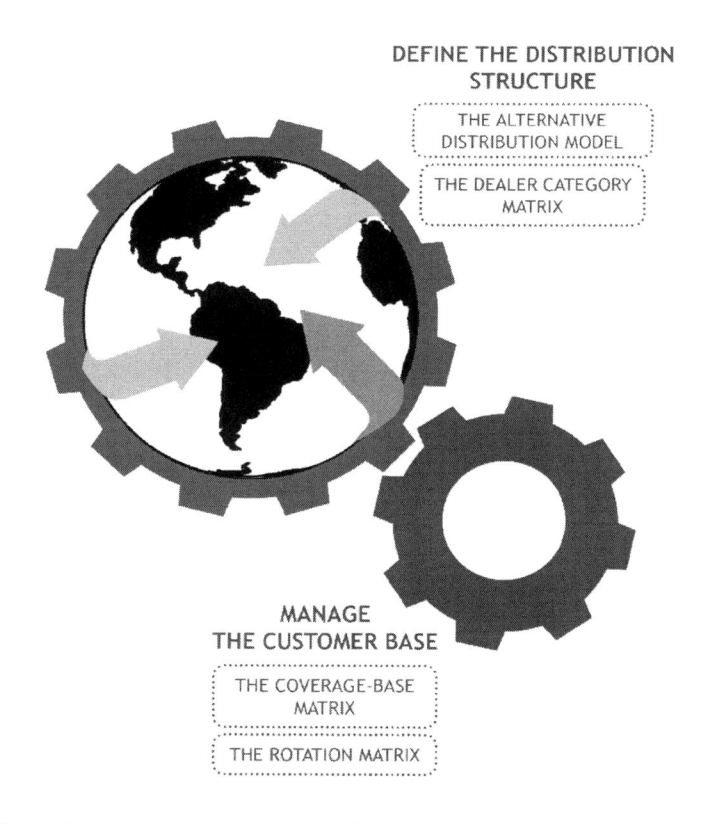

DEFINE THE DISTRIBUTION STRUCTURE

THE ALTERNATIVE DISTRIBUTION MODEL

THE DEALER CATEGORY MATRIX

MANAGE THE CUSTOMER BASE

THE COVERAGE-BASE MATRIX

THE ROTATION MATRIX

B2B Marketing managers are fully involved in the design of the distribution model, which must fit with the value proposition. The sales VP manages the revenue generation and the distribution structure, while the marketing VP regularly introduces new products and analyzes customer behavior in order to optimize and propose new models.

What is specific to B2B?

In B2B, the distribution value addition is larger than in B2C. Its activities include finding customers, advising, designing customer solutions, negotiating, partnering with other suppliers, delivering, assisting in product use start-up, training and supporting users, as well as maintaining, informing, and managing close relations and other future supports. The model may require a combination of several actors, with different profiles, which need different management types. Some suppliers just deliver products to distributors. Others help them acquire the business field knowledge, the product and services sales practice, the management of the customer-installed base, the organization of the customer experience. In the relation supplier-distributor, the balance between support and negotiation can be limited to one conversation on price per year and all other conversations concerns support. Four tools help define a distribution structure and customer base support. In another chapter, other tools will concern the sales support.

Define the distribution structure
- Tool 58: The Alternative Distribution Model
- Tool 59: The Dealer Category Matrix

Manage the customer base
- Tool 60: The Coverage-Base Matrix
- Tool 61: The Customer Rotation Matrix

Tool 58: The Alternative Distribution Model helps to design the distribution mix

DEFINITION

The *value-added reseller* (VAR) not only buys and sells products, but transforms them and/or adds services to package and/or customize a solution.

The Alternative Distribution Model visualizes the main distribution possibilities from manufacturer to customer, and helps to choose the mix of distribution channels. The distributor is in a better position to sell bundles, a global trend that is appreciated by customers, if it is close to a real customization (Sharma & Iyer Gopalkrishnan, 2011). The tool is used differently for the domestic market compared to the export market. For the domestic market, five solutions exist: selling to distributors, which sell to customer end users (Path A); selling to an intermediary (e.g., wholesaler), which sells to a distributor (Path B) or a VAR, which sells to the customer (Path C). The VAR not only buys and sells products, but also transforms them and/or adds services to package a solution. In specific businesses, the final customer requires global solutions. The fourth path is a sale to a VAR (Path D), and the fifth is direct to customers (Path E).

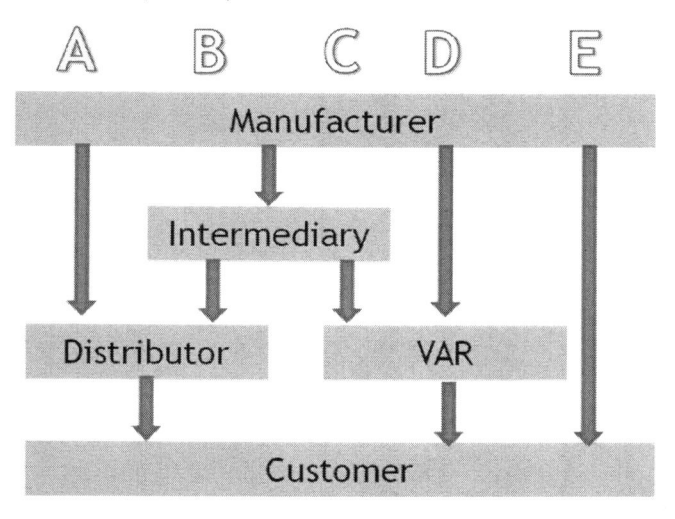

FIGURE 11.1 *Alternative Distribution Model in Home Markets.*

The choice of a distribution mix varies based on the industry and firm strategy. Each model has its benefits and drawbacks, so a mix of solutions is often chosen. Decision factors include customer requirements, the resources needed, required controls, flexibility for changes, and the margin. For example, the choice between distributors and VARs depends on the requirements of the customer segment and impacts the company positioning.

TABLE 11.1 *Benefits and Drawbacks of Direct and Indirect Distribution Networks.*

DISTRIBUTION MODEL	DIRECT	INDIRECT
Benefits	Price control Product margin Service revenue Market knowledge Expertise control Brand awareness Focus Large account deals	Low investment Distributor installed base reach Distributor complementary range Large coverage SME penetration
Drawbacks	Financial risk Cost Coverage limitations Set-up time	Margin lost Dependence Competitor products Price war between distributors Risk of lack of focus Multiple sites lack of coordination

With export markets, the path must include actors with considerable export know-how. This know-how can belong to the manufacturer, which sells directly to customers (Path A), to local distributors (Path B), or to VARs (Path G). The manufacturer can also sell to nationally based intermediaries or foreign intermediaries. Foreign export intermediaries sell directly to customers (Path D) or to distributors or VARs (Path F). The last possibility is that the manufacturer has a subsidiary in a foreign country, with direct foreign investment (DFI). In such cases, the exporter staff can sell to the subsidiary, which can then sell to customers (Path I) or to distributors or VARs (Path H).

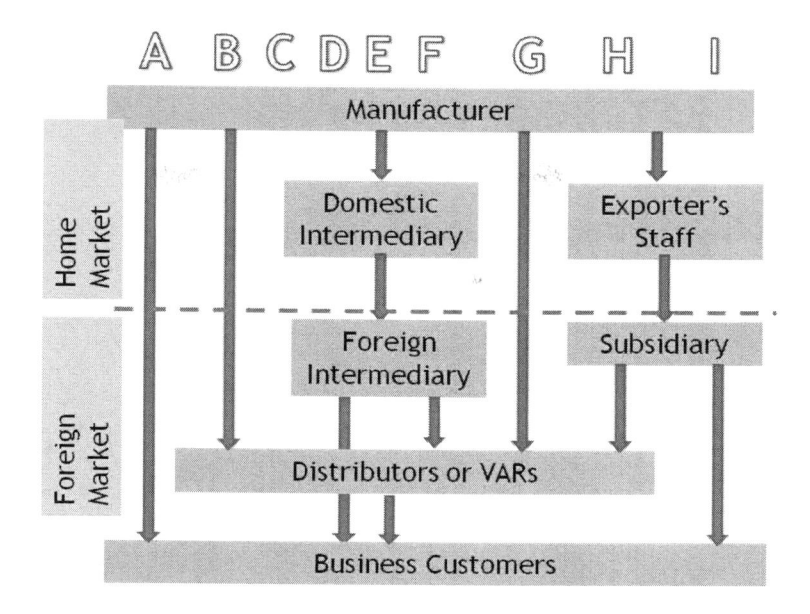

                    A   B C D E F   G   H   I
```
                         Manufacturer
                              │
                    ┌─────────┴──────────┐
                    ▼                    ▼
              Domestic              Exporter's
              Intermediary          Staff
Home Market
- - - - - - - - - - - - - - - - - - - - - - - - -
                    ▼                    ▼
              Foreign               Subsidiary
              Intermediary
Foreign Market      ▼
              Distributors or VARs
                    │
                    ▼
              Business Customers
```

FIGURE 11.2 *Alternative Distribution Model in Export Markets (Tamer-Cavusgil et al., 2014).*

How to use the tool?

The figures and table give an indication of the benefits and drawbacks of the different distribution formats. A short list of viable scenarios can be generated based on the business field. The Value Chain Analysis is necessary to measure the profits generated by different players as well as the benefits they bring to the end user. Comparing investments based on different scenarios will suggest the best distribution solution.

Strengths and limitations of the tool

This tool is effective when the different factors of each distribution possibility are evaluated. It helps to select, for example, a direct distribution for large companies, and indirect distribution for small and medium-sized companies. A limitation of the tool is that it requires accurate and up-to-date local information in order to model the different scenarios. Another limitation is that the models need to be constantly adapted, which requires a distribution intelligence system. Transitions from direct networks, which can appear to be too expensive, to indirect networks, which may lack the product expertise—or vice versa—should be done smoothly in order to minimize negative consequences to customers.

Tool 59: The Dealer Category Matrix helps to adapt the distribution support

DEFINITIONS

Market reach is the ability to contact targeted customers and process sales operations.

The Dealer Group Matrix helps to define profiles of dealers in an area according to two criteria: (a) the need for technical support, and (b) the need for marketing support. Technical support includes technical training, equipment, Level 2 diagnostics and repair when the distributor cannot make them, availability of experts, etc. Marketing support includes sales training, lead generation, sales tools, salespersons' presence to close specific deals, etc. The four types in the matrix drive different management and contract policies, including target revenue, transfer prices, invitations to conferences, contests, awards, etc. A Dealers require a low level of marketing and sales support and have a lot of market reach expertise; they negotiate high margins and gross high levels of revenue. In the opposite corner, starter dealers (C Dealers) require both support and will not benefit from low prices from the supplier. B1 dealers can produce revenue, but need technical support; B2 dealers require marketing support. Support resources will define the price policy. This tool is more accurate than the usual segmentation of dealers, which is based only on gross revenue.

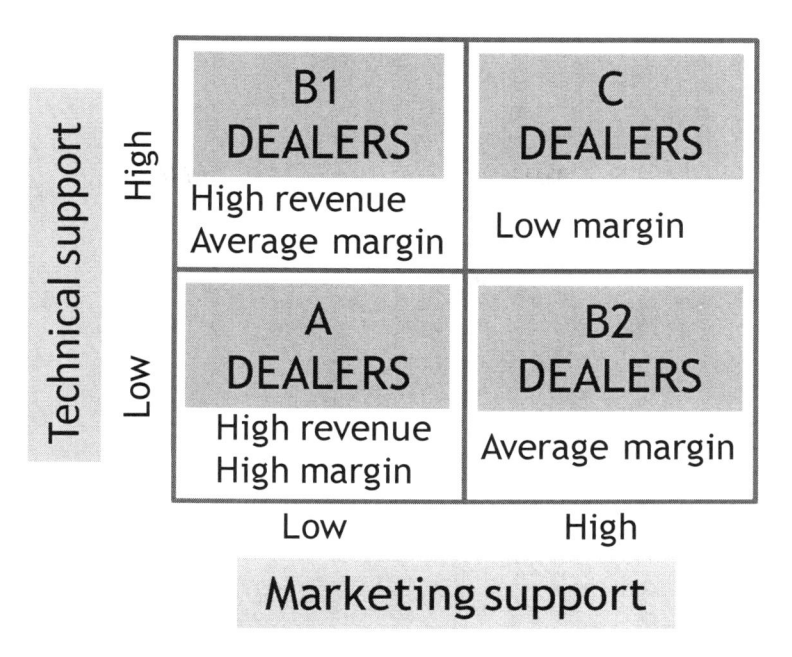

		Low Marketing support	High
Technical support	High	**B1 DEALERS** High revenue Average margin	**C DEALERS** Low margin
	Low	**A DEALERS** High revenue High margin	**B2 DEALERS** Average margin

FIGURE 11.3 *The Dealer Group Matrix.*

How to use the tool?

First, technical and marketing resources are listed, and their importance is evaluated, particularly in terms of cost. The two indicators marketing and technical support are created from this list of resources. Then, each distributor is analyzed using this criteria. The selected distributors are split into the four categories and decisions can then be made about each of them according to available resources and targeted revenue.

Strengths and limitations of the tool

This tool is beneficial when a supplier has many dealers and must optimize its distribution management budget. Splitting dealers into homogeneous categories helps to create different scenarios based on the categories. Other criteria may also be relevant: exclusivity of the supplier product, specific segment penetration, size of the account, domestic or foreign and product range sold. Marketing managers can define the best criteria for evaluating their distribution policy. A limitation of the tool is the resources required to analyze the distributor and the quality of their information.

Tool 60: The Coverage-Base Matrix anticipates the market reach

DEFINITIONS

The *customer base* is the list of customers who have bought products from the company and have an existing relationship with the company. The *coverage* is the list of customers where the company distribution network is active to sell.

In contrast to the sales organization, which is more devoted to producing revenue for the year, the B2B marketing efforts are divided between revenue production and growth of the customer base. The second objective helps to build future years' revenue. The Coverage-Base Matrix highlights the importance of the sales effort based on customer status.

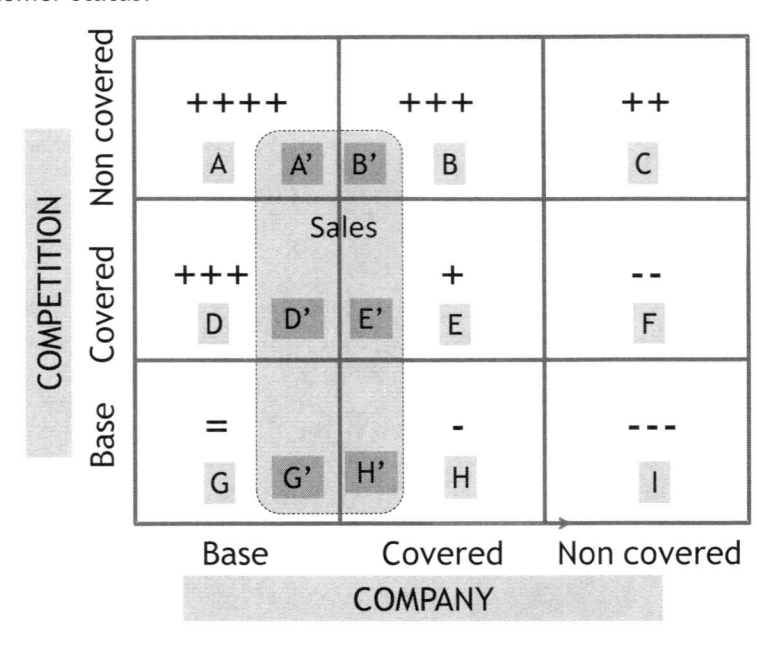

FIGURE 11.4 *The Coverage-Base Matrix.*

Customer status is divided into two dimensions: (a) belonging to the base, and (b) coverage of the company or competition. In Figure 11.4, + or − are used to represent the ease of sale. The letters correspond to figures of sales in the squares.

For example, sales are easiest at the customer base where the competition does not cover the particular product or service (Area A). At the common covered area (D, E, G and H) of the two companies, the competition is equal but sales are more difficult for non-customers (H for the company, D for competition). Companies make all efforts to retain current customers and not lose them to the competition. The customer base of the company is equal to A + D + G. Coverage includes its installed base and is equal to A + B + D + E + G + H. Sales in the installed base of the competition are represented by E'. The matrix aids in balancing investments. First, based on the evaluation, a decision must be made regarding whether to fight competition (D + E + F + G + H + I) or extend the coverage outside the competition base (E + F). Second, efforts for sales in highly competitive areas (G' + H' + D' + E') or in base expansion areas (B' + E' + H') should be rewarded in the form of incentives to the sales forces.

How to use the tool?

This tool requires a CRM process in order to identify the nine customer statuses in relation to the company and competition. Based on the business field, database management may require buying addresses and recording customer relations, as well as getting salesforce and technician feedback. Then, the policy is defined for each customer status, and is tested and evaluated.

Strengths and limitations of the tool

This tool is useful in that it can identify where efforts are exerted to win deals. Marketing and sales managers can use the matrix to define coverage, set commission policies for sales staff, and plan sales training. A limitation of the tool is that sales experts and/or direct practice may be necessary to understand the realities of the field; also, the matrix may vary based on local market factors.

Tool 61: The Customer Rotation Matrix helps to build a sales expectations plan

DEFINITIONS

The *attrition rate* or *customer churn* refers to the percentage of customers lost due to competition, bankruptcies, mergers, and acquisitions. The *cross sale* is the sale of additional products after the first sale to a customer. It can take place at a much later time. *Product churn* is the replacement of equipment.

The Customer Rotation Matrix is a powerful tool to simulate the global market sales and the customer status dynamics. It separates the buyers into three categories: (a) the customers of the company, (b) the customers of the competition, and (c) the prospects who never bought. Additional categories may be added for customers who bought from several suppliers. The events are split into five types: (a) the first purchase, (b) the replacements or product churn, (c) the cross sales (i.e., sales of additional products), (d) the attrition (i.e., the loss of the customers to competition or end of product use). There is also a category of customers where no event took place. The matrix depicts the movements generated by the companies or the competition and their quantities.

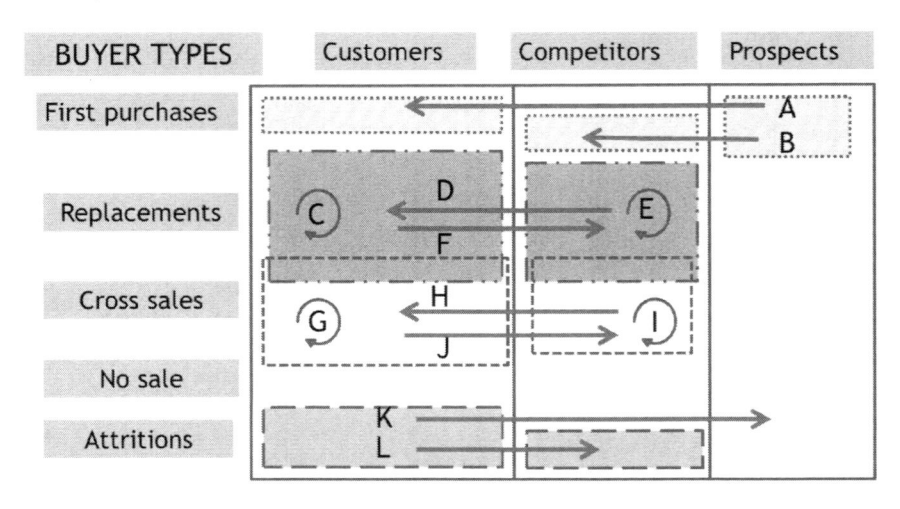

FIGURE 11.5 *The Customer Rotation Matrix.*

For example, the first purchase made by the company is made visible by the arrow A, and that made by competitors with the arrow B. Replacements on the company installed base made by the company are represented by the arrow C and made by competition by the arrow D, etc. Twelve arrows, A through L, represent the different movements. A quantity or revenue is attached to each of them; they collectively give the global picture of the market.

The tool is more valuable in equipment industries. In other industries, raw material, consumables, etc. the product churn does not exist, but first purchase, cross sale, and attrition do exist.

How to use the tool

The process starts with the construction of the database in the CRM, including competition customers and prospects who never bought the type of product. In real life, the database is not exhaustive, but instead, contains a reasonable target of addresses. It is close to 100% of the customer base and lower for competitive customers and prospects and varies with the business field. Then, for each type, the volumes of the different customer rotations mentioned in the tool are estimated, which can be translated into revenue. Outside the analysis of previous years, market surveys and distribution consultation are necessary for new products.

Strengths and limitations of the tool

The matrix can be used for both past years and present years and simulate the future budget and 3-year exercises. It can be an exercise for either a particular segment or the total market. A limitation, however, lies in the ability to obtain the data. A detailed intelligence activity of competition and customers must be organized.

CHAPTER 12
HOW TO MANAGE THE CUSTOMER EXPERIENCE

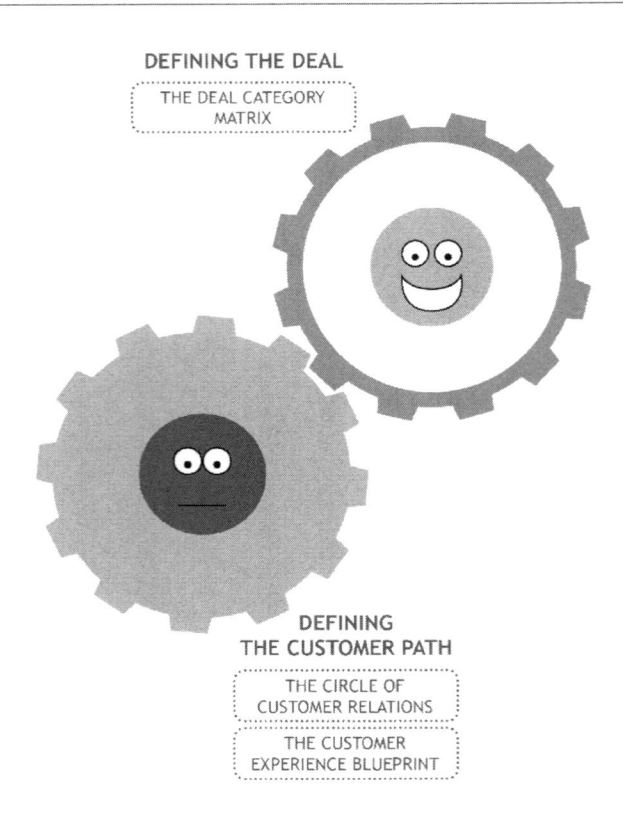

DEFINING THE DEAL
- THE DEAL CATEGORY MATRIX

DEFINING THE CUSTOMER PATH
- THE CIRCLE OF CUSTOMER RELATIONS
- THE CUSTOMER EXPERIENCE BLUEPRINT

Organizations' buyers define their methods of purchase. The people, processes, and decision criteria are the result of their internal considerations and their external experience with suppliers. Marketing managers are in charge of designing a customer path that is suitable to members of the buying center.

What is specific to B2B

In B2C, the consumer culture theory (Arnould & Thompson, 2005) invites marketing managers to understand contextual, symbolic, and experiential aspects of consumption—particularly their hedonic, aesthetic, and ritualistic dimensions. In B2B, the contextual and experiential factors are important and vary considerably by the organization, the business field, and, in particular, the type of deal at hand. With three tools, this chapter will focus on understanding the deal and designing the blueprint according to three buyer profiles.

Defining the deal
- Tool 62: The Deal Category Matrix

Defining the customer path
- Tool 63: The Circle of Customer Relations
- Tool 64: The Customer Experience Blueprint

Tool 62: The Deal Category Matrix anticipates the sales effort with purchase processes and sales types

DEFINITIONS

The *tender* or *bid* is an invitation to submit a formal quoted proposal contract for products or services with information about the supplier. It can be the proposal document itself. The *customer churn* is the loss of customers because of stop of purchase or switch to another supplier. The *product churn* is the customer equipment replacement. A *cross sale* is the sale of an additional product to the customer who bought the first one. The *product listing* is the referencing of products to buyers made by a parent organization; it can be a recommendation or a compulsory list with negotiated prices. The *reverse auction* is an auction in which the winner offers the lowest price.

The number of purchase process types increases with the communication technologies available and the complexity of the customer organizations. Buyers' process choices include face-to-face meetings, Internet purchases from a supplier, dual decision-making with a product listing by a parent organization followed by purchase, and reverse auctions. With each type, the benefits perceived by the customers are different. For example, the terms of neutrality and independence will vary (Truong, Thuang, Senecal, & Rao, 2012). On the other hand, the sales type varies from a customer acquisition in the first sale, a repeat sale of the same product, a churn with a different product, or a cross sale. The Deal Category Matrix helps to understand

155

the complexity, the price pressure, and the speed of the deal. It suggests a process according to product complexity (see Figure 12.1).

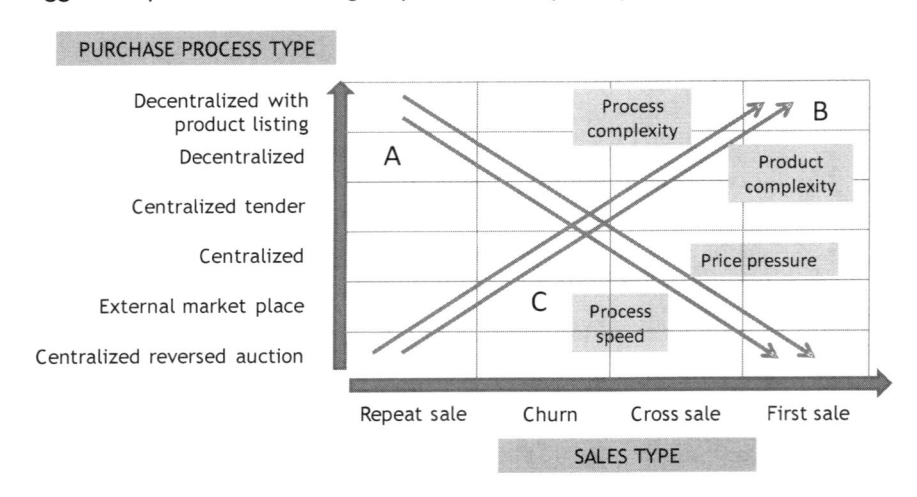

FIGURE 12.1 *The Deal Category Matrix.*

A deal in which the customer wants to replace an existing solution should have a simple product to use an external marketplace (Case C). In Case A, the repeat deal is not quick because it is decentralized. Case B is a first sale; it is decentralized. Thus, the product will be well adapted to the local need.

How to use the tool

First, a segmentation of customers and prospects is made according to the sales process. The six types each need to be evaluated in terms of number of customers. Then, the types of deals are analyzed in quantities and revenue. Next, the decisions emerge: The picture allows one to identify the attractive customers—either because the sales process and sales type make the deal simple, or because the revenue is high. This allows one to lower the priority, discount, and improve sales efforts with other types of customers.

Strengths and limitations of the tool

The tool is a grid to get a first gauge of the sales efforts that needs to be localized. Product complexity can vary greatly depending on the business field. For example, the product listing can be a tough negotiation in some business fields. Other factors may be added by each

B2B company to sales type and purchase process type to anticipate the price pressure or transaction speed.

Tool 63: The Circle of Customer Relations introduces the enterprise CRM strategy

DEFINITIONS

Awareness and contact is a phase in which the customer knows the supplier brand and has intent to engage with it. *Mutual education* is a phase in which the customer and the supplier inform each other to decide and prepare a deal. *Decision and transaction* is the phase of the purchase. The *support phase* refers to supplier operational help to customers after the deal. *Nurturing* is an activity to maintain customer awareness and interest after a deal is completed.

The intended nature of relationships with customers is key to constructing the CRM strategy. The Circle of Customer Relations is a tool that helps define customer relationships according to the enterprise business field. It proposes five relationships and invites one to assess their quality, their type (i.e., collaborative or contentious), and their intensity according to the type of deal. The intensity reflects the communication and sales efforts. The relations generate a cycle—awareness, education, transaction, support, and nurturing—which should remain in continuous flux.

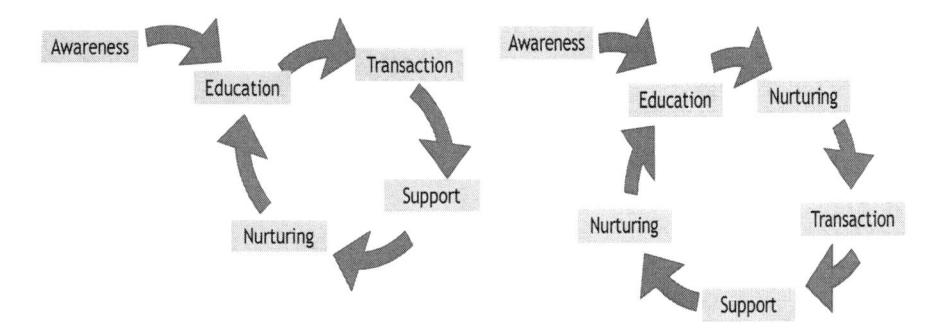

FIGURE 12.2 *The Circle of Customer Relations (Two Examples).*

Nurturing replaces the awareness activity after the first deal. It is a permanent necessity; buyer turnover may occur, the customer may have new needs, or the supplier or its competition may have new products or services. In the case on the left, the sales cycle is so long between the first face-to-face meeting and the transaction that a nurturing is necessary and organized by marketing to keep customer interested.

TABLE 12.1 *The Circle of Customer Relations (Example).*

EXPERIENCE	AWARENESS	EDUCATION	TRANSACTION	SUPPORT	NURTURING
CUSTOMER OBJECTIVE	Know the supplier	Know the solutions	Buy the best solution	Optimize usage	Be up-to-date
SUPPLIER OBJECTIVE	Reach the customer	Know the customer	Sale	Help usage	Maintain the interest
QUALITY KPIs	Cost of lead	% sale	Cost of transaction	% satisfaction	% second purchase
NATURE • Collaborative	X	XXX		XX	XX
• Contentious			XXX	X	
INTENSITY • First sale	XXX	XXX	XXX	XXX	X
• Churn	X	XX	XX	X	X
• Cross sale	X	XX	XX	XX	X
• Repeat sale	X		X		X

In this example, the first sale is critical and requires the most effort, with a strong contentious transaction phase. The churn and cross sale are equal, and some repeat deals exist with limited energy. The education phase is also important due to the complexity of the products.

How to use the tool

The phases of the cycle need to be adapted to the business field. Some specific phases may be added, such as product test, for example. Then, the significant objectives, KPIs, and the type of sale are decided. Lastly, the nature and intensity of the relationship are evaluated. Finally, the tool will allow for the splitting of communication and sales resources.

Strengths and limitations of the tool

The tool generates a global view of CRM, and triggers a common understanding of the resource allocation according to the five types of relations within the four types of deals. A limitation of the tool is that insight is needed in order to understand the customer's buying process

Tool 64: The Customer Experience Blueprint describes the intent of contact path

DEFINITIONS

The *blueprint* is the series of physical or electronic contacts between the customer and the supplier and its partners. The *proof of concept (POC)* is a live test of the product in order to ensure its technical adaptation. The *request for information (RFI)* is a formal document issued by a buyer to select suppliers. The *request for proposal (RFP)* is a formal document issued by a buyer to select a product.

The customer experience is designed by the marketing managers. It needs to be efficient to conclude the deal and must be adapted to the customer's media preference. The Customer Experience Blueprint provides four patterns for creating a blueprint. It describes the steps, the mode, and the people in contact on both customer and supplier sides. It also identifies the marketing quality criteria of greatest importance and shows moments with risk (R) or with wait (W). Tables 12.2 through 12.5 demonstrate four different patterns. The first one is the Tender Pattern, the second the Technical Pattern, the third is the 2.0 Pattern, and the last the Marketplace Pattern. In real life, a mix of these patterns is typically generated.

TABLE 12.2 *The Customer Experience Blueprint (Tender Pattern).*

BLUEPRINT	Awareness Exhibition	Education Consultation	Education Visit	Education RFI	Transaction Short list	Transaction RFP	Transaction Date	Purchase	Support Installation	Support Payment
Quality	% lead		% date	% listed			% purchase		% success	
Customer location				X R	X R		x R	x R	x R	X
Branch			X							
Exhibition	X									
Website		X								
Technician		X	X		X	X			X	
Buyer	X	X	X	X	X	X	X	X		X
BU director					X		X			
Salesperson	X		X	X		X	X			
Technician						X	X		X	
Admin.				X						X

In the Tender Pattern, the process of purchase is formal and includes the RFI and RFQ documents. In between, a short list of eligible suppliers is selected in a formal meeting. Before and after the document publications, meetings take place primarily at the customer's premises. Public authorities may be obliged to follow this process.

TABLE 12.3 *The Customer Experience Blueprint (Technical Pattern).*

BLUEPRINT	Awareness			Education				Transaction			Support			Education
	Key word	Consultation	Request a date	Give a date	Date 1	Date 2 Demo	Date 3	POC	Purchase	Delivery	Payment	Failure	Repair	Churn
Quality	% click				% date	% demo		% sale	% success		% payment	MTTR		
Customer location			x		x			x R	xR	x	x W		x W	x
Branch							x R							
Website	x R	x W		x								x		
User	x			x	x	x		x		x		x		x
Buyer		x	x	x	x		x		x		x		x	
Consultant		x						x						
Salesperson					x	x	x	x	x					x
Director							x		x					
Technician					x		x			x		x	x	x
Admin.			x	x					x		x	x		

In the Technical Pattern, the process includes a visit for a demonstration at the supplier branch and a POC at the customer premises. In this model, the buyer hires an external expert consultant who consults beforehand and is present at the POC. This person makes product evaluations.

In the 2.0 Pattern, the customer prefers conversation on the Internet. S/he debates on professional social media with peers and shares experiences with bloggers, and reads white papers published by suppliers. S/he follows demonstrations online and makes ROI calculations with salespeople. S/he accepts a date in her/his office very late, after an installation and to investigate other products.

TABLE 12.4 *The Customer Experience Blueprint (2.0 Pattern).*

BLUEPRINT	Awareness		Education				Transaction			Support		Education
	LinkedIn	Blog	Research	White paper	Online demo	ROI caluc.	Date request	Date	Purchase	Integration	Sat. call	Date cross
Quality				% download	% date	ROI		% POC			% sat.	% sales
Customer location	x	x	x		x		x W	x		x W	x	X
Branch									x			
Website			x	x	x	x R			x			
User	x	X			x R		x	x		x	x	x
Buyer			x	x	x	x		x	x		x	X
Peer	x	X										
Salesperson				x	x		x					x
Director								x	x			
Technician				x	x					x		
Admin.							x		x	x	X	

TABLE 12.5 *The Customer Experience Blueprint (Marketplace Pattern).*

BLUEPRINT	Awareness	Education			Transaction				Support		Nurturing
	LinkedIn Company page	Research	RFI + RFP	Quotation	Comparision	Info precision request	Purchase		Information	Satis. call	New product
Quality			% recieved		% selected		% sales			% sat.	% sales
Customer location					x				x W	x	
Website	x	x	x	x W			x				
email						x			x		x
User			x		x				x	x	x
Buyer	x	x	x		x		x			x	x
Salesperson			x	x		x	x				x
Technician support				x		x			x		
Admin. support				x		x	x		x	x	

In the Marketplace Pattern, the customer decides to look for a marketplace in LinkedIn, and with a keyword, finds pages of suppliers. S/he selects some of them and leaves a document containing a synthesis of the RFI and RFP. Then the buyer receives quotations, selects the best, and makes a choice. The purchase is made on the marketplace website (or not). Complementary information and post-sales support are made via email. In this pattern, the physical contacts do not exist. This process uses the help of a marketplace to find suppliers. It may require a commission in order to be effective.

How to use the tool

Several customer blueprints are designed per segment and tested. They can include a range of media in the first phase and combine a mix of the steps suggested by the three patterns. In practice, the blueprints are tested and some steps are adapted according to the quality measurements.

Strengths and limitations of the tool

The tool suggests generating multiple customer paths after a customer insight exercise. Every B2B company will mix many media which brings coherent and complementary—though not identical—information. Imagining the path does not mean the customer will follow it; thus, the jump from one media source to another may be easy and anticipated.

CHAPTER 13

HOW TO MODEL THE SALES MEETING AND SUPPORT THE SALESPERSON

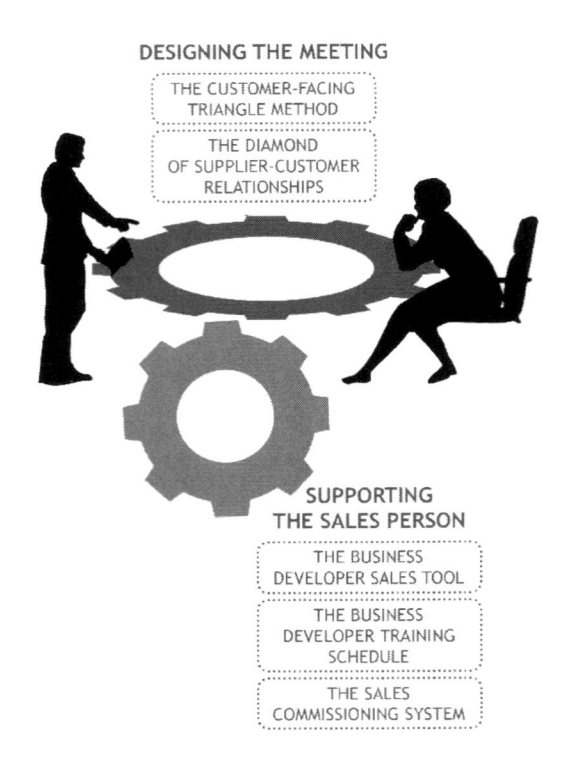

DESIGNING THE MEETING
- THE CUSTOMER-FACING TRIANGLE METHOD
- THE DIAMOND OF SUPPLIER-CUSTOMER RELATIONSHIPS

SUPPORTING THE SALES PERSON
- THE BUSINESS DEVELOPER SALES TOOL
- THE BUSINESS DEVELOPER TRAINING SCHEDULE
- THE SALES COMMISSIONING SYSTEM

Marketing managers organize the scenario surrounding the contact between the buyer and salesperson. Both parties want to simultaneously understand the opportunities that each brings to the table and control the meeting; thus, a sales contact is a mix of collaboration and conflict. Modeling the phases of the meeting is key to maximizing the chances of concluding the deal.

What is specific to B2B?

The deal is a process including a succession of communication between buying center and sales center members. Indeed, face-to-face meetings can be more efficient than phone or email exchanges. Regardless of the speed of contact, certain phases are necessary to ensure that the benefits and value proposal are well evaluated. For example, technical exchanges may be necessary to build the solution. In order to smooth relations, marketing managers should ensure that the salesperson understands the purchase process as well as technical aspects. Sales personnel must set up the contacts between the two organizations and know how to respond to buyers' objections. Five tools are proposed to marketing managers for this purpose.

Designing the meeting
- Tool 65: The Customer-Facing Triangle Method
- Tool 66: The Diamong of Supplier-Customer Relationships

Supporting the salesperson
- Tool 67: The Business Developer Sales Tool Series
- Tool 68: The Business Developer Training Schedule
- Tool 69: The Sales Commissioning System

Tool 65: The Customer-Facing Triangle Method supports the sales meeting monitoring

DEFINITIONS

An *objection* is a customer comment against the proposed solution or the supplier, which most of time requires a response from the salesperson. An *alternative conclusion* is a proposal made to the customer to choose among several closely related solutions.

The conversation between sales personnel and buyers remains inside a triangular "supplier-customer-value" proposition. The B2B marketing managers provide a vision of the sales process, including the management of the sales meeting. The Customer-Facing Triangle method divides the meeting into seven steps. The opening phase is where a presentation of the supplier is made and should end with an implicit agreement on its credibility. This step is also the opportunity to check the customer identity and purchase role. Then, rapport is established, where the salesperson and buyer get to know each other and agree on both the purpose of the meeting and on the necessary exchange of information. Then, the probing phase is the opportunity to make deep discoveries about the customer's organization, motivation, priorities, and buying process. Next, the salesperson will move to a clear mutual agreement on the needs and expected benefits that will be addressed. At the fifth step, a choice of alternative solutions will be proposed and objections answered. Before negotiating the price, a precise presentation of the support and means deployed to the customer is made. Lastly, the conclusion phase is the time to help the customer make a choice.

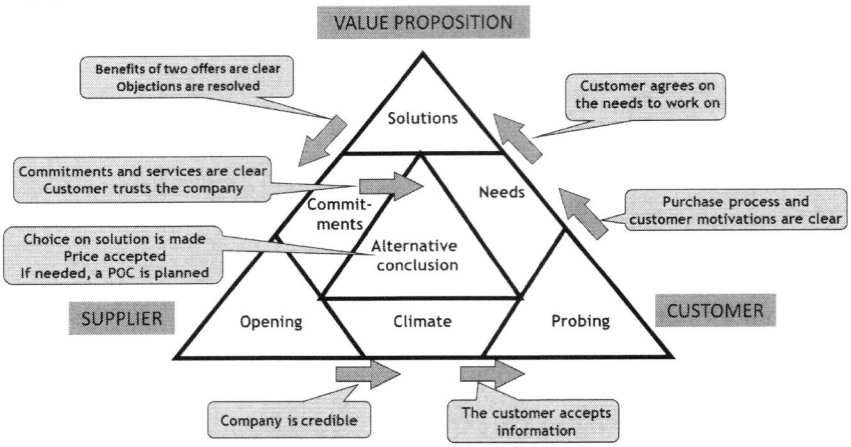

FIGURE 13.1 *The Customer-Facing Triangle Method.*

Using this method, the solution will only be presented after a clear understanding and agreement on the customer identity and need has been reached. This will ensure that the customer has been given time to assess her/his need(s), has built the purchase scenario, and has visualized the benefits.

How to use the tool

The tool is used to build the phases of the sales meeting. Each phase includes well-chosen questions in the probing step, and arguments in the following three steps. The tool is used also to respond to potential arguments and defend the price in the case of a negotiation fight. Figure 13.1 depicts these arguments. This tool requires preparation and training. The tool is global and may be used at different paces when the customer buying center cannot be moved altogether from one step to the next.

Strengths and limitation of the tool

With this tool as a guide, the sales meeting is well-monitored and does not move too quickly to the product presentation or price negotiation. The proposal is well-focused due to mutual understanding and synchronization. The tool is powerful for new sales personnel and new products. Marketing can provide a customized support at each phase of the sales meeting. A limitation could be the tendency to stereotype groups of customers; as such, it is important to remain flexible with each individual customer.

Tool 66: The Diamond of Supplier-Customer Relationships structures the interrelationships of the deal

The Diamond of Supplier-Customer Relationships attempts to forecast the necessary collaborative contacts of the deal process. Many times the deal is concluded with contacts between two persons only. In reality, there is likely a complex exchange of information among many individuals. Technicians, legal consultants, IT persons, and accounting managers must create technical agreements that buyers or account manager may not be able to write themselves. The type of information exchange is agreed upon between the salesperson and the buyer, who will provide the internal contacts, organize and participate in meetings with the two parties, and check their output. This tool lists the persons who must liaise between the two companies and the purpose of the meeting or contact in order to facilitate the supplier's proposal. For each contact, an objective is given and an output is provided in minutes. The tool is also used after the deal for the deployment of the solution in the customer organization.

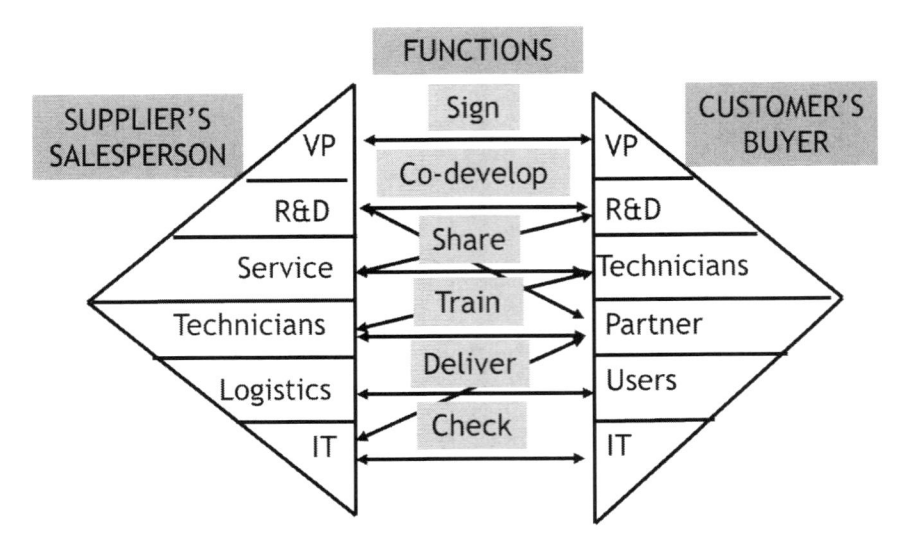

FIGURE 13.2 *The Diamond of Supplier-Customer Relationships (Example)*.

In Figure 13.2, the co-development is organized between R&D departments, followed by technical sharing and training with customer technicians and a partner of the customer. The integration and delivery require contacts between IT departments and the supplier's logistics with the customer's future users.

How to use the tool

The salesperson and purchase manager need to first list the functions that require other members from the two organizations in preparing the deal and the transaction. They will then find the names of the persons and ask for their agreement to contribute, if the process does not already exist. Then, they will organize the contacts at the right time. If the process is very involved, the salesperson manages the operation with project tools: agenda, meeting minutes, action checklist, reminders, etc.

Strengths and limitations of the tool

The benefits of the tool include a vision of the collaboration and series of green lights on the way to the final signature, and thereafter. The limitation comes often from the restriction of the buyer who acts as a barrier to contacts inside her/his company. The salesperson has to convince her/him to open her/his doors. At the opposite end, another risk is when the appointed people are not mobilized to close the deal. For example, legal support may be more motivated by risk elimination, regardless of the result of the negotiation. The tool can be updated and used for the necessary remaining interconnections after the deal.

Tool 67: The Business Developer Sales Tool Series lists the array of on-demand tools that support the sales meeting and customer decision

DEFINITIONS

The *sales cycle* is the time and series of events between the initial contact with a customer and the transaction that completes the sale. The *business developer* is a person who seeks business opportunities using all means of leveraging, including direct sales, managing distributors, lobbying, and influencers or partnerships. *Customer education* is the sales phase when the customer learns about the business field, technologies, suppliers, purchase processes, benefits, and products. The *value proposition* is the customer's intended perception of a supplier's offerings.

The sales meeting in B2B can last from a few seconds to a few days, and the sales cycle may last a few years. At different phases of the meeting, the salesperson must provide information, ask the customer questions, and educate the customer on technical, organizational, financial, and legal topics. Additionally, after the meeting, the same information is necessary when the salesperson is not present. The Business Developer Sales Tool Series lists tools that help educate the customer, present the company, and present the offer value and tools focused on his or her final decision. Both physical and electronic supports are then given. One tool concerns the salesperson's monitoring of the meeting preparation and management, and another the management of distributors.

SUPPLIER PRESENTATION	VALUE PROPOSITION	CUSTOMER DECISION SUPPORT
Business statement	Product/service range	Testimonials
Targeted customers	Product/service usage	Business cases
Positioning	Product sample	Product benefits
Values	Product specification sheets, performance, features	Purchase ROI
Organization	Product/service comparison	Deployment organization agreement
Financial results	Product/service videos	Deployment schedule
Knowhow	Product simulations	Sales contract
Infrastructure	Proposal design and pricing software	Service level agreement
Distribution network	Price list	Leasing contract
Partnerships	Packages of products	Contact list
References		Satisfaction survey results
Coverage		

FIGURE 13.3 *The Business Developer Sales Tool Series (Part 1).*

CUSTOMER EDUCATION	PRESENTATION SUPPORTS	SALESPERSON MONITORING
Business field actors	Product to demonstrate	Prospect lists
Market evolution	Video	Phone computer-aided guide
Technologies	PowerPoint, Excel, Word, etc.	Face-to-face guide
Types of solutions	Software on tablet	Customer analysis guide
Customer applications	Website tools	Customer application check
Customer usages	Invitations	Customer contracts synthesis
Global customer benefits	Private area in exhibitions	Competition comparison
	White paper	Reminders to contact customers
	Short customer quiz	Route of visits
	Computer-aided guides	CRM content and use
	Scripts	Commissions and incentives
	Quizzes	

FIGURE 13.4 *The Business Developer Sales Tool Series (Part 2).*

A group of B2B sales tools aims at enhancing the supplier's credibility, which helps facilitate the decision-making process when the purchase is critical.

How to use the tool

The choice of sales tools is made with the customer buying process analysis and business developer consultations. They take into account the business field actors and customer relations with influencers, manufacturers, and distributors. Each of them should give a value to the buyer during and after the meeting. For example, when the purchase managers have separate decision meetings, the sales tools must be easy enough to use without the salesperson's presence. Tools become the salesperson. Many are cheap and easy to produce. Others take time and money. The efficiency of them and real use is controlled.

Strengths and limitations of the tool

Sales tools promote professionalism, precision, and confidence in sales meetings. Newly hired individuals can benefit greatly from using them. In practice, the limitation comes from the business developers themselves, who tend to rely on their conversation and neglect the tools after some period. Thus, regular reminders of their benefit may be necessary.

Tool 68: The Business Developer Training Schedule helps to develop sales skills

DEFINITIONS

Blended learning is a mix of both online and classroom learning sessions. The *training module* is the minimum training sessions necessary to achieve the target knowledge or know-how. *Complex selling* concerns the sales which involve multiple partners, co-creation with the customer, high value of purchase and risk.

B2B companies spend a lot of energy training the sales force. Together, the technical nature of the products, the width of the ranges, the complexity of purchase processes, and the turnover of the sales force all converge into a large training effort. The marketing department therefore which knows the customer, the range, and the market can take a legitimate role. It delivers the materials and, at best, the training methods and training sessions. The Business Developer Training Schedule proposes a series of content and training modes or tools. Here, traditional sales techniques and organization modules are mentioned with a focus on possible new distance training modes. An area concerns the specific sales techniques required with large accounts, auctions, or marketplaces.

TRAINING MODES & TOOLS

- Classrooms
- Web conferences
- Independent learning documents
- Learning management systems
- e-Learning software
- Serious games
- Videos of sales
- Negotiation sketches
- Videoed sketches
- Quizzes
- Best practices forums
- Experts blogs
- Trainee field coaching

VALUE PROPOSITION

- Market knowledge
- Competition
- Targeted customer profile
- Product use
- Product features
- Product arguments
- Demonstrating products
- Defining solution
- Pricing solution
- Product benefits
- Customer TCO calculation
- Customer ROI calculation
- Deal profit calculation

FIGURE 13.5 *The Business Developer Training Schedule (Part 1, Example).*

SALES TECHNIQUES

- Personal networking
- Canvassing
- Telephone scripts
- Sales meeting management
- Use of sales tools
- Needs probing
- Answering objections
- Writing responses to tenders
- Sales center management
- Playing with contract clauses
- Financing and leasing solutions
- End of lease contract management
- Sales analysis
- Business ethics

ORGANIZATION

- Customer life management
- Customer portfolio management
- CRM content analysis
- Dates scheduling
- Revenue forecast
- Customer value
- Lead management
- Inbound, outbound, offline media

SPECIFIC SALES

- LNA purchase processes
- Consulting
- Partnership management
- Contractual negotiations
- Sales escalation process
- Customer-supplier coordination
- Deployment management
- Deal profit calculation
- Exhibition sales
- Marketplace management
- Auction sales management

FIGURE 13.6 *Example of the Business Developer Training Schedule (Part 2).*

Training modules have widely moved from market and product knowledge to abilities to value offers to customers (i.e., TCO, ROI, benefits, global solutions, deployment). They include skills to navigate inside and outside the organization, CRM use, lead management linked to each type of media, and personal networking. Complex selling for large accounts is an important module that needs to be custom built based on the business field.

How to use the tool

In order to build a training schedule, it is critical to stay up to date with the knowledge and best practices of the sales force. The training program depends on the customer targets, the selling methods, the product complexity, and the budget available. Usually, the modules utilize a blended learning technique involving classrooms, online conferences, e-learning software, videos, and tests, which provide repetition of the concepts covered without boring the sales force. Modules are short, with components of around 20 minutes each, and interesting quizzes with solutions may be used to ensure the acquisition of the necessary knowledge. All modules are tested, and after the launches, they are evaluated. The library of modules needs regular updates, however, which is expensive if they are too numerous.

Strengths and limitations of the tool

Training is permanent and not limited to product launch events. The tool utilizes the 13 modes and 46 types of modules in order to provide the maximum number of choices for the best suitable program. The limitation involves the sales force's available time. Training outside working hours is not popular with sales personnel, while training during working hours may be not popular with sales managers. Thus, kickoff, launch, and team meeting events can include training sessions, completed with regular, short modules.

Tool 69: The Sales Commissioning System optimizes sales force productivity

DEFINITIONS

The *incentive system* refers to all operations aimed at maintaining and promoting motivation in the sales force in order to produce revenue and profit. Commissioning refers to variable money earned by the sales force.

The incentive system is key to success for B2B distribution organizations. The greatest motivating factor for sales personnel is money. The Income Commissioning System is a tool that helps to decide the criteria for earning, as well as the time for giving incentives. It drives the sales force in the direction of the company marketing policy. The first criterion is sales frequency. Fixed income will be higher if the frequency is low. The second criterion is sales amount. Commission rate will be lower if the amount is high. Commission also varies based on target revenue. Below a certain revenue, the commission can be low or non-existent; over a certain percentage, commission can increase or decrease. The range of variation can be large if the sales frequency is low, or narrow if it is large. The three other criteria are specific to the business field and help to prioritize the type of sale. For example, typical "diseases" that can be cured by commissioning the sales force include the following: (a) need to canvass new customers, (b) insufficient sales frequency, and (c) unsatisfactory mix of products, (d) limitation to a specific segment or area. Sale force can be incentivized with quarterly or annual bonuses.

TABLE 13.1 *The Income Commissioning System Principles.*

CRITERIA	Level	Fixed income	Commission rate	Commission bracket	Monthly bonus	Quarterly bonus	Annual bonus
Sales frequency	High Low	Low High		Narrow large	High Low		
Sale value	High Low		Low High			High	High
Multiple Product sales	High Low	Low				High	High
Canvass need	High Low	Low				High	High
Product mix	Fine Unbalanced					Low High	Low High

Table 13.1 is an example of a company with frequent sales and low value; the company needs to improve customer acquisition and increase product mix sales. So two bonuses were designed to improve this situation.

TABLE 13.2 *The Income Commissioning System Example.*

% RESULT TO REVENUE TARGET	<80	80-100	101-120	121-140	>140
Commission on monthly revenue target	3%	4%	5%	6%	6%
Quartely bonus $ • Number of new clients > 10 in the quarter • Number of multiple sales > 5 in the quarter	0 0	500 500	5000 5000	5000 5000	5000 5000
Annual bonus in % of revenue	0	0	0.5	1	1.5

How to use the tool?

The commission system should be analyzed on a yearly basis. In the first step, the company's strategic objectives are set, including the following: target revenue, specific product to push based on the company's margin, customer acquisition, etc. Then, the system is built, leaving several options to discuss among management. The system is also adapted based on the sales personnel, account managers, size of the account, and type of salary or commission—fixed, monthly, yearly, etc. It is completed with other incentives such as contests for a trip, an event invitation, or presents which the sales people enjoy.

Strengths and limitations of tool

This tool is effective at motivating the sales force. It can monitor revenue targets and areas for improvement with considerable accuracy. Companies often make the commission system extremely complex, with several specific commission rates per product. Sales personnel should be able to easily evaluate the amount they earn at the time of customer sign-up. A limitation is the long annual cycle of the system. Thus, regular additional promotional discounts, contests, and incentives for new product launches should take place every month.

CHAPTER 14
HOW TO DECIDE THE MEDIA MIX AND CUSTOMER EXPERIENCE

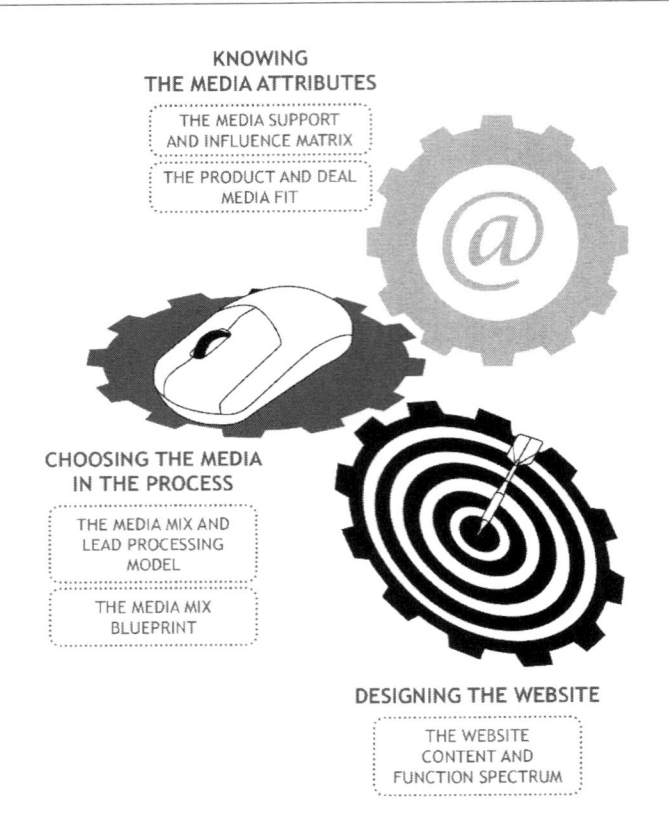

KNOWING THE MEDIA ATTRIBUTES
- THE MEDIA SUPPORT AND INFLUENCE MATRIX
- THE PRODUCT AND DEAL MEDIA FIT

CHOOSING THE MEDIA IN THE PROCESS
- THE MEDIA MIX AND LEAD PROCESSING MODEL
- THE MEDIA MIX BLUEPRINT

DESIGNING THE WEBSITE
- THE WEBSITE CONTENT AND FUNCTION SPECTRUM

The selection of media is an ongoing try-and-test marketing activity, requiring knowledge of the advantages of each type of media, creativity, and campaign experience. Well-chosen B2B communication agencies can provide both. They provide the ROI for each type of campaign they have produced, can adapt them in real time and thus, their relation with marketing is vital.

What is specific to B2B?

In B2B, the communication must reach the customers, and often influencers, prescribers, distributors, regulators, partners, etc. The information given to buying center members need to be relevant at the phase of the purchase process, contextual, and helpful to the recipient. This process can be very long with specific phases that should all be supported by the media plan. The buyer's time is limited and, therefore, he or she prefers a minimizing of intrusive communications which can interrupt the work. This evolution generates a redirection of choice to inbound media. The objectives of communication are less often to get immediate online sales, but more to generate leads which will be processed. The central media is the company website. Five tools are proposed to decide media and customer experience.

Knowing the media attributes
- Tool 70: The Media Support and Influence Matrix
- Tool 71: The Product and Deal Media Fit

Choosing the media in the process
- Tool 72: The Media Mix and Lead Processing Model
- Tool 73: The Media Mix Blueprint

Designing the website
- Tool 74: The Website Content and Function Spectrum

Tool 70: The Media Support and Influence Matrix qualifies the media choice

DEFINITIONS

A *white paper* is a document describing the state of a market or technology, or suppliers' best practices. The *cost of lead* is the average communication expenditure to generate a lead.

The number of media types increases regularly and marketing managers look for an optimization of their use benefit to cost. There is no universal B2B solution for a given mix of media. The Media Support and Influence Matrix supports this decision utilizing two qualitative criteria: (a) the support, and (b) the influence impact. The first concerns the ability to adapt to the B2B content of the message, which must be rational and credible; it can also be detailed and technical, utilizing the language of the buyers' business field. The second concerns the influence efficiency given the audience size.

TABLE 14.1 *Media Support Comparison.*

MEDIA SUPPORT	Social proof	Authority Trust	Affinity Reciprocity	Adequation Precision	Consistency Duration	Reach Frequency
Expert Blog	X	X		X	X	XXX
White paper		XXX		XXX	XXX	X
Testimon. video		X	X	X	XX	X
User forum	XXX	XXX	XXX	XX	X	X
Social media	XXX	X	XXX	X	X	XX
E-mail		X				XXX
Newsletter		XX	X		XX	XX
Microblogging					XX	XX
Product video		X		XX	XXX	XXX

The need for support for the content can be crucial and can eliminate some media. If trust of an authority is important to push a new technology, a white paper and a user forum can help. If the precision is a key factor, a product video is supportive. It may be in opposition to the influence and volume necessity.

TABLE 14.2 *Media Influence Comparison.*

MEDIA INFLUENCE	Non intrusive	Quantitative	Buzz ability	Info richness	Participative	Low cost
Expert Blog	XXX	X	X	XX	XX	XX
White paper	XXX	X	XX	XXX		XXX
Testimon. video	XXX	X	XX	X		XX
User forum	XXX	XX	XXX	XX	XX	X
Social media	XXX	XX	XXX	XX	XXX	X
E-mail		XXX				
Newsletter	XX	XX	X	X		XX
Microblogging	X	XX	XX	X	X	XX
Product video	XXX	X	X	XX	XX	XXX

The influence can be evaluated by the quantity, the buzz, and degree of intrusiveness. The cost and the richness of the information delivered also contribute to the overall influence.

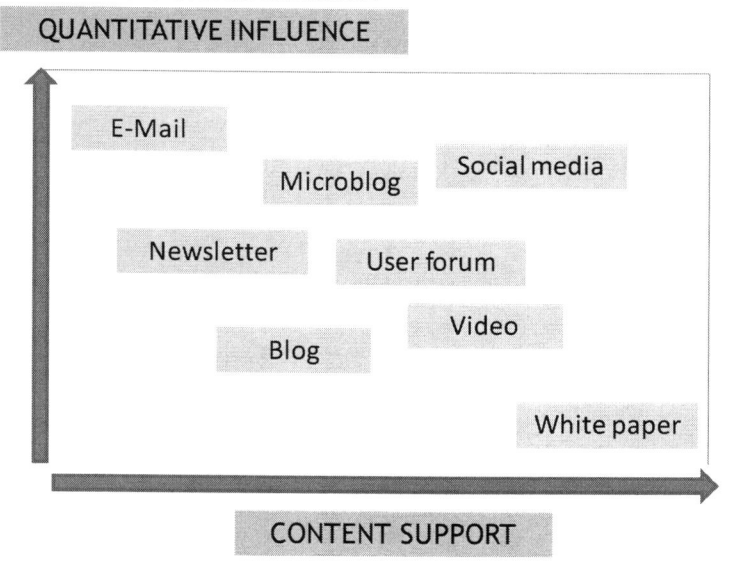

FIGURE 14.3 *Media Influence and Content Matrix.*

An example of a support–influence media distribution is provided in Figure 14.3.

How to use the tool

The marketing manager needs to update the media list. New media appears regularly and attributes may change. S/he can use the two tools by choosing the factors that are pertinent to the business. Other media can be added. No one individual medium is compulsory. It is important to look at similar businesses and use benchmarking to enhance the effectiveness of this tool.

Strengths and limitations of the tool

This tool helps to understand the impact of each media type and select which ones to utilize. The ability to examine media across two dimensions—support and influence—helps in the highly subjective world of communication. A limitation of the tool is that after implementing media campaigns, other criteria become more important, in particular the cost of lead, the lead transformation rate, and the cost of sales, which vary considerably by product and deal type.

Tool 71: The Product and Deal Media Fit Tool outlines the product complexity and deal size as selection criteria

DEFINITIONS

Off-line media are media that do not involve the use of Internet or telephone. *Inline media* refers to Internet media. *Inbound media* are media the customer chooses to use; *outbound media* are unsolicited media sent to customers, such as intrusive messages from the supplier.

In the previous tool, media were assessed based on their influence on customers and required content support. The Product and Deal Media Fit Tool suggests the use of two other criteria: (a) the complexity of the product, and (b) the size of the deal. It includes three categories of media: (a) off-line, (b) inline outbound, and (c) variations of inline inbound.

TABLE 14.3 *The Product and Deal Media Fit.*

		Simple product or small deal			Complex product or large deal		
		LNA	SME	SoHo	LNA	SME	SoHo
Off-line	Face-to-face				x	x	x
	Local branch				x	x	x
	Exhibition				x	x	
	Press				x		
Inline Inbound	Search	x	x	x	x	x	x
	LinkedIn				x	x	x
	Facebook		x	x	x	x	
	Video sites	x	x	x	x	x	x
	Photo sites				x	x	x
	Slide sites				x	x	x
	Website	x	x	x	x	x	x
	Blog	x			x	x	
	Marketplace	x	x	x	x	x	x
	Forum				x	x	x
Inline Outbound	Email		x	x		x	x
	Banner		x	x		x	x
	Microblogging				x		
	Newsletter	x	x	x	x	x	x
	SMS				x	x	x
	Telemarketing					x	x

Some tools are compulsory, such as websites, while others are only useful for complex products or large deals.

How to use the tool

The list of media should be regularly updated with the most popular types used by the targeted companies. The evaluation of fit may also be revisited according to local preferences. Positioning media within the tool will help to eliminate the least efficient types. The different media types can then be further sorted using the two criteria of the <u>Media Support and Influence Matrix</u>.

Strengths and limitations of the tool

This tool points out that the size of the deal and type of product trigger the selection of different types of media. In choosing the best media fit, the tool will also take into account the individual customer's preference. A limitation of the tool is that it is necessary to frequently update the list of available media as well the criteria for selecting different media types.

Tool 72: The Media Mix and Lead Processing Model integrates four types of media into one global lead process

DEFINITIONS

Inbound media involves using the Internet in a non-intrusive way: Customers decide the type of contact in which they would like to engage, such as blogs, search engines, or social media. *Outbound media* refers to pushing messages to the customer inline, such as banners, email, and SMS via mobile phones. By extension, *off-line inbound media* are events, exhibitions, or branches which customers can visit, and *off-line outbound media* are telemarketing calls to propose dates or telesales.

The amount of media increases regularly and B2B customers enjoy the choice of multiple communication channels. The Media Mix and Lead Processing Model organizes a global process from the four types of media to sales, either made directly or through the sales force. For online media, the heart of the process is the website or specific applications on the site, tablets, or mobile phone. Whether online or off-line, the system should be able to support the sale immediately or direct a lead to the sales force. The tool proposes 10 types of media; however, the list is neither compulsory nor exhaustive. Defining the list involves tests as well as an evaluation of the processing cost.

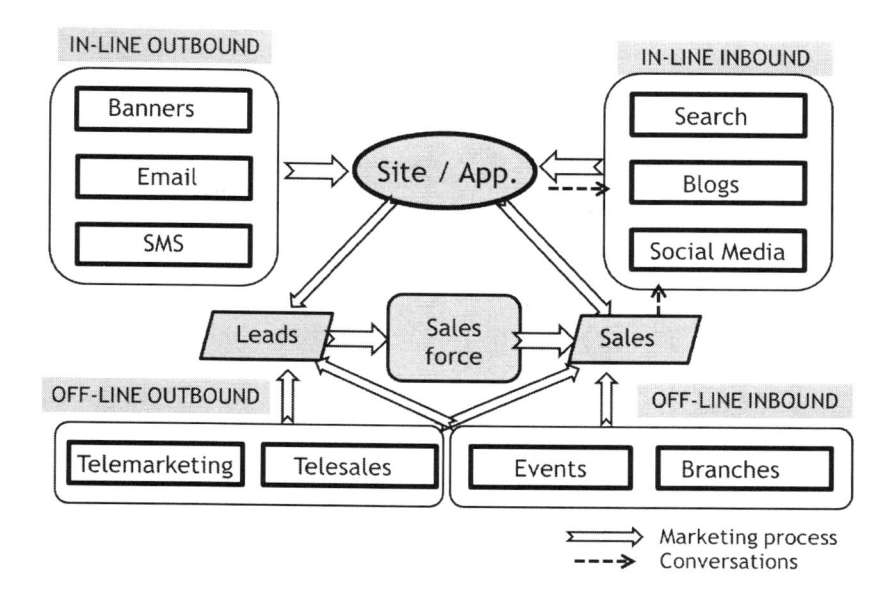

FIGURE 14.4 *The Media and Lead Processing Model.*

The benefit of the tool is the full integration of all communication into one process—which is visible in the CRM—in order to improve the flow with customers. It increases the sales productivity and the ROI of the campaign. A limitation is the heterogeneity of the media, which requires a means to automatically or manually store all of the different types of messages.

How to use the tool

This tool helps to create a list of the most interesting online and off-line media. Other tools in this chapter can be used in this first step. Then, the lead management process is designed, which includes the customer relations record and lead workflow. Inside the same global format, the lead processing can vary per customer segment, per product, or per type of deal. In particular, the choice of telesales, sales per Internet, face-to-face sales is not the same for simple versus complex products. After the lead process is established, the administration workflow is put in place.

Strengths and limitations of the tool

This tool helps to define a global process for lead management and ensures coherence between the sales networks and media. It also helps track the origin of sales and allows for better calculation of the ROI of campaigns. The limitation lies in the complexity of the network and the multiplicity of media; the process should be continuously adapted to account for these factors.

Tool 73: The Media Mix Blueprint helps to choose the media mix inside the four phases of customer experience

DEFINITIONS

The *blueprint* is a schedule of the events and contacts related to the customer experience. *Education* is the phase in which the customer has a need and seeks information in order to make a decision. *Nurturing* is the phase in which the customer has only made contact, or made a purchase a while ago and is given valuable information to keep him/her interested and aware of the supplier. *Outbound media* refers to intrusive messages that are not desired by the customer. *Inbound media* refers to media that are not intrusive, and are received after the customer makes contact.

The number of media increases continuously and the profile for each type varies. Media can be selected by following the five phases of the customer experience. The Media Mix Blueprint provides a sketch of inbound and outbound media for each of the five phases: awareness, education, transaction, support, and nurturing. The phases have different needs and the each media capability should be maximally utilized. The blueprint is monitored in order to improve customer experience.

```
INBOUND

| Video         | Blog          |             |             | Forum        |
| WoM           | Site          |             |             | Social media |
| Search        | Forum         | Marketplace | Video       | Video        |
| Social media  | Social media  | Site        | Site        | Site         |
| **Awareness** | **Education** | **Transaction** | **Support** | **Nurturing** |
| Face-to-face  | Webinar       | Phone       | Microblogging | Newsletter  |
| Banner        | Newsletter    | Face-to-face| Email       | Email        |
| Email         | Exhibitions   |             | SMS         | Webinars     |
| Phone         | Events        |             |             | Events       |
|               |               |             |             | Face-to-face |

OUTBOUND
```

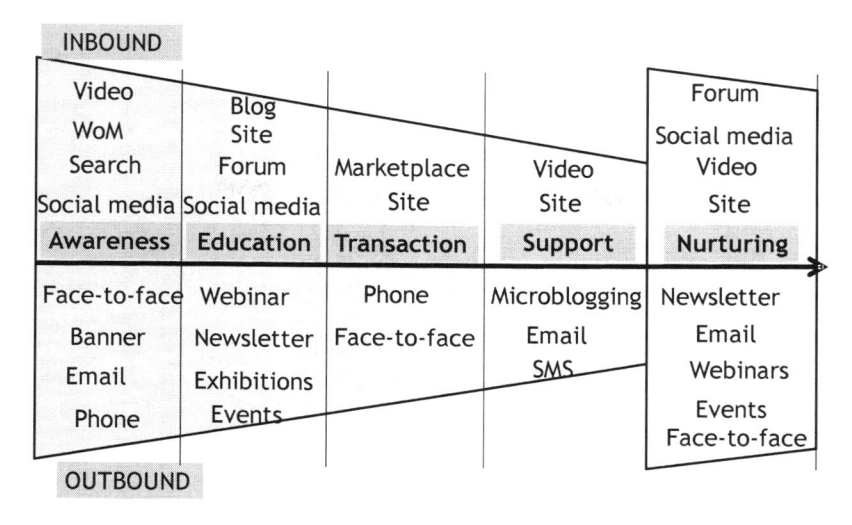

FIGURE 14.5 *The Media Mix Blueprint (Example With Short Sale Cycle).*

The number of preferred media is large in the first and second phases, where communication covers many subjects and the media must match with the variable customer communication preference. Detailed qualitative information is collected and global conversations take place. In Phases 3 and 4, media become restricted; communication is straight forward in order to reach a limited number of objectives. In Phase 5, nurturing, media coverage is expanded in order to address a greater number of interests.

```
INBOUND

| Video         | Blog          | Forum        |                 |              |
| WoM           | Site          | Social media |                 |              |
| Search        | Forum         | Video        | Marketplace     | Video        |
| Social media  | Social media  | Site         | Site            | Site         |
| **Awareness** | **Education** | **Nurturing**| **Transaction** | **Support**  |
| Face-to-face  | Webinar       | Newsletter   | Phone           | Microblogging|
| Banner        | Newsletter    | Email        | Face-to-face    | Email        |
| Email         | Exhibitions   | Webinars     |                 | SMS          |
| Phone         | Events        | Events       |                 |              |
|               |               | Face-to-face |                 |              |

OUTBOUND
```

FIGURE 14.6 *The Media Mix Blueprint (Example With Long Sale Cycle).*

In this second example, the time between the first contact, education, and the transaction is long, such that a nurturing phase must be placed in between.

How to use the tool

The phases of the customer experience need to be agreed upon. Then, the choice of the media can be tested. The tool proposes a series of media per phase. It is optimal for customers to choose the media, which can subsequently be introduced into the CRM process. The program of communication can then be set up with objectives for leads, revenue, a schedule, and a budget.

Strengths and limitations of the tool

This tool shows the effective types of media based on the customer status. It highlights the education and nurturing phases of the customer experience, which are key to B2B and must be designed. A limitation is that because not all types of media are necessary, the tool must be adapted based on the business field and the company positioning.

Tool 74: The Website Content and Function Spectrum builds the enterprise web strategy

DEFINITIONS

The *value proposition* is the customer's perception of the benefits of product acquisition and use after accounting for the total cost. The *community of practice* is a group of customers who exchange their experiences with products.

The B2B website is the basis of the enterprise web strategy. It can include a very large number of functions and content. The Website Content and Function Spectrum delivers the scope of possibilities, organized into three perspectives: (a) the company, (b) the value proposition, and (c) the customer. B2B companies include product and company information on their website, which in continuously updated. The value proposition angle includes the product information and all means of understanding it.

TABLE 14.4 *The Website Content and Function Spectrum.*

	CONTENT	FUNCTIONS
Company	Company references Company mission statement Company annual report Distribution network description Manufacturing and R&D facilities Sustainable development policy Company partners	Newsletter registration Dealer extranet access Link to partners' sites Link to a LinkedIn page Link to Facebook page Link to Twitter Company news
Value proposition	Product education information Product features Product catalog Product prices Product video demonstrations Product detailed specifications Service specifications Customer full solution Product use course slides Product comparative chart	Home page access per product Extranet customized information Help me choose my product tools Product solution configurator Customer ROI benefit calculation Private customer catalog Customer intranet catalog Product download User manuals download Free trial
Customer	Technology white paper Business field information Customer segments information Product benefits Best use of the product Video testimonials Customer business cases Frequently asked questions Checklists Guides Expert blog Expert reports for download Best practices videos	Home page access per segment Home page access per application Opportunity assessment tool Purchase online Web conferences Join the community Forum for customers Information request form Online chat Find a dealer tool Event and exhibition invitations Contact us Call me back

The customer perspective is sometimes poor. The tool suggests website information and functions to ensure that the buyer sees the benefits of the product. The website should facilitate customer education and ultimately lead to the selection of a company for products or services, purchase, and support. The quantity of website content and functions increases regularly and becomes an important differentiation factor. In particular, the 2.0 tools provide opportunities to familiarize the customer with the community of practice, to ask questions to peers in forums, and to join conferences online. The presence of customers is also growing in video testimonials, in segment need descriptions, and in business cases.

How to use the tool

All the functions and content suggested by the tool can be evaluated in terms of the benefit and cost of generation and update. Tracking page visits will demonstrate the customer's interest in the web functions and particular information. The content list is not exhaustive and may adapted as needed.

Strengths and limitations of the tool

The website is an important step in the customer experience blueprint. The tool is flexible, providing a number of options for content. It helps B2B companies to look professional, regardless of the size. Thus, one must choose carefully according to the customer profile, the different purchase processes, and the information searched. A limitation of the tool is that customer insight is necessary in order to limit expenditures and to focus on the content that is most likely to be read as well as the functions that are most likely to be utilized.

CHAPTER 15

HOW TO MANAGE THE CUSTOMER LIFECYCLE

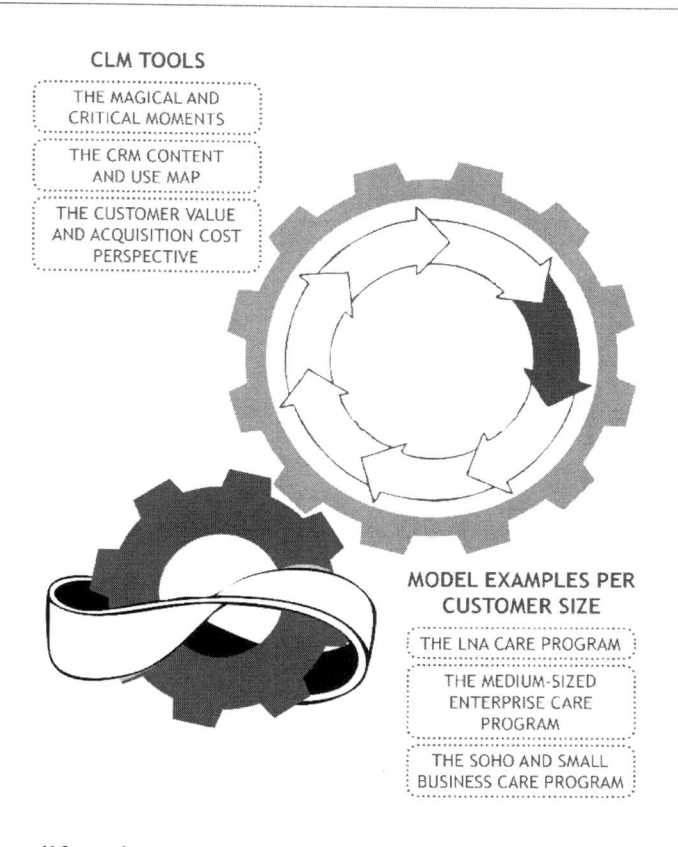

CLM TOOLS
- THE MAGICAL AND CRITICAL MOMENTS
- THE CRM CONTENT AND USE MAP
- THE CUSTOMER VALUE AND ACQUISITION COST PERSPECTIVE

MODEL EXAMPLES PER CUSTOMER SIZE
- THE LNA CARE PROGRAM
- THE MEDIUM-SIZED ENTERPRISE CARE PROGRAM
- THE SOHO AND SMALL BUSINESS CARE PROGRAM

Customer lifecycle management (CLM) is the identification and creation of customer events over the customer life in order to generate business performance. CLM requires a global vision of customer life, which allows for effective monitoring of relationships. CLM includes all types of communication (e.g., messages, phone calls) with main office employees of the supplier, as well as experiences with products and services.

What is specific to B2B?

In B2B, the relationships last longer than in B2C. The nature of contacts varies among sales, marketing, customer service, administration, and the supply chain. Thus, the CLM is particularly rich. Given the complexity, there is a risk of employees not understanding one another. As such, it is important for marketing managers to look closely at the CLM and adapt their models accordingly. This chapter proposes six tools to improve CLM.

The CLM tools
- Tool 75: The Magical and Critical Moments
- Tool 76: The CRM Content and Use Map
- Tool 77: The Customer Value and Acquisition Cost Perspective

Models examples per customer size
- Tool 78: The LNA Care Program
- Tool 79: The Medium-Sized Enterprise Care Program
- Tool 80: The SoHo and Small Business Care Program

Tool 75: The Magical and Critical Moments Tool helps to identify customer opportunities and prevent attrition

DEFINITIONS

Customer lifecycle management (CLM) is the series of processes based on customer experience events beginning from acquisition to the termination of the relationship, which manage customer satisfaction and maximize revenue and profit. *Attrition* is the loss of customers. *Magical moments* are events that generate revenue. *Critical moments* are events that can potentially end a relationship with a customer.

In B2B, CLM includes several possible events over a long period of time. Marketing managers anticipate these events, publish processes, and train the sales force to manage them. The Magical and Critical Moments Tool details a list of common events. *External events* are generated by suppliers or other actors in the environment, and *internal events* appear as a result of the customer. The series of events includes who should trigger and be responsible for particular actions in the CLM process.

CUSTOMER EVENTS			PROCESS	
EXTERNAL EVENTS	STATUS	RESPONSIBLE	ACTION	
ACQUISITION CAMPAIGNS	M	MARKETING	Batch lead generation and management process	
NURTURING MESSAGES	M	MARKETING	Contact salesperson	
CROSS CAMPAIGNS	M	MARKETING	Batch lead generation and management process	
REPLACEMENT CAMPAIGNS	M	MARKETING	Batch lead generation and management process	
COMPETITION CAMPAIGNS	C	MARKETING	Reactive marketing campaign and alert salesperson	
NEW REGULATION	M/C	MARKETING	Specific information campaign and alert salesperson	
EXHIBITIONS	M/C	MARKETING	Sales on the stand or lead management process	
INTERNAL EVENTS	STATUS	RESPONSIBLE	ACTION	
PURCHASE CHANGE	M/C	MARKETING	Alert salesperson	
EQUIPMENT AGING	M/C	MARKETING	Alert salesperson	
BREAKDOWNS	M/C	CUST SERVICE	Alert salesperson at the second occurrence	
END-OF-SERVICE CONTRACT	M/C	MARKETING	Alert salesperson	
END OF LEASE	O	MARKETING	Alert salesperson	
PROJECTS	M/C	SALESPERSON	Identify salesperson and contact customer	
NEW BUYER	M/C	SALESPERSON	Identify salesperson and contact customer	
NEW USER	M/C	SALESPERSON	Identify salesperson and contact customer	
ACTIVITY CHANGE	M/C	SALESPERSON	Identify salesperson and contact customer	
PRODUCT USE CHANGE	M/C	CUST SERVICE	Alert salesperson	
NEW ORGANIZATION	M/C	SALESPERSON	Identify salesperson and contact customer	
MOVE	M/C	SALESPERSON	Identify salesperson and contact customer	
MERGER/ACQUISITION	C	SALESPERSON	Identify salesperson and contact	
PAYMENT DELAY	C	FINANCE	Alert salesperson	
ETC.				

FIGURE 15.1 *The Magical and Critical Moments Process (Example)*.

Many internal events exist, which can be technical, organizational, or relative to the customer's activity. The "C" indicates that it is a critical moment, and the "M" a magical moment. Some events can be both.

How to use the tool

A list of external and internal events needs to be generated by marketing managers with customer surveys and consultation with sales force. The processes are then built into the CRM system with event tracking, alerts, designated action, and feedback on the results. The goal should be maximum automation, though the process should be flexible enough for the salesperson to choose different options based on his or her knowledge of the customers.

Strengths and limitations of the tool

Rigorous use of the tool will help to identify customer opportunities and minimize attrition. The tool can complement typical quantitative campaigns. A limitation of the tool is the ability to detect internal customer events. Fortunately, the sales staff can be trained to use effective questioning tools and to optimize the frequency of contact. A second limitation may be the multiplication of processes. Ultimately, the workflow should be easy to understand.

Tool 76: The CRM Content and Use Map shows the data and the abilities of the CRM

DEFINITIONS

Customer relationship management (CRM) is the system for managing customer relationships and tools to generate them. *Nurturing* is the activity of communication to maintain the customer's interest between the first contact and the purchase, or between one purchase and the next.

A company's CRM program aims at optimizing relationships with customers. Though CRM adoption by B2B companies is promising, it requires a large effort with contributions from all employees in contact with customers. The CRM Content and Use Map presents customer data that can be used for targeting, generating campaigns, selling, or nurturing. It also provides the type of reporting, which can be modified, as well as tools for marketing managers.

CUSTOMER PROFILE

Identity
Size
Business field SIC or NAICS
Structure of subsidiaries
Addresses of sites
Organigram of managers
Purchase center contacts & roles
Purchase criteria
Purchase procedure
Total purchase budget
Strategy, global need
Credit score

PRODUCTS & SERVICES SOLD

Products sold models, options, customizations
Dates of installation
Integration operations
Customer system description
Maintenance online and on-site visits
Volume of use
Usage status
Diagnosis reports
Competition products models & age
Dates of preventive maintenance
Financing status, end of leasing

RELATIONS

Non-disclosure agreements
Contacts with the sales force, the technicians, the administration
Contacts generated by the campaigns
Suppliers contacts for each contact
Visits
Customer requests and answers
Community participation
Satisfaction survey responses
Newsletter registration
Navigation on specific webpages

FIGURE 15.2 *Example of a CRM Content and Use Map (Part 1).*

DEALS

Purchase orders and payments
Sales contracts
Service contracts
Service level agreements
Information about contracts with competition
Projects
Specific needs
Leads on track
Proposals
Favorable status of the decision makers
Sales forecast
ROI of the deal

CRM REPORTING

Sales per segment
Number of campaigns
ROI of campaigns per source
Sales per product
Sales per salesperson
Number of leads per source
Leads per sales person
Lead transformation rate
Website visits
Sales visits per type
Acquisition & retention rate
Replacement rate
Cross-selling rate

CRM TOOLS

Campaigns for acquisition, cross selling, replacement, retention
Campaigns for nurturing
Invitation to events
Reminders after customer web visits
Alerts for consumables
Alerts to sales staff
Alerts for end of contracts or leasing
Alerts for end-of-service contracts
Salesperson activity scheduling
Salesperson diagnosis
Product forecast
Revenue forecast

FIGURE 15.3 *Example of a CRM Content and Use Map (Part 2).*

All the CRM data is linked; the campaigns are related to deals, which are related to sales and to products such that the CRM is used by the marketing, customer service, sales, or supply chain departments. The CRM information allows for all types of campaigns—acquisition, product churn, competition churn, cross selling, and retention.

How to use the tool

CRM use includes global campaigns, deals tracking, nurturing campaigns, and CLM alert management. At each point of contact, individuals primarily in charge of customer relations should introduce the information. This task is time-consuming and sales personnel must be convinced of the short- and long-term benefits of the process. Support to top management is also vital in order to implement the procedures. Successful CRM implementation is ensured by limiting CRM content to what is most efficient at the beginning; additional content can be added later on.

Strengths and limitations of the tool

The tool allows one to leverage the market potential. For example, the best time to contact customers, the best offer, and revenue targets can all be deduced from the CRM information. A limitation of the tool is the reliance on sales personnel. Together with the marketing campaigns, sales people are the ones who provide content information to customers. As such, the quality of information is key.

Tool 77: The Customer Value and Acquisition Cost Perspective steers the CLM

DEFINITIONS

Customer perceived value proposition is the prospective customer's evaluation of the costs and benefits of acquiring a product (Kotler & Keller, 2013). At the opposite end of the spectrum, *customer value to the supplier* is the prospective supplier's evaluation of the costs and benefits of acquiring a customer.

The customer value to the supplier is a question of perspective. The Customer Value and Acquisition Cost Perspective tool presents levels of customer value to be used in supplier calculations. The choice to work with particular customer segments depends on the perspective of the individual making the evaluation, as well as the ability to calculate value with reasonable accuracy. The tool proposes a calculation that includes four types of cost associated with customer acquisition.

CUSTOMER VALUE VARIATIONS	ExP	Expected Profit	Forecasted ExR – TC of the average life time
	ExR	Expected Revenue	Forecasted revenue over the average life time
	PaP	Past Profit	PsR – TC of the past years with the customer
	PsR	Past Revenue	Revenue of past years with the customer
	PYP	Present Year Profit	PYR – TC of the year customer deals
	PYR	Present Year Revenue	Total revenue for the year with the customer
	PDP	Present Deal Profit	PDR – TC
	PDR	Present Deal Revenue	Revenue from the present deal
TOTAL COSTS	TC	Total Costs	DC+IC+GC+DD+TC+SfC+CC of the customer deal
LANDED PRODUCT COSTS DC+IC+GC	DC	Direct Costs	Attributable costs to the purchased products
	IC	Indirect Costs	Per product R&D or other supply chain costs
GENERAL COSTS	GC	General Costs	Other general administrative costs per product
DEALS & CUSTOMER ACQUISITION COSTS DD+TC+SfC+CC	DD	Deal Discount	Discount given to get the deal
	TC	Technical Costs	Average technical costs to close the deals
	SfC	Sales force Contacts	Cost of quota bearer divided by # deals
	CC	Communication Costs	Communication budget divided by # deals

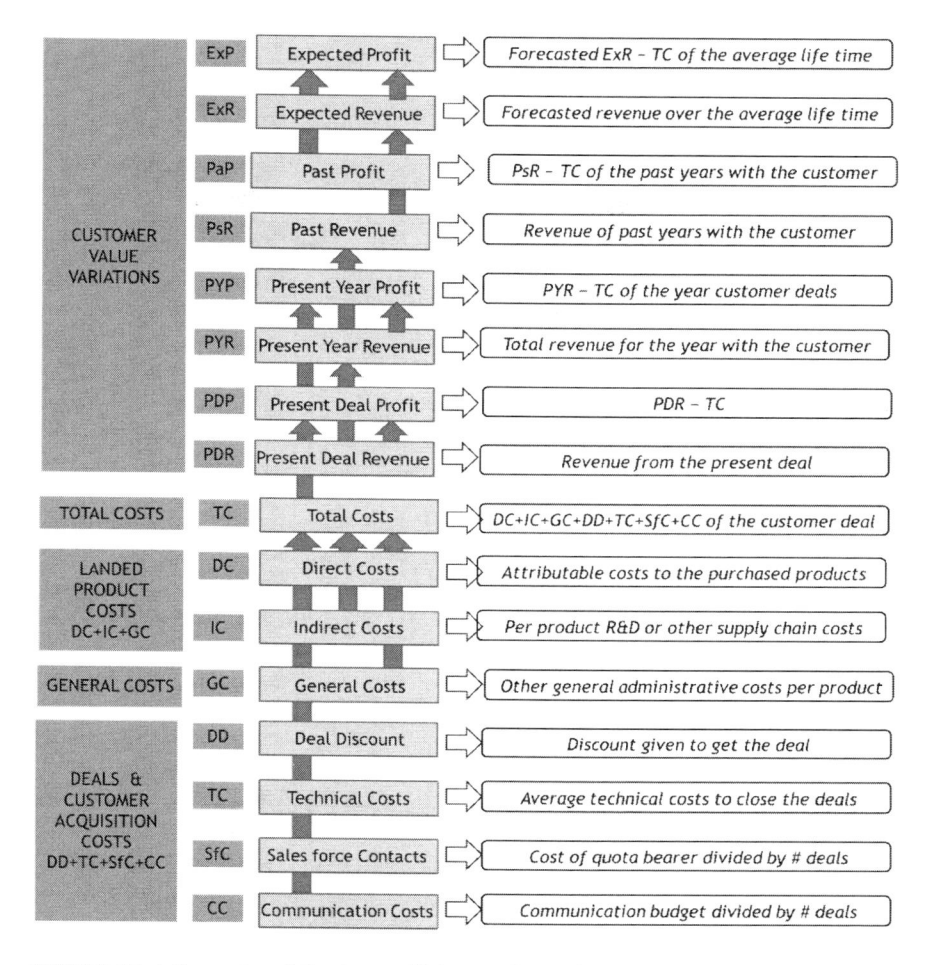

FIGURE 15.4 *Example of Customer Value and Acquisition Cost.*

In the simplest model, the ongoing revenue from the customer constitutes the customer value. This is the perspective of the salesperson. In the second model, the sales manager's perspective, value is based on two criteria: (a) present year revenue from the customer, and (b) profits. Profit calculations should include discounts given. Past and future revenue and profits over the average customer's lifetime constitute the marketing perspective. Total past revenue, which should be easy to calculate, is also interesting information to include in CRM for campaign generation.

How to use the tool

The cost of customer acquisition is made by taking the average of figures for communication costs, sales discounts, and technical costs at the level of one customer or at the level of a segment. When lifetime value is calculated, all of the revenue sources are added—including initial products and services sold, such as consumables, replacements, and cross sales. In the same way, the four types of costs are added to get the total cost of first deal and all subsequent deals. Once calculated, the customer value can be used as a segment criterion to generate revenue or profit strategies. It is also used by sales force to target specific customer bases.

Strengths and limitations of the tool

This tool helps to allocate marketing and sales resources based on expected revenue and profits for the life duration of a particular customer or segment. It helps to operational aspects of the business model, leading to strategic decisions. A limitation of the tool is the ability to evaluate revenue and cost with enough accuracy at the deal and segment levels.

Tool 78: The LNA Care Program is designed to handle the demanding requirements of large and national accounts

DEFINITIONS

Large and national accounts (LNAs), are customers who represent an important revenue opportunity from the supplier's perspective. Some countries include intermediate size enterprises, which vary in size between 250 and 500 employees (with sometimes up to 5,000 depending on the country), and *large enterprises*, which have either over 5,000 employees or generate a revenue over $1 billion.

Large enterprises are demanding customers. Contractually, they request a high level of commitment from the supplier. However, they are also large deal opportunities. The sales and marketing challenge is linked to their size and it requires an understanding of the enterprise's purchasing process and multiple needs. The LNA Care Program defines the marketing and sales activities needed to attract this type of buyer. It includes customized solutions, sales organization, and marketing support. As many LNA deals include special products and services, the tool also describes the transversal process necessary to ensure that promises are met.

CUSTOMIZED SOLUTION

MANAGEMENT SERVICES & SUPPORT
Consultancy
Fleet management
Consolidated information access
Deployment support

CUSTOMIZED SYSTEMS
Solution with custom-made design
Management of multiple providers
Web services

USER SERVICES
Configuration & integration
Response time and recovery commitments
On-demand training
Large user communities

FLEXIBLE PRICING
Global solution pricing
Long-term commitments
Penalty management

SALES ORGANIZATION

SPECIAL SALES CENTER
Bid management team for bid tracking and response support
Centralized level, tenders, auctions, marketplace management
Purchase criteria identification
Lobbying resources
Legal support

VERTICAL STRUCTURE
Salesperson per business field
World business coordination

PROJECT MANAGEMENT
R&D design resources
Service technical support

REPORTING
LNA deals world reporting
Sales tactics sharing

FIGURE 15.5 *The LNA Care Program (Part 1).*

MARKETING SUPPORT	TRANSVERSAL PROCESS
EXTENDED CRM	**PRE-SALE SUPPORT**
Customer world installed base	Solution design team
Competition installed base	R&D commitment
Consolidated business visibility	Service commitment
Share of wallet	Supply chain commitment
World alerts	Admin commitment
EVENTS	Legal support
Conferences, road shows, PR, VIP webinars	**DEPLOYMENT SUPPORT**
	Project Manager
SALES TOOLS	Organization document
Business cases, testimonials	**POST SALES SUPPORT**
LNA web area, white papers	Customized procurement
LNA SALES TRAINING WITH HR	Schedule of meetings
Complex selling	Customized invoicing
DEALS SUPPORT	**CUSTOMER INFORMATION ACCESS**
Complementary range	Consolidated activity reports
Solution proposal, ROI	Private catalog ordering
Partner contracting	Financial status

FIGURE 15.6 *The LNA Care Program (Part 2).*

LNA marketing support is close to the sales force and in direct contact with customers at the time of acquisition events or negotiations. The support differs per deal and continues after the deals.

How to use the tool

Figures 15.5 and 15.6 cover a number of areas of the care program. The customer analysis made by the main account manager will help to determine which activities are necessary. Each program activity needs to be evaluated in terms of information, cost, and revenue expectations. In particular, the transversal process is unavoidable once customization appears outside the existing product specifications. It is thus preferable to propose partially secure offers to LNAs rather than to overpromise global solutions.

Strengths and limitations of the tool

This tool shows the investments needed to ensure sales and marketing quality. For large deals or complex products, the effort may be more important than a discount on the price. LNA sales cannot be free test exercises. Thus, a limitation is the sales cycle and uncertainty of the deal. Such efforts often take several years before the first profitable sale and forecasted return.

Tool 79: The Medium-Sized Enterprise Care Program helps to define marketing activities for both the sales force and customers

DEFINITIONS

Medium enterprises are companies between 10 and 20, 50 and 250, or 500 and 1,000 employees, depending on the country's conventions. They can be also defined as companies with a revenue typically between $10 million and $1 billion. *Micro-segments* are small groups of customers with many common attributes, which justifies dedicated campaigns (Shapiro & Bonoma, 1984). *CRM information quantity* refers to the number of customers in the database. *CRM information depth* refers to the volume of information per customer in the database. *CRM information quality* is the percentage of missing or incorrect information in the database.

Though numerous, medium enterprises represent an opportunity for considerable revenue. Their size triggers specific needs and a certain number of people is needed to manage the CRM process. In effect, marketing faces both quantitative and qualitative challenges. The activities shown in the Medium Enterprise Care Program include CRM data management, which is more complex than in the case of a small business; and campaign and multimedia communication management, which has many variations. The tool also shows how activities interface with the sales force, which can be particularly involved.

CRM DATA MANAGEMENT

DATA OBJECTIVES
Resources available for data management
Quantity: % Customers in database
Quantity: % Prospects in database
Depth: Data per customer
Quality of data: % incorrect/missing

DATA SOURCING PROCESS
  Service source
  Sales people
  Campaigns
  Social media
  External files purchase

QUALIFICATION & UPDATES
Web, ERP, service automate CRM
Qualification campaigns
Cleaning duplications
Normalization

YEARLY CAMPAIGNS

ANALYSIS
Segmentation and profiling

OPPORTUNITIES
  Acquisition
  Retention
  Replacement churn
  Cross Selling
  New product launches

TARGET
Profiles
Timeslots

EXTENSIVE ANNUAL PROGRAM
Schedule
Budget
Copy strategy

CAMPAIGN DESIGN
Blueprint
Offers

ROI EVALUATION

FIGURE 15.7 *The Medium-Sized Enterprise Care Program (Part 1)*.

COMMUNICATION MIX

MULTIMEDIA SCENARIOS EXAMPLES:
- Email + web page + purchase online
- Telesales + purchase on the phone
- Telemarketing + exhibition + visit + purchase
- Newsletter + web page + customer call + visit
- Telemarketing + visit
- LinkedIn group participation + email + visit
- LinkedIn direct contact + email + call
- Adwords + web page + form + call
- User community event invitation + participation + call
- Email + catalog + web pages + telesales

SALES FORCE INTERFACE

PROGRAM INFORMATION
Campaign announcement

MANAGEMENT INVOLVEMENT
Revenue target
Timing, salesperson availability

COMPLEMENTARY TRAINING
Spot training reminder tool

LEADS SPOONFEEDING
Lead quantity monitoring

CLM AND NURTURING CAMPAIGNS
CRM update
On-demand messages, follow-up

TRACKING OF RESULTS
Per lead revenue
Per sales person
ROI

CAMPAIGN FEEDBACK
Target and media tuning

FIGURE 15.8 *The Medium-Sized Enterprise Care Program (Part 2)*.

The marketing activity of medium-sized enterprises is divided into micro-segments for customer targeting, message design, and sales force animation. The same customers are frequently contacted with a spectrum of media and different offers.

How to use the tool

The choice of CRM data content is the starting point for all marketing activities, but it requires a lot of information. It is important to decide on a balance of information; for instance, too much information quantity may lead to disappointment in quality. In order to divide the effort, categories for data importance can be created. Data collection can also span a longer period to ensure that it is not overwhelming. The data will help to define the micro-segments, to identify campaigns based on the type, and to create scenarios for multimedia communication. It is necessary to test the campaigns among small groups of customers before expanding them to larger segments.

Strengths and limitations of the tool

This tool helps to oversee the global activity processes from the database to the sales force. It displays the types of campaign programs and the importance of the sales force's support. This activity is valuable as soon as the quantity of targeted mid-sized companies is large enough. Otherwise, simplified programs are necessary to lower the cost.

Tool 80: The SoHo and Small Business Care Program helps to manage quantitative marketing activities

DEFINITIONS

Small office/home office (SoHo), or *micro-enterprises*, are terms used to describe companies that have 0 to 9 employees. *Small businesses* have between 10 and 19, 49 and 500, or 1,000 employees depending on country statistics and conventions. Both are also defined as enterprises with an annual revenue of below $10 million. *Scoring* refers to assigning a value to customers, usually in points, which measures future sales potential based on a mix of heterogeneous criteria.

Millions of SoHo and small businesses exist in the United States, as well as in Europe, Japan, etc. Marketing activities focused on this target face the challenge of being profitable with quantitative operations that have small revenue opportunities per deal. The SoHo and Small Business Care Program plans special cost-based scoring and blueprint programs to increase sales probabilities. It includes customer automation, nurturing, and retention processes, which can benefit from online technology.

OPPORTUNITIES IDENTIFICATION	BLUEPRINT

AQUISITION SCORING
Revenue and profit scoring
Industry codes
Location
Size
Business field criteria
Need
Offer
REPLACEMENT SCORING
Installed base
Competitive base
CROSS SELLING SCORING
Installed base
Competitive base
NEW PRODUCT SCORING
Mix acquisition, replacement
	PREFFERED DISTRIBUTION
	• **WEBSITE**
	  Purchase online
	• **MARKETPLACES**
	  Referencing
	• **TELESALES**
	  Call with or without web support
	• **DISTRIBUTOR BRANCHES**
	• **LIMITED VISITS TO CUSTOMERS**
	QUICK DECISION OFFERINGS
	  Simple packages, all-included
	COST-BASED SCENARIO
	  e.g., Mail + telesales
	  e.g., Newsletter + web demo + purchase online
	  e.g., Customer visit to local point of sale

FIGURE 15.9 *The SoHo and Small Business Care Program (Part 1)*.

Due to the large number of SoHos and small businesses, this tool helps to organize the flow of communication to very specific targets. Small business decision makers have no time to buy and thus, the offerings and purchase processes need to be simple, direct, and fast.

CUSTOMER AUTOMATION	NURTURING AND RETENTION
WEB-SUPPORTED CUSTOMER USER SUPPORT Manuals Security procedures and contact Product demonstration Chat and mail support Forum FAQ **BUYER SUPPORT** Transaction information Delivery information Account information Option to update information **PROCUREMENT** Supplies adapted to products Best products **HOTLINE** User assistance	**SALE CYCLE** Duration Dead periods per customer Scheduling nurturing messages **RED FLAG ALERTS** Purchase change Customer calls Payment delays **REMOTE WIN-BACK PROCESS** Call scripts Training Specific offer **SATISFACTION SCREENING** **REMOTE PREVENTIVE PROGRAMS** Fragile customer segmentation Newsletter and mail Call campaigns

FIGURE 15.10 *The SoHo and Small Business Care Program (Part 2).*

How to use the tool

The tool invites one to start with the construction of a contact database, which is typically purchased from brokers. Next, statistical analyses generate the different scorings. There is a learning process and the initial campaigns will be large. Nonetheless, as sales increase, the scoring will improve and become more accurate, leading to more efficient campaigns. The blueprint scenarios will be tested as well. Automation helps to reduce administrative costs. Specific post-sale communication programs are needed to manage customer relations.

Strengths and limitations of the tool

This tool helps to direct marketing managers to preferred customer addresses and proposes lifecycle management processes. When combined with precise tracking of the customer acquisition cost, it allows one to manage the large volume of communication necessary while maintaining profitability. A large volume of addresses is necessary in order to perform the scoring, as well as a follow-up of expenditures per customer. The limitation will come from a focus that is restricted to core buyers using high scoring. When this limit is reached, monitoring the scoring for a larger target can be considered.

CHAPTER 16
HOW TO SELECT AND CONDUCT SURVEYS

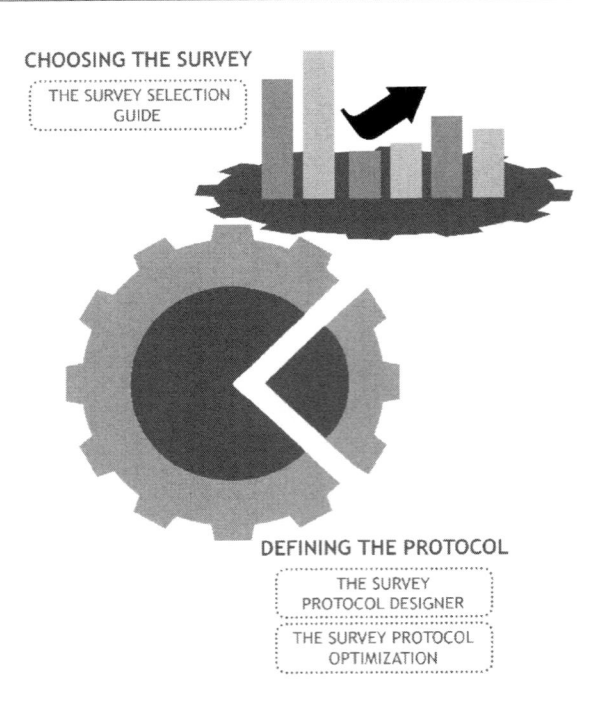

CHOOSING THE SURVEY
- THE SURVEY SELECTION GUIDE

DEFINING THE PROTOCOL
- THE SURVEY PROTOCOL DESIGNER
- THE SURVEY PROTOCOL OPTIMIZATION

Surveys are considered strategic and operational marketing activities. Customer behavior, market size, and product acceptance are among the topics which regularly require surveys before making decisions about the value proposition, the targeted segments, distribution, or the customer relationship. B2B marketing managers must maintain accurate, up-to-date knowledge about the field and conduct regular surveys. Survey results depend on the specific methodology employed and the quality of data collection process.

What is specific to B2B?

In B2B, surveys are used more broadly. Technologies, business field, distribution value, and lead generation are important factors that add to the usual topics of customer need and behavior. Because of the cost of surveys and B2B customers' availability, the methods used differ; for instance, qualitative methods and expert consultations are often employed. The small sample size, however, may limit the generalizability of the results. In practice, though the same survey may meet several objectives, several surveys are necessary to triangulate the results. Once a research question is defined, the choice of survey is made and the protocol is defined. Three tools are proposed to help B2B marketing managers.

Choosing the survey
- Tool 81: The Survey Selection Guide

Defining the protocol
- Tool 82: The Survey Protocol Designer
- Tool 83: The Survey Protocol Optimization

Tool 81: The Survey Selection Guide helps to choose from 34 survey types based on the scope and level of analysis

DEFINITIONS

Triangulation refers to the use of several survey methods to answer a research question. The *customer blueprint* refers to customer's series of events and contacts with the company before, during, and after the purchase. The *business field* is the list of the actors in the market that influence the company strategy. The *lead* is an event that shows a customer's interest in the company products. *Co-marketing* is a communication program shared with one or several partners. *Ergonomics* is the science of improving customer interfaces with the product. *LNA* stands for large and national accounts, and refers to a company generally over 5,000 employees. A *benchmark* is a performance comparison with a non-competitor for a certain activity.

B2B managers face several day-to-day decisions that require ongoing research initiatives. The scope of surveys is very large; they can be done internally or externally. Survey protocols can vary considerably and the costs can therefore range from almost nil to millions of dollars. The Survey Selection Guide suggests a range of survey types organized according to the level, perspective, and survey objectives. To select the type of marketing survey, move from left to right and top to bottom.

For example, if the survey intends to examine the environment at the company level, technology, business field, or image surveys can be conducted. If the objective is to define the strategy, once the environment is known, business model, segmentation targeting, and positioning surveys are necessary. If the go-to-market needs to be surveyed, the environment can trigger an evaluation of customer and distribution satisfaction; to evaluate strategy, distribution model or customer blueprint surveys are needed; on the operations side, lead generation or web strategy surveys can be conducted.

	Environment	Strategy	Operations
Company level	Technology	Business mod.	Alliances
	Business field	Segmentation	Co-marketing
	Competition	Positioning	Profitability
	Image awaren.	Targetting	Benchmark
		Diversification	
Value proposition	Offerings	Creativity	Product test
	Price intelligence	Product def.	Price test
		Service def.	Ergonomy
Go-to-market	Customer sat.	Distribution	Lead generation
	Distribution sat.	Cust. blueprint	Sales force
	Buying process	Conquest	LNA
		Loyalty	Web strategy
		Retention	Post launch

FIGURE 16.1 *The Survey Selection Guide.*

This tool proposes 34 survey types. Multiple survey types may be needed. For instance, the question "What should the future product specifications, the target, the large account penetration strategy, and web strategy be?" cannot be addressed by only one survey. The best method is to triangulate data—to use two or three survey types and make a comparison of the results.

How to use the tool

Select a survey by first answering the following questions: (a) What is the real issue to be investigate? (b) What is already reasonably well-known? (c) What is the missing information? and (d) What survey can cover several burning questions? The two dimensions suggested by the tool—company, value proposition, and the go-to-market on one side, and environment, strategy, and operations on the other side—allow one select several surveys. The time and cost surveys will lead to the final selection of instruments.

Strengths and limitations of the tool

This guide includes 34 survey types to address precise questions. For example, if the objective is to measure the market to target, segmentation, business field, and distribution surveys may be selected. The three methods will yield different results and the final figure will be an estimation. A limitation of this tool is that it may require knowledge of how to conduct a pilot survey. Another limitation is the time and resources needed to create the surveys.

Tool 82: The Survey Protocol Designer helps to choose the best mix of data collection methods

DEFINITIONS

The *protocol* of a survey is the series of methods used to collect and process data in order to obtain results.

Usually, the survey initially uses qualitative methods in order to understand the scope of the topic, then it uses quantitative methods to make accurate measurements. The Survey Protocol Designer provides a description and the attributes of 10 survey methods (see Tables 16.1 and 16.2). Depending on the budget, time, scope, and accuracy of the results, a protocol may include a mix of methods. The intrusiveness of the method is also an important consideration. If the survey is particularly intrusive, participants may modify their responses, which negatively impacts the results.

TABLE 16.1 *The Collection Methods.*

COLLECTION METHOD	DESCRIPTION AND PRECAUTIONS
Documentary research	Very large but heterogeneous and often inaccurate information. Multiple checks are needed.
Face-to-face interviews	Unavoidable in B2B to evaluate the range of customer issues. They are efficient in qualitative surveys with non-directive or semi-directive methods. They can be used for directive quantitative surveys as well.
Focus groups	Small groups of persons interviewed together. They are efficient for insights from a homogeneous group of customers, competitive buyers, users, experts, salespersons, etc. Heterogeneous groups are used for idea generation.
Phone interviews	Frequent in B2B, they must raise interviewees' interest to go over just a few questions. They can be qualitative or quantitative.
Online surveys	Processed over internet, they have a great abandonment rate, which can be improved with a prior phone agreement.
Pure observation	With the agreement of the participants, this method includes observation by a non-anonymous person, a mystery customer, or a camera. Pure observation is effective for understanding product manipulations, user errors, customers' physical behaviors.
Participative observation	In this method, the observer lives the same experience and shares it verbally with the customer. This method is effective for understanding customer reasoning, actions, habits, language, etc.
Life path	The interviewer observes and questions the customers at each point of engagement—from purchase to product use and elimination—to assess customer experience. Because this method is typically intrusive, it is rarely used in B2B.
Nethnography with pure observation	This method includes simple observation of conversations in social media. It is efficient for understanding opinions, but requires checking the person's profile.
Nethnography with participative observation	In this method, the observer share opinions and ask for feedback from community members.
Online focus group	Distance online focus groups use 2.0 tools (i.e., chat, web conference, teleconference, forum, blogs, and bulletin board).
Big data	Collection of massive heterogeneous online data related to product use. High performance statistical processing software is needed. Big data outlines global trends.

For example, when the budget and time are limited, and the scope of requirement is not very large, the protocol can include online participative observation followed by an online survey. If the scope requirement is large, then the online participative observation can be replaced by a physical focus group.

TABLE 16.2 *Comparative Attributes of the Collection Methods.*

COLLECTION MODE ATTRIBUTES	Intrusive	Sample choice	Qualitative results	Quantitative results	Easy data processing	Accurate	Fast	Cheap
Documentary research	No	No	Yes	Variable	No	Variable	No	No
Face-to-face interviews	Very	Yes	Yes	No	Yes	No	No	No
Focus groups	Very	Yes	Yes	No	Yes	No	No	No
Phone interviews	Yes	Yes	Poor	Yes	Yes	Yes	Yes	Yes
Online surveys	Yes	Yes	Poor	Yes	Yes	Yes	Yes	Yes
Pure observation	No	Yes	Yes	No	No	No	No	No
Participative observation	Very	Yes	Yes	No	No	No	No	No
Life path	Very	Yes	Yes	No	No	No	No	No
Nethnography pure observ.	No	No	Yes	No	No	No	Yes	Yes
Nethnography part. observ.	Yes	No	Yes	No	No	No	Yes	Yes
Online focus group	Yes	Yes	Yes	No	Yes	No	Yes	Yes
Big data collection	No	No	Yes	Yes	No	Yes	No	No

How to use the tool

The possible survey protocols are first sorted with the attributes proposed by the tool. For example, is the choice of the sample compulsory? Is the protocol intrusive? How accurate should the results be? The remaining protocols are evaluated.

Strengths and limitations of the tool

Evaluation is made in terms of cost, time, and performance, with the eventual support of a survey consulting company. This process will help to select the best survey methods. The tool proposes a number of collection methods, and suggests combining a mix of methods in order to generate both qualitative and quantitative results. The limitation, however, lies in the ability to find the expertise needed to collect and analyze data. Outsourcing the survey is the usual solution, but this poses the challenge of choosing an appropriate consultant. Consultants typically need time to become familiar with the business field.

Tool 83: The Survey Protocol Optimization Tool proposes three protocols

Marketing managers choose protocols based on available resources (i.e., time and money), which can lead to the selection of quick validation, standard, or in-depth surveys. The Survey Protocol Optimization Tool proposes three generic protocols based on the available time and budget. For example, the quick check survey will limit external activities to well-chosen qualitative contacts; the standard survey will include a focus group and online quantitative pool; and the in-depth survey suggests a crowdsourcing of ideas, several focus groups per segment, semi-quantitative phone interviews, and an online quantitative survey. The accuracy and robustness of the results will vary based on the choice. For example, the protocols will be adapted based on the nature of the survey and the availability of the contacts.

TABLE 16.3 *The Survey Protocol Optimization.*

Quick check survey	Standard survey	In-depth survey
Few days Below $5k	Few weeks $5-50k	Few months Over $50k
• Internal and external documentary research • Community observations • Forum questions • Internal face-to-face interviews • External experts phone interviews	• Internal and external documentary research • Community observations • Forum questions • Internal and external face-to-face qualitative interviews • Focus group • Online quantitative survey	• Internal and external documentary research • Community observations and participation • Crowdsourcing of ideas • Forum questions • Internal and external face-to-face qualitative interviews • Several focus groups • Phone semi-quantitative survey • Large online quantitative survey per segment • Conclusions validated with experts phone interviews

The quick check will provide spontaneous confirmation for intuitive ideas, while the in-depth survey searches for counter ideas, reconsiders the question, provides quantitative figures, and validates the results from several angles.

How to use the tool

The tool invites one to think differently about survey protocols. The three surveys—quick, standard, and in-depth—can be designed to respond to specific needs and to develop targeted solutions. The cost of each type should be compared to their relative performance; for example, the accuracy and robustness of conclusions.

Strengths and limitations of the tool

Each survey technique yields a number of ideas for addressing the question, and each can be useful to validate insights. Whatever the technique, the uncertainty posed by the question is reduced if the quality of the survey is high. The three formats provide increasing validity to the responses provided, given the multiple samples of participants and different collection methods. The limitation comes from an expectation of results that are not in line with the resources allocated to the survey. Another limitation is that the question may be particularly difficult to address with the targeted sample of participants.

CHAPTER 17

HOW TO DESIGN AND MONITOR THE MARKETING ORGANIZATION

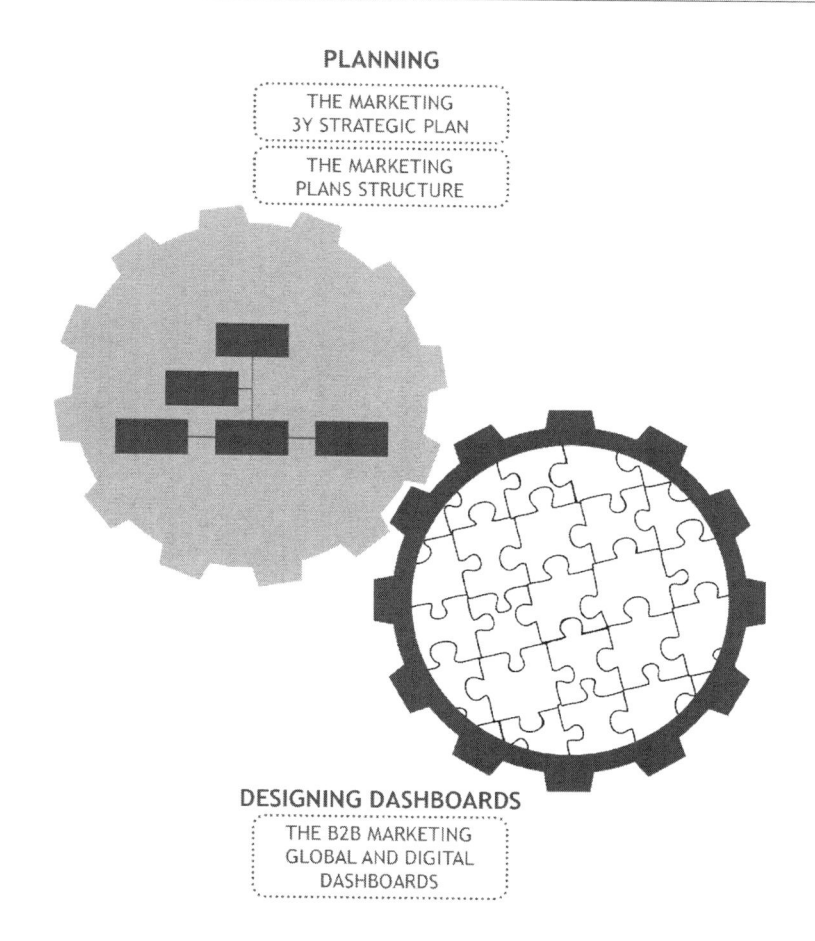

PLANNING
THE MARKETING 3Y STRATEGIC PLAN
THE MARKETING PLANS STRUCTURE

DESIGNING DASHBOARDS
THE B2B MARKETING GLOBAL AND DIGITAL DASHBOARDS

As with any organization, the marketing structure and objectives are designed according to priorities and available resources. The size of the product range, the pace of new product generation, the quantity of communication campaigns, and the number of customer segments are among the factors that determine the activities and functions.

What is specific to B2B?

In B2B, the activities of marketing and sales may overlap, and may need to be frequently reorganized (Biemans & Maja Makovec, 2007; Kotler, Rackham, & Krishnaswamy, 2006; Matray, 2012). The closeness of R&D and marketing and product complexity trigger specific strategic marketing organization. Some activities are overdeveloped in B2B, including for instance, sales team support (i.e., supplying leads), sales tools creation, complex account database management, and training. The mechanics of all marketing activities and document production must be clear and coherent, and their performance must be easy to evaluate.

Three tools are proposed to support this process.

Planning
- Tool 84: The Marketing 3Y Strategic Plan
- Tool 85: The Marketing Plans Structure

Designing dashboards
- Tool 86: The B2B Marketing Global and Digital Dashboards

Tool 84: The Marketing 3Y Strategic Plan proposes a framework for marketing strategy over a 3-year period

DEFINITIONS

The *key performance indicator* (KPI) is a figure on the company dashboard measuring activity efficiency.

The yearly marketing activities are defined in a document that serves as the guidebook for the executive staff as well as the marketing team or the board. The Marketing 3Y Strategic Plan provides a 3-year view of marketing activities and suggests nine specific phases. After an executive summary, an external and internal analysis is made, along with a synthesized SWOT analysis—which contains the hypothesis and

possible scenarios. Then, the strategic objectives are given, followed by the operations, resource needs, financial forecast, and reporting.

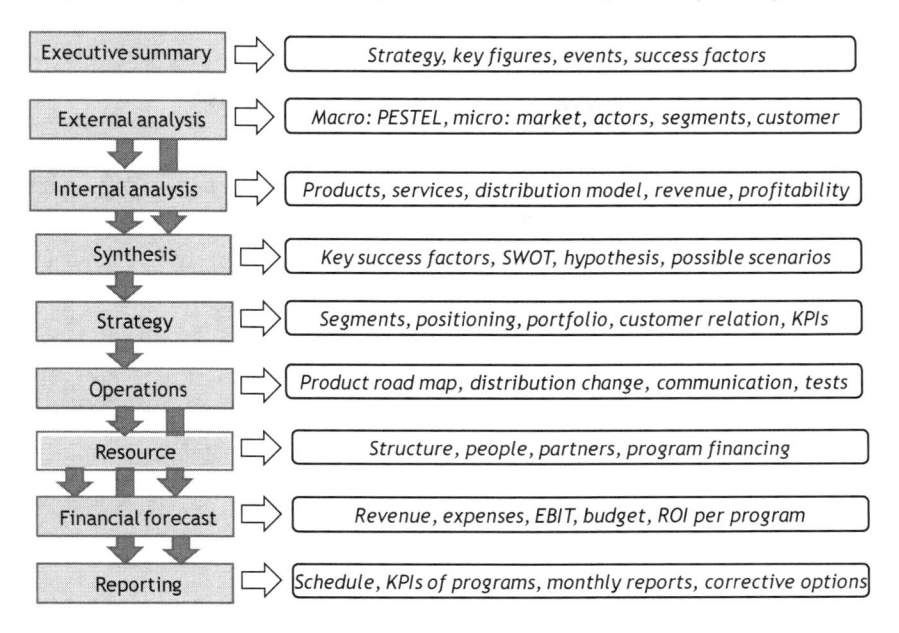

Executive summary	Strategy, key figures, events, success factors
External analysis	Macro: PESTEL, micro: market, actors, segments, customer
Internal analysis	Products, services, distribution model, revenue, profitability
Synthesis	Key success factors, SWOT, hypothesis, possible scenarios
Strategy	Segments, positioning, portfolio, customer relation, KPIs
Operations	Product road map, distribution change, communication, tests
Resource	Structure, people, partners, program financing
Financial forecast	Revenue, expenses, EBIT, budget, ROI per program
Reporting	Schedule, KPIs of programs, monthly reports, corrective options

FIGURE 17.1 *The Marketing Strategic 3y Plan Content.*

The strategic plan provides the main purpose and introduces other, more detailed plans. The strategic plan represents the best know-how of the marketing team; it is generated with a lot of internal and external consultation and research. It contains a synthesis of observations made over the course of the year.

How to use the tool

This tool provides a global framework. The proposed phases and content need to be adapted to the business field and company status. Some phases or stages may be added, particularly when new activities are scheduled. The 3YP construction requires iterative consultations with R&D for the product road map, sales department for the revenue targets, and the financial department for the financial forecast.

Strengths and limitations of the tool

A 3Y marketing plan provides direction for the company. Its quality will determine the success of the company. It cannot be created by persons who have no experience or have a superficial knowledge of the business. By contrast, having individuals with shorter tenures on the team may help to reconsider existing strategies.

Tool 85: The Marketing Plans Structure outlines the interconnections among plans and ensures the coherence of marketing activities

Marketing managers take on a considerable number of activities, which need to be tightly synchronized. The Marketing Plans Structure is a tool that defines eight typical, interlinked B2B plans, including their objectives and progress measurements. First, the 3-year plan defines the global company objectives, with qualitative strategic targets and key performance indicators such as revenue, EBIT, EBITDA, earnings per share, and resources (i.e., R&D expenditures, employees, etc.). Out of this plan, the product portfolio road map is created. This serves as the basis for the strategic marketing activities with products, revenue, and profitability per segment. It will also feed the operational plan, which gives the go-to-market 3-year directions: distribution, customer relation model, and communication models with revenue and profitability targets per network. Of the two strategic and operational plans, five annual plans are employed: (a) the customer life management 360° vision, (b) the lead generation campaigns, (c) product launches, (d) dealer events, and (e) sales training. They are described with other tools in this book. The marketing dashboard encompasses information about all of the plans and compares their results with their objectives.

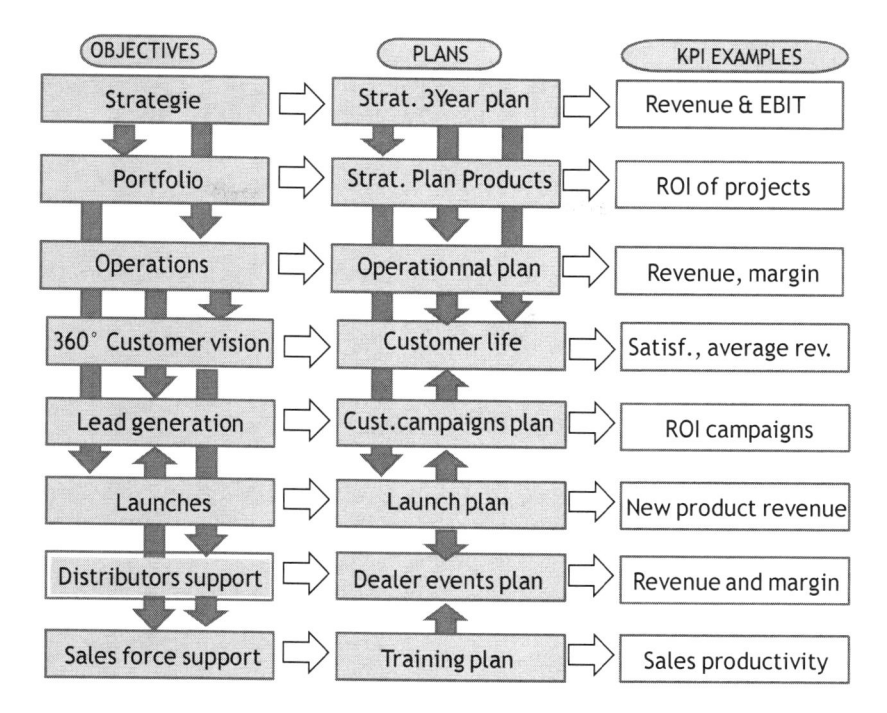

OBJECTIVES	PLANS	KPI EXAMPLES
Strategie	Strat. 3Year plan	Revenue & EBIT
Portfolio	Strat. Plan Products	ROI of projects
Operations	Operationnal plan	Revenue, margin
360° Customer vision	Customer life	Satisf., average rev.
Lead generation	Cust. campaigns plan	ROI campaigns
Launches	Launch plan	New product revenue
Distributors support	Dealer events plan	Revenue and margin
Sales force support	Training plan	Sales productivity

FIGURE 17.2 *Marketing Plans Structure.*

In B2B, support to the distributors, lead generation, and support to the sales force are often the most important marketing activities. As such, they require specific plans and KPIs.

How to use the tool

In practice, plans are often developed using previous years' plans, with adaptations for the next year. This method will lead to incremental improvements. Another way is to hold a general brainstorming session regarding the business model, customer targets and relations, and value propositions. After defining the business strategy, a second brainstorming session on operations will help to promote radical change and improve cross communications.

Strengths and limitations of the tool

This tool helps to collapse the different marketing activities into one mechanism. The plans are delineated, making the marketing value chain coherent. The tool has to be adapted to each company based on marketing resource allocation. For example, a company with a small sales force but an important program of co-marketing activities with partners could limit its training plan and instead create a yearly partnership plan. The limitation of the tool comes from the marketing resources needed to produce the plans. Small B2B enterprises often prefer to concentrate their marketing activities on short-term operations.

Tool 86: The B2B Marketing Global and Digital Dashboards collect indicators to track marketing efficiency

DEFINITIONS

The *bounce rate* is the percentage of website visitors whose visits end at the home page. The *customer attrition rate* refers to the percentage of customers lost. *Outbound calls* are phone calls made by the supplier, while *inbound calls* are those made by the customer. The *salesperson portfolio* is the list of customers who have already been contacted by the salesperson and who may buy in the near future. The *sale cycle* is the duration between the first customer contact and the purchase. The *cross-selling ratio* refers to the percentage of customers who buy more than one product or service. The *net promoter score* is the percentage of very satisfied customers (rated 9 to 10) minus the percentage of not satisfied customers (rated 0 to 6). The *engagement index* measures employees' level of commitment to the company and to customers. The *lead-to sale rate* is the percentage of leads converted to a sale.

Any company activity requires a measurement of performance; some marketing activities can even be tracked and their efficiency evaluated (e.g., the lead generation). Others are more difficult to track, however, given the flow of corporate communication. The B2B Marketing Global and Digital Dashboards lists over 60 indicators, which serve as the basis of the dashboard. It separates strategic activities, sales support, customer life, service, and web activities.

STRATEGY
- Market share
- Market share per segment
- Installed base size per segment
- Distribution coverage rate
- # New customers
- Attrition rate (% of lost customers)
- # Products launched compared to competition
- ROI of new product projects
- Revenue growth compared to competition
- Average revenue per customer life
- Average customer value
- Average gross margin

GLOBAL LEAD GENERATION
- # total leads and per media type
- Average cost of lead per media type
- # Outbound total calls
- # Inbound total calls
- # Calls per telesales person
- # Dates per teleactor
- Lead-to-sales rate

SALES
- Total sales and per product
- Revenue per quota bearer
- # Visits per salesperson
- # Visits per telesales person
- Service-to-product attachment rate
- % Deals won
- Average # of deals in portfolio
- Average duration of sales cycle
- Average revenue per deal
- Average discount per deal

CUSTOMER LIFE
- Average customer lifetime
- Satisfaction net promoter score
- Cross-selling ratio
- Replacement ratio
- Recommendation ratio
- Average number of products per customer

SERVICE
- Employee satisfaction index
- Employee engagement index

FIGURE 17.3 *Example of a Global B2B Marketing Dashboard.*

Services with human contacts may heavily involve employee relations with customers. Additionally, the marketing organization may have specific programs and efficiency measurements, including trainings, events, animations, and certifications (Coleman, de Chernatony, & Christodoulides, 2011).

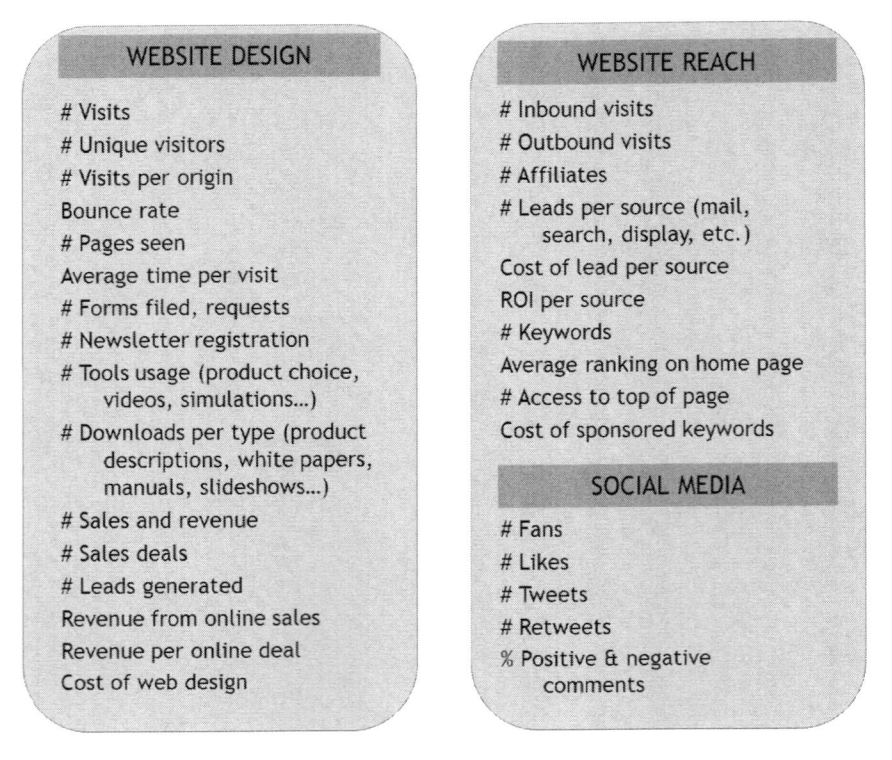

WEBSITE DESIGN	WEBSITE REACH
# Visits	# Inbound visits
# Unique visitors	# Outbound visits
# Visits per origin	# Affiliates
Bounce rate	# Leads per source (mail, search, display, etc.)
# Pages seen	Cost of lead per source
Average time per visit	ROI per source
# Forms filed, requests	# Keywords
# Newsletter registration	Average ranking on home page
# Tools usage (product choice, videos, simulations…)	# Access to top of page
# Downloads per type (product descriptions, white papers, manuals, slideshows…)	Cost of sponsored keywords

	SOCIAL MEDIA
# Sales and revenue	# Fans
# Sales deals	# Likes
# Leads generated	# Tweets
Revenue from online sales	# Retweets
Revenue per online deal	% Positive & negative comments
Cost of web design	

FIGURE 17.4 *The Digital B2b Marketing Dashboard (Example).*

Internet service providers offer many technical measurement figures. Each have their own definitions, which should be understood.

How to use the tool

The analytics of web activities are made easier with the automated generation of data by Internet providers and search engines. Various sources are consolidated and the most interesting figures are sorted out to limit the size of the dashboard. Much of the information on the dashboard is automatically generated from the CRM. This critical data comes partly from entries from the sales force. The effort may be burdensome and subsequently neglected if the benefits of the dashboard are not made clear when initially introduced.

Strengths and limitations of the tool

The dashboard is the basic management tool that helps to orient the strategy and operations. The data quality and quantity should be controlled, and there should be a well-balanced effort between the costs and benefits of data generation. A limitation of the tool is that figures in dashboard tend to be continuously added, while the time available to evaluate them decreases. In practice, only a few figures are closely examined, and these should have a robust quality.

CONCLUSION

The tools used by marketing managers are key to understanding company performance. The tools outlined in this book provide structure, enhance clarity, and offer a range of choices. They provide sound criteria for decision-making. They help to allocate resources, improve customer relations, and increase profitability, all of which are critical to company survival. Academic research and consulting companies are valuable resources to find the best tools. Despite the popularity of tools in business schools, the number actually used in practice is very small.

Each marketing manager finds his or her own means of solving problems. This book provides a number of flexible B2B marketing tools to promote decision-making. It always recommended to first search for information, which helps to identify the best tools and serves as the basis for any decision. Readers are invited to adapt these tools based on their business context. They can also define specific criteria when utilizing the tools.

In this edition, I have tried to compile the most useful and generic tools. In future editions, additional tools used in the field or proposed by researchers will also be included. With the evolution of supplier value propositions and means of communication, new decision models appear regularly. The number models will continue to increase to account for complex decisions—both strategic and operational—in the global market. In the same way, new tools will be needed to support such models.

REFERENCES

American Marketing Association. (2015) *Dictionary of the American Marketing Association*. Retrieved from https://www.ama.org/resources/Pages/Dictionary.aspx?dLetter=B

Ansoff, H. I. (1987). *Corporate strategy*. London, United Kingdom: Penguin.

Armstrong, J. S., & Brodie, R. J. (1994). Effects of portfolio planning methods on decision making: Experimental results. *International Journal of Research in Marketing, 11*, 73-84. doi:10.1016/0167-8116(94)90035-3

Arnould, E. J., & Thompson, C. J. (2005). Consumer culture theory (CCT): Twenty years of research. *Journal of Consumer Research, 31*, 868-882. doi:10.1086/426626

Bateson, G. (1956). The message 'this is play.' In B. Schaffner (Ed.), *Group processes: Transactions of the second conference* (pp. 145-242). New York, NY: Josiah Macy, Jr. Foundation.

Biemans, W. G., & Maja Makovec, B. (2007). Designing the marketing-sales interface in B to B firms. *European Journal of Marketing, 41*, 257-273. doi:10.1108/03090560710728327

Blythe, J., & Zimmerman, A. (2013). *Business to business marketing management: A global perspective* (2nd ed.). New York, NY: Routledge.

Brenann, R., Håkansson, H., & Johanson, J. (1992). A model of industrial networks. In B. Axelsson & G. Easton (Eds.), *Industrial networks: A new view of reality* (pp. 28-34). London, United Kingdom: Routledge.

Brock, J. K.-U., & Zhou J. Y. (2012). Customer intimacy. *Journal of Business & Industrial Marketing, 27*, 370-383. doi:10.1108/08858621211236043

Brown, B. P., Zablah A. R., Bellenger, D. N., & Donthu N. (2012). What factors influence buying center brand sensitivity? *Industrial Marketing Management, 41*, 508-552. doi:10.1016/j.indmarman.2011.06.008

Business model. (n.d.). In *Oxford dictionaries*. Retrieved July 27, 2015, from http://www.oxforddictionaries.com/definition/english/business-model

Cham Kim, W., & Mauborgne, R. (2004, October). Blue ocean strategy. *Harvard Business Review*. Retrieved from https://hbr.org/

Coleman, D., de Chernatony, L., & Christodoulides, G. (2011). B to B service brand identity: Scale development and validation. *Industrial Marketing Management, 40*, 1063-1071. doi:10.1016/j.indmarman.2011.09.010

Coombes, P. H., & Nicholson, J. D. (2013). Business models and their relationship with marketing: A systematic literature review. *Industrial Marketing Management, 42*, 656-664. doi:10.1016/j.indmarman.2013.05.005

Cooper, R. (2008). Perspective: The Stage-Gate idea-to-launch process—update, what's new, and NexGen Systems. *Journal of Product Innovation Management, 25*, 213-232. doi:10.1111/j.1540-5885.2008.00296.x

Cova, B., & Salle, R. (2008). Marketing solutions in accordance with the S-D logic: Co-creating value with customer network actors. *Industrial Marketing Management, 37*, 270-277. doi:10.1016/j.indmarman.2007.07.005

Ernst & Young. (2015). *A spiral approach to business model innovation.* Retrieved from http://www.ey.com/GL/en/Issues/Driving-growth/Growth-through-innovation---The-innovation-spiral

Gebauer, H., Paiola, M., & Saccani N. (2013). Characterizing service networks for moving from products to solutions. *Industrial Marketing Management, 42*, 31-46. doi:10.1016/j.indmarman.2012.11.002

Hakansson, H., & Snehota, I. (2003). *Managing business relationships.* Hoboken, NJ: Wiley.

Hambrick, D. C., MacMillian, I. C., & Day, D. L. (1982). Strategic attributes and performance in the BCG matrix—a PIMS-based analysis of industrial product business. *Academy of Management Journal, 25*, 510-531. doi:10.2307/256077

Hamel, G., & Prahalad, C. K. (1996, July/August). Competing for future. *Harvard Business Review.* Retrieved from https://hbr.org/

Hill, T., & Westbrook R. (1997). SWOT analysis: It's time for a product recall. *Long Range Panning, 30*, 46-52. doi:10.1016/S0024-6301(96)00095-7

Kano, N., Seraku, N., Takahashi, F., & Tsuji, S. (1984). Attractive quality and must be quality. *Hinshitsu, Journal of the Japanese Society for Quality Control, 14*(2), 39-48. Retrieved from http://www.jsqc.org/en/

Kline, S. J., & Rosenberg, N. (1986). An overview of innovation. In R. Landau & N. Rosenberg (Eds.), *The positive sum strategy: Harnessing technology for economic growth* (pp. 207-305). Washington, DC: National Academy Press.

Kotler, P. (1972). *Marketing management: Analysis, planning, and control* (2nd ed.). Upper Saddle River, NJ: Prentice-Hall.

Kotler, P., & Keller, K. L. (2013). *Marketing management* (14th ed.). Upper Saddle River, NJ: Pearson Education.

Kotler, P., Rackham N., & Krishnaswamy S. (2006, July/August). Ending the war between sales and marketing. *Harvard Business Review.* Retrieved from https://hbr.org/

Lecocq, X., Demil, B., & Warnier V. (2006). Le business model, un outil d'analyse stratégique [The business model, a strategic analysis tool]. *L'Expansion Management Review*, *123*, 96-109. Retrieved from https://www.cairn.info/revue-questions-de-management-2013-1.htm

Lovelock, C., & Wirtz J. (2010). *Services marketing: People, technology, strategy* (7th ed.). Upper Saddle River, NJ: Prentice Hall.

Malaval, P., & Benaroya, C. (2013). *Marketing business to business*. Upper Saddle River, NJ: Pearson Education.

Matray, M. A. (2012). *Etude de la relation entre la vente et le marketing et son impact sur la performance de vente* [Translation: Study of the relationship between sales and marketing and its impact on sales performance] (Doctoral dissertation, l'IAE-Paris Panthéon Sorbonne). Retrieved from http://www.gregoriae.com/index.php?option=com_content&view=article&id=4774%3Athese&catid=40%3Apublications&Itemid=97&type=1&lang=en

McCarthy, J. (1960). *Basic marketing: A managerial approach*. Burr Ridge, IL: Irwin.

Osterwalder, A., & Pigneur Y. (2010). *Business model generation: A handbook for visionaries, game changers, and challengers*. Hoboken, NJ: Wiley.

Parasuraman, A. (2000). Technology readiness index (TRI): A multiple-item scale to measure readiness to embrace new technologies. *Journal of Service Research*, *2*, 307-320. doi:10.1177/109467050024001

Porter, M. E. (1985). *Competitive advantage: Creating and sustaining superior performance*. New York, NY: Free Press.

Sharma, A., & Iyer Gopalkrishnan, R. (2011). Are pricing policies an impediment to the success of customer solutions? *Industrial Marketing Management*, *40*, 723-729. doi:10.1016/j.indmarman.2011.06.002

Tamer-Cavusgil, S., Knight G., & Riesenberger, J. (2014). *International business: The new realities*. Upper Saddle River, NJ: Pearson Education.

Treacy, M., & Wieserma, F. (1995). *The discipline of market leaders: Choose your customers, narrow your focus, dominate your market*. London, United Kingdom: Harper Collins.

Truong, D., Thuong, T. L., Senecal S., & Rao S. (2012). Electronic marketplace: A distinct platform for business-to-business (B-to-B) procurement. *Journal of Business-to-Business Marketing*, *19*, 216-247. doi:10.1080/1051712X.2012.638467Shapiro, B., & Bonoma T. (1984, May). How to segment industrial markets. *Harvard Business Review*, *62*(3), 104-110. Retrieved from https://hbr.org/

Ulaga, W., & Reinartz, W. (2011). Hybrid offerings: How manufacturing firm's combine goods and services successfully. *Journal of Marketing, 75*(3), 5-23. doi:10.1509/jm.09.0395

Vargo, S. L., & Lusch, R. F. (2004). Evolving to a new service dominant logic for marketing. *Journal of Marketing, 68*(1), 1-17. doi:10.1509/jmkg.68.1.1.24036

Abbreviations

1:1 - one to one
4SR - solution and return, seduction and reach, support and relation, sustainability and responsibility
6P - product, price, place, promotion, process, people
ADL - Arthur D. Little
ARA - actor, resource, activity
B2A or B to A - business to administrations
B2B or B to B - business to business
B2B2C or B to B to C - business to business to consumers
B2C or B to C - business to consumers
B2E or B to E - business to employees
B2U or B to U - business to user
BCG - Boston Consulting Group
C2C or C to C - consumer to consumer
CLM - customer life management
CRM - customer relationship management
CTO - chief technical officer
DMU - decision making unit
EBIT - earnings before interest and tax
EBITDA - earnings before interest, tax, depreciation and amortization
IMP - industrial marketing and purchase group
KPI - key performance indicator
LNA - large and national account
MTBF - mean time between failures
MTTR - mean time to repair
NPS - net promoter score
PESTLE - political, economic, social, technological, legal, and ecological
PLM - product life management
POC - proof of concept
RFI - request for information
RFP - request for proposal
RFQ - request for quotation
ROI - return on investment
SoHo - small office/home office
SPECTRED - political, economic, social, technological, legal, ecological, demographic
SWOT - strengths, weaknesses, opportunities, threats
TCO - total cost of ownership
TRI - technology readiness index
VAR - value-added reseller
WoM - word of mouth

Glossary

1:1 media is media developed for personal interactions with consumers (e.g., personal messages).

Achieved price is the list price minus all various discounts.

Added value of a company is its revenue minus its purchases, sometimes called the *gross margin*. More broadly, added value refers to all of the benefits a company brings to its customers beyond the benefits brought by suppliers.

Adjacent individuals or organizations are external persons or organizations connected via collaborative Internet tools.

Alternative conclusion is a proposal made to the customer to choose among several close solutions.

Attrition rate or customer churn refers to the percentage of customers lost due to competition, bankruptcies, mergers, or acquisitions.

Awareness and contact is a phase when the supplier brand is known by the customer with the intent to contact it.

B2A means business to administrations, a part of B2B limited to business conducted with public authorities, including federal, national, state, and local authorities.

B2B or B to B are acronyms for business to business, which is the business of selling products or services to organizations.

B2B2C refers to companies that produce products and sell them to other companies, which further develop the products and sell them to consumers.

B2C or B to C means business to consumers; it is the business of selling products or services to individuals.

B2E means business to employees, which refers to products developed specifically for employees.

B2U means business to user, where the products are sold to administrations and used by citizen.

Benchmark is a comparison of a practice or performance with a non-competitor organization.

Blended learning is a mix of both online and classroom learning sessions.

Blue team is the process of presenting a project to a person familiar with this type of exercise in order to get a feedback.

Blueprint is a schedule of the events and physical or electronic contacts of the customer experience before and after sales with the supplier and its partners.

Bounce rate is the percentage of website visitors whose visits end at the home page.

Brainstorming is a creativity method which is based on a set rules for idea generation (i.e., no censorship, no judgment, listening, respect on others' ideas) and spontaneity.

Brand Identity Charter is a document that provides the rules for usage of all the brand identity attributes, including graphical elements like the logo and colors, and verbal elements such as the baseline and positioning.

Brand premium is the bonus or penalty to customers' product price perception based on trust of the brand.

Business developer is a person who seeks business opportunities using all means of leveraging, including direct sales, managing distributors, lobbying, and influencers or partnerships.

Business field is the list of the actors in the market which influence the company strategy.

Business field or ecosystem is the group of actors or professional organizations whose actions impact the enterprise strategy and results.

Business model is the plan for the successful strategy and operations of a business, including sources of revenue, intended customer base, products, alliances, and financing details.

Business plan is a document that helps make decisions about launching a business project as well as stop-or-go decisions at major milestones.

Buying center, or decision making unit (DMU) is the group of individuals that consists of all organizational members internal or external to the company who are involved in any way, to any extent, in any phase of a specific buying decision (American Marketing Association, 2015).

C2C means consumer to consumer; it is the business of direct sales between consumers.

Ceiling price is the maximum possible price that will still win a deal.

Closed-loop marketing is the process of bridging marketing and sales activities.

Co-marketing is a communication program shared with one or several partners.

Commissioning refers to variable money earned by the sales force.

Community of practice is a group of customers who share their experiences regarding products.

Company Tier 1 is a direct provider.

Complex selling concerns sales that involve multiple partners, co-creation with the customer, or high value of purchase and risk.

Core competencies of an enterprise are the technical knowledge bases needed to differentiate the business and employ the business model (Hamel & Prahalad, 1996).

Cost of lead is the average communication expenditure to generate a lead.

Coverage is the market space in which the enterprise is able to sell to and provide services to customers.

Critical moments are events that could end the relationship with the customer.

Criticality is the level of impact of the purchase on customer performance.

CRM information depth is the volume of information per customer in the database.

CRM information quality is the percentage of missing or incorrect information in the database.

CRM information quantity is the number of customers in the database.

Customer life management (CLM) refers to the procedures for managing customer events.

Customer relationship management (CRM) is the system and management of customer contacts.

Cross sale is the sale of additional products after the first sale to a customer. It can take place at a much later time.

Cross-selling ratio refers to the percentage of customers who buy more than one product or service.

Crowdsourcing is a method for sourcing information or ideas from a large number of people using collaborative Internet tools.

Customer acquisition cost refers to the total cost of sales, communication, discount, and pre-sales technical support necessary for the first deal.

Customer attrition rate refers to the percentage of customers lost.

Customer base is the list of customers who have bought products from the company and have an existing relationship with the company.

Coverage is the list of customers where the company distribution network is active to sell.

Customer churn is the loss of customers because of stop of purchase or switch to another supplier.

Customer education is the sales phase when the customer learns about the business field, technologies, suppliers, purchase processes, benefits, and products.

Customer engagement index is an index of the customers' activities and conversations in favor of the brand.

Customer installed base is the number of products in use by a customer.

Customer intimacy is the ability to know the customer organization and employees well enough to quickly, appropriately, and accurately respond to their needs.

Customer lifecycle management (CLM) is the series of processes based on customer experience events beginning from acquisition to the termination of the relationship, which manage customer satisfaction and maximize revenue and profit.

Customer perceived value proposition is the difference between the prospective customer's evaluation of all the costs and benefits of acquiring the product (Kotler & Keller, 2013).

Customer predictability is the ability to predict customer purchases. Product value is the customer perception of the benefits of a product.

Customer relationship management (CRM) is a system including a database of the customer relationships and tools to generate them.

Customer value to the supplier is the difference between the prospective supplier's evaluation of all the costs and benefits of acquiring the customer.

Customization is the design of tailor-made products or services for each customer.

Decision maker is a person who must give his or her agreement to allow the purchase.

Decision making unit, DMU, or buying center is the group of organizational members, internal or external to the company, who are involved in any way, to any extent, in any phase of a specific buying decision (American Marketing Association, 2015).

Defensive project intends to keep the customer base.

Deployment is the service of delivery, integration, and start-up.

Differentiation is the way in which a company makes a different value proposition to customers than the competition.

Direct distribution is made up of manufacturer's employees and indirect distribution through external distributors.

Distribution business model is a business model focused on finding and selling to customers.

EBIT is the earnings before interest and tax, a key profit key indicator.

EBITDA is the earnings before interest, tax, depreciation and amortization, a key profit key indicator.

Education is the phase when the customer has a need and seeks information to make a decision.

Employee engagement index measures employees' level of commitment to the company and to customers.

Ergonomics is the science of improving customer interfaces with the product.

Floor price is the minimum possible price offered by a supplier.

Horizontal integration is the strategy of buying competitors and capturing their market share.

Hybrid offerings include both products and services.

Ideation is the process of idea generation.

Inbound calls are those generated by the customer.

Inbound media are media where the customer decides to use, such as blogs, search engines, or social media.

Incentive system refers to all operations aimed at maintaining and promoting motivation in the sales force in order to produce revenue and profit.

Incremental innovation involves minor product improvements.

Indirect distribution is made to external distributors.

Influencer is a person who influences members of the buying center without being a decision maker.

Initiator is a person who requests the equipment and generates the purchase process.

Inline media uses Internet technology.

Installed base is the number of products in use sold to customers.

Intelligence is a program of business field analysis concerning competition, technology, partnerships, etc.

Intrusive messages are unsolicited messages from the supplier.

Kano survey is a questionnaire used to evaluate the importance, preference, indifference, or opposition to each feature of a product, service, or support (Kano et al., 1984).

Key performance indicator (KPI) is a business metric used to evaluate activities that impact the success of the enterprise.

Large and national accounts (LNA) are customers who represent an important revenue opportunity from the supplier's perspective. LNAs include *intermediate size enterprises*, which vary in size between 250 and 500 employees (with sometimes up to 5,000 employees, depending on the country), and *large enterprises*, which have either over 5,000 employees or generate a revenue over $1 billion.

Lead is an event that demonstrating the customer's interest in the company products.

Lead-to-sale rate is the percentage of leads converted to a sale.

License business model is a model in which supplier authorizes the use of an asset, such as software, a patent, or a trademark.

List price is the public price, or catalog price.

Localization is the adaptation of products, services, and support to local context.

Magical moments are events that may generate revenue.

Market drivers are the key motivating factors influencing customers to purchase.

Market of a product or service is the total revenue of all the products of the same type sold in 1 year in a specific area.

Market reach is the ability to contact targeted customers and process sales operations.

Medium enterprises are companies between 10 and 20, 50 and 250, or 500 and 1,000 employees, based on the country's conventions. They can be also defined as companies with a revenue typically between $10 million and $1 billion.

Meta message is a piece of abstract information that needs interpretation, such as cues or propositions about relationships among communicators (Bateson, 1956).

Micro-enterprises are companies that have 0 to 9 employees.

Micro-segments are small groups of customers with many common attributes, which justifies dedicated campaigns (Shapiro & Bonoma, 1984).

Mutual education is a phase when the customer and the supplier inform each other in preparation for a deal.

Mutualization business model is a model in which the enterprise gives back its profit to shareholders or associated members.

Net promoter score (NPS) is percentage of very satisfied customers (rated 9 to 10) minus the percentage of not satisfied customers (rated 0 to 6).

Nurturing is the communication activity needed to maintain the customer's interest between the first contact and the purchase, or between one purchase and the next.

Nurturing phase is the phase when the customer has had only one contact with the supplier, or made a purchase a while ago, and is given valuable information to keep him/her interested and aware of the supplier.

Objection is a customer comment against the proposed solution or the supplier, which most of time requires a response from the salesperson.

Off-line media are media that do not involve the use of Internet or telephone, such as events, conferences, exhibitions, or branches where customers can visit.

Offensive project intends to extend the customer base.

Offering height is the number of segments addressed.

Offerings depth is the number of redundant products that answer to the same customer need.

Offerings length is the total number of products sold.

Offerings width is the number of complementary products or services sold to the same segment.

Open innovation is based on alliances.

Operations are the "how to sell" actions.

Outbound calls are phone calls generated by the supplier

Outbound media are unsolicited media sent to customers, such as banners, email, and SMS via mobile phones.

Penetration is a strategy used to capture the maximum market share.

Positioning is the level at which customer needs are addressed.

Prescriber is a person who suggests to the buyer a specific product.

Pricing committee tracks the lost or won deals and their particulars, and proposes price tactics to the account manager.

Producer business model is a model in which the enterprise creates and produces a product or service.

Product churn is the replacement of an equipment.

Product cycle is represented by a curve with the number of sales over the life of the product, including the second-end market and recycling of material.

Product listing is the referencing of products to buyers made by a parent organization; it can be a recommendation or a compulsory list with negotiated prices.

Product marketing specification is a document that describes what the product should do for customers, including the benefits, usage, functions, performance, and features.

Product platform is the architecture of a product, which can be used for several products.

Product synergy is potential savings due to common efforts in R&D.

Product technical specifications is a document that describes how the product is made, including its components, architecture, and system.

Proof of concept (POC) is a test of the product in real life by the customer before purchasing.

Protocol of a survey is the series of methods used to collect and process data in order to obtain results.

Pull innovation is based on customer need.

Purchase synergy is the potential savings in purchase activities.

Push innovation is based on technology.

Radical innovation generates major customer behavior changes.

Reverse auction is an auction in which the winner offers the lowest price.

Request for information (RFI) is the first document of a tender and asks suppliers interested in a deal to contact the customer and complete the company information.

Request for quotation (RFQ), or request for proposal (RFP), is a second document of a tender to select a product, which asks for a detailed offer and prices to respond to a specific need.

Sale cycle is the duration between the first customer contact and the purchase.

Salesperson portfolio is the list of customers who have already been contacted by the salesperson and who may buy in the near future.

Sales synergy is potential savings due to the sale of several products at the same sales meeting with customers.

Scoring refers to assigning a value to customers, usually in points, which measures future sales potential based on a mix of heterogeneous criteria.

Segmentation is the process of subdividing a market into distinct subsets of customers who behave in the same way or have similar needs (American Marketing Association, 2015).

Skimming is the strategy of market leaders to keep high price and maximize profit per customer.

Small businesses have between 10 and 19, 49 and 500, or 1,000 employees depending on country statistics and conventions. They are also defined as enterprises that have a revenue below $10 million.

Small office/home office (SoHo), or micro-enterprises, are terms to describe companies that have 0 to 9 employees.

Solution ensures a result or benefit to the customer over a certain period of time. It may include products, chargeable services, or free support.

Start-up service is the service to help customers starting to use a product.

Strategic learning is the acquisition of a knowledge or know-how perceived as vital for the future.

Strategy defines "what" and to "whom" to sell. It includes the segmentation, identification of the target market, positioning, marketing mix elements, and expenditures (American Marketing Association, 2015).

Supply chain includes manufacturing and deployment to the customer premises or system.

Support phase corresponds to supplier operational help to the customer after the deal.

Switching costs are the customer technical and organizational costs of change from one supplier to another.

Total cost of ownership (TCO) includes all customer costs generated by the purchase, such as products, services, supplies, process adaptations, people training, up to the time of the purchase manager

Technology access is the process to acquire technology knowledge and use.

Technology platform is a group of technologies built for a series of products.

Tender office, or Bid Desk, is in charge of tracking the tender publications, contacting all concerned managers to get their replies, and writing the responses.

Tender or bid is an invitation to submit a formal quoted proposal contract for products or services with information about the supplier. It can also be the proposal document itself.

Tier 2 is a provider to one of Tier 1 providers.

Tier 3 is a provider to a Tier 2 provider, and so on.

Triangulation survey is the use of several survey methods to address a research question.

Triangulation refers to checking information or making estimations by using several sources.

Value-added reseller business model is a model in which the enterprise buys products and services, finds customers, adds services (i.e., customization), and sells a solution.

Value addition chain is a chain of activities that a firm employs in a specific industry in order to deliver a valuable product or service to the market (Porter, 1985).

Value proposition is the customer's intended perception of a supplier's offerings.

Value-added reseller (VAR) not only buys and sells products, but transforms them and/or adds services to package and/or customize a solution.

Vertical integration is the strategy of buying suppliers or customers to capture their profits or secure the relationship.

Virtual organizations are structures that are working from a distance.

Voice of the customer refers to customers' frustrations, wishes, dreams, and fears.

White paper is a document describing the state of a market or technology, or suppliers' best practices.

Printed in Great Britain
by Amazon